The DMC Book of
EMBROIDERY

Melinda Coss

The DMC Book of
EMBROIDERY

Melinda Coss

COLLINS & BROWN

First published in Great Britain in 1996 by
Collins & Brown Limited
London House
Great Eastern Wharf
Parkgate Road
London SW11 4NQ

The acknowledgements that appear on page 190 are hereby made a part of
this copyright page.

1 3 5 7 9 8 6 4 2

British Cataloguing-in-Publication Data
A catalogue record of this book is available from the British Library.

ISBN 1-85585 273-X, hb
ISBN 1-85585 279-9, pb

Conceived, edited and designed by Collins & Brown Limited

EDITOR: Liz Dean
CONSULTANT EDITOR: Maggi McCormick
ART DIRECTOR: Roger Bristow
DESIGNER: Alison Lee
PHOTOGRAPHY: Lucinda Symons (style shots);
    Mark Gatehouse (stitched samples)
ROOM SETS: Steve Gott
ILLUSTRATIONS: Coral Mula
ADDITIONAL ILLUSTRATIONS: Amanda Patton

Printed in Italy

CONTENTS

 # INTRODUCTION

Learning to stitch is a step-by-step procedure that almost anyone can master with ease, given a little time and patience. This book is designed to show you all the stitches and techniques you will need.

EMBROIDERY IS A wonderfully creative pastime, and it is also a therapeutic outlet for the often stressful business of living. Add to that the sheer pleasure of being surrounded by beautifully coloured threads and an array of richly textured fabrics, and you will soon begin to understand exactly why embroidery is undergoing such a strong revival.

This book is an invaluable stepping stone into this fascinating world. It explains exactly what a beginner needs to know before commencing a stitching project, and it also answers questions for experienced needleworkers by giving clear, detailed information on all the stitches, equipment, and techniques that you will need for a wide variety of stitching methods.

Whether you wish to decorate a piece of clothing or embroider a plain tablecloth, this book gives advice on the threads and the fabrics available and recommends which to use. For those of you who wish to explore traditional skills and re-create their effects, there are step-by-step demonstrations of the necessary techniques and advice on the relevant materials you will need.

How to Use This Book

This book is divided into three main sections: basic stitches, the stitch library, and special skills.

Basic stitches (pages 20-43) As with all skills, the best place to start is at the beginning. If you learn to work the ten basic stitches illustrated in this section, you can create simple, straightforward designs with ease, as demonstrated by

Left: Detail of crewelwork cushion
(see project on page 124)

the five projects that follow the stitches. The basic stitches form the basis of many of the stitches in the stitch library.

The stitch library (pages 44–109) The stitch library shows how to work more than 85 different embroidery stitches, step by step. This library is divided into six stitch families – straight stitches, satin stitches, cross stitches, knotted stitches, looped stitches, and laced stitches. Each family is colour-coded to make it easier for you to find all the stitches you need, and they are arranged in order of increasing difficulty.

At the beginning of each stitch family is a stitched example, a kind of embroidery sampler. A traditional way of learning different stitches is to create a sampler by working small areas of various stitches on a piece of cloth. The stitching can be worked according to a planned design, as shown in this book, although many of the most beautiful samplers are composed simply of random blocks of practice stitches. These samplers make an ideal starting point, and are an enjoyable way to learn new stitches and practise familiar ones.

The examples here show all the stitches in the family, so you can see the effects that the stitches create, and how different stitches can work together to create pattern and texture.

The projects in this section range from a simple geometric place mat to a decorative woollen Valentine blanket.

Special skills (pages 110–177) The special skills section provides an opportunity to use some new techniques and materials. Beadwork, monogramming, couching and goldwork, ribbon embroidery, and crewelwork are included, along with additional step-by-step stitches and techniques to learn. There are also two

inspiring projects for every skill, and these range from a simple beadwork evening bag and a ribbon-embroidered cardigan to a Jacobean-style needlecase and a monogrammed scarf.

For those who wish to create their own images and projects, there is a design section to encourage experimentation with a range of shapes, textures, and colours (pages 12–17). This section explains how to enlarge and reduce motifs, and how to transfer them from paper to fabric using a variety of simple techniques. To help with this process, there are pages of motifs throughout the book. All are annotated with stitch suggestions, and they are ready to be traced and interpreted in your own embroidery designs.

There is also information on how to finish your projects professionally, from laundering to storage. Step-by-step sequences demonstrate how to hem, block, and mount your work, and also show how to make your own trimmings such as tassels and fancy cords.

Whether you would like to recreate a traditional piece of work or express yourself in a contemporary way, the following pages will show you how. Let this book help you to discover new and old skills and enjoy the time-honoured pleasures of embroidery.

Left-handed Stitchers

If you are left-handed and have difficulty with any stitch diagrams, place the book in front of a mirror and read the diagrams from the reflection. In some instances, the easiest solution is to change the direction of working a stitch.

Materials and Equipment

Choosing the right materials can make the stitching process easier and your finished piece more effective.

THERE IS A vast range of needles, threads, fabrics, and many other needlework materials available to embroiderers today. Here follows a selection of those most commonly used.

Needles

The choice of needle for a particular project depends upon the fabric and thread being used. The thickness of the thread determines the size of the needle's eye, and the weave of the fabric determines its point. The needle should be large enough to take the thread without strain and should also glide easily through the fabric.

Threads

Some DMC threads are designed to enhance stitching. Others, particularly the heavier variety of threads, are used for surface decoration and should be couched onto your fabric (page 128). Certain threads are used for specific techniques, such as goldwork, ribbon embroidery, and crewelwork, and these are described in depth in the relevant special skills sections (pages 110–177). Standard embroidery threads are shown on page 9 (opposite), and most of these are available in a large choice of plain colours and a number of interesting random-dyed and variegated colours.

There are also several varieties of alternative threads available, such as textured silks, ribbons, and wool and cotton threads, coloured with natural and synthetic dyes. Try them out to develop your individual style.

Sewing thread is also needed to transfer and finish projects. For finishing work, use a thread to match the fabric. For transferring designs using the tacking method, use a contrasting thread to show design lines.

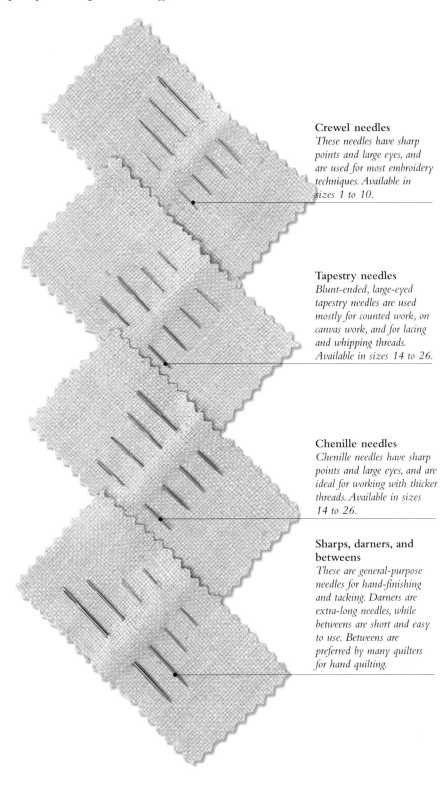

Crewel needles
These needles have sharp points and large eyes, and are used for most embroidery techniques. Available in sizes 1 to 10.

Tapestry needles
Blunt-ended, large-eyed tapestry needles are used mostly for counted work, on canvas work, and for lacing and whipping threads. Available in sizes 14 to 26.

Chenille needles
Chenille needles have sharp points and large eyes, and are ideal for working with thicker threads. Available in sizes 14 to 26.

Sharps, darners, and betweens
These are general-purpose needles for hand-finishing and tacking. Darners are extra-long needles, while betweens are short and easy to use. Betweens are preferred by many quilters for hand quilting.

Stranded cotton

This shiny thread consists of six strands which can be divided or blended with different coloured threads and threaded together in the needle.

Cotton perlé

This high-sheen, twisted mercerized cotton is excellent for textured effects. Normally used as a single strand, it is available in skeins and in thicknesses, from No.3 (thick) to No.12 (thin).

Coton à broder

This is suitable for fine embroidery such as open work, cutwork, satin stitching, and monogramming and composite stitches. Available in sizes 12, 16, 20, 25, 30, and 35 and a broad range of colours in regular thicknesses.

Persian yarn

This is available in a stranded form which can be used as single strands.

Tapestry wool

Used in needlepoint on canvas, tapestry wool is also good for couching techniques. Available as a single strand.

Crewel wool

This fine, 2-ply yarn can be used singly or in multiple strands, and is used widely in crewelwork (page 112).

Flower thread

This has a fine, matt finish which gives a softer edge than stranded cotton or cotton perlé. It comes in a single strand and a reasonable colour range, yet does tend to attract dust and dirt.

Linen thread

This traditional thread is strong and textured with a natural effect.

Silk and rayon threads

Used to create very high sheen. Pure silk is prized by traditional embroiderers. Silk snags easily on rough fabric and fingernails, and wears thin quickly.

Soft embroidery cotton

Thicker than flower thread, this is effective in bold peasant designs on quite coarse fabric, or for matt effects. A good lacing or whipping thread in composite stitches (page 101).

Metallic thread

Metallic thread can be threaded with other threads to highlight a simple or complex stitch, particularly with couched cotton or wool threads (page 131). For goldwork threads, see page 129.

Frames

With most embroidery techniques, it is a great advantage to keep the fabric taut during stitching. There are various frames available (see right).

Fabrics

Embroidery can be worked on a vast range of fabrics, which can be divided into two main groups: evenweave fabrics and plain weave fabrics.

Evenweave fabrics The exact number of threads per inch on evenweave fabric is referred to as the "count". If your stitches are evenly spaced and of equal size, the higher the fabric count, the more stitches there are to the inch – so higher-count fabrics mean more, and smaller, stitches. Evenweave fabrics are useful for stitches where spacing is crucial, as stitches can be placed by simply counting threads.

Plain weave fabrics This group includes furnishing and dress fabrics in smooth and textured varieties, such as velvets, satins, slub silks, and even heavy wools.

The fabric needs to be heavy enough to support your threads and light enough to enhance your stitching. Work a small area to test the balance first.

Some fabrics stretch; iron lightweight interfacing on the back of the fabric before stitching to reduce movement. Some iron-ons use a gummy adhesive which is hard to stitch through, so test first. Stable fabrics are best for novices.

Consider the purpose of your work, and check the manufacturers' cleaning instructions for fabric and thread to make sure they are similar.

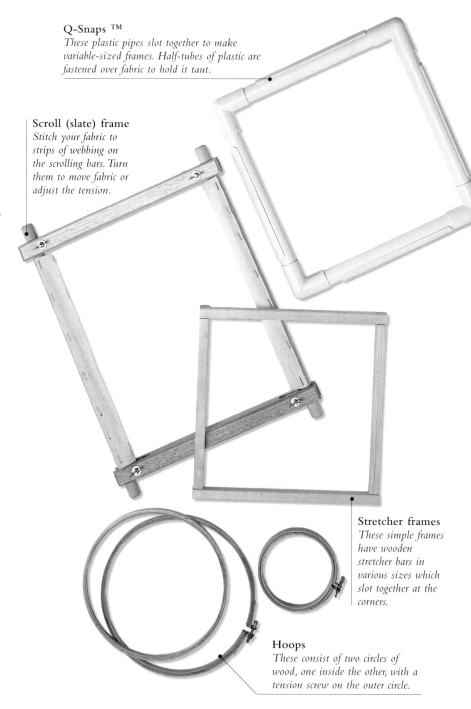

Q-Snaps ™
These plastic pipes slot together to make variable-sized frames. Half-tubes of plastic are fastened over fabric to hold it taut.

Scroll (slate) frame
Stitch your fabric to strips of webbing on the scrolling bars. Turn them to move fabric or adjust the tension.

Stretcher frames
These simple frames have wooden stretcher bars in various sizes which slot together at the corners.

Hoops
These consist of two circles of wood, one inside the other, with a tension screw on the outer circle.

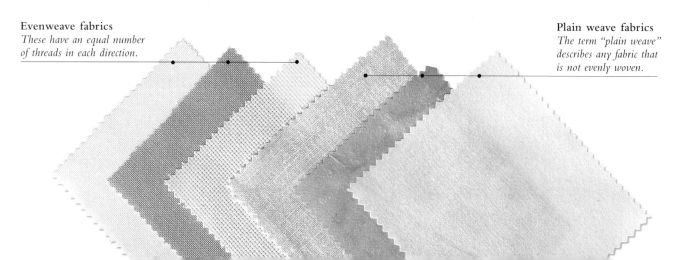

Evenweave fabrics
These have an equal number of threads in each direction.

Plain weave fabrics
The term "plain weave" describes any fabric that is not evenly woven.

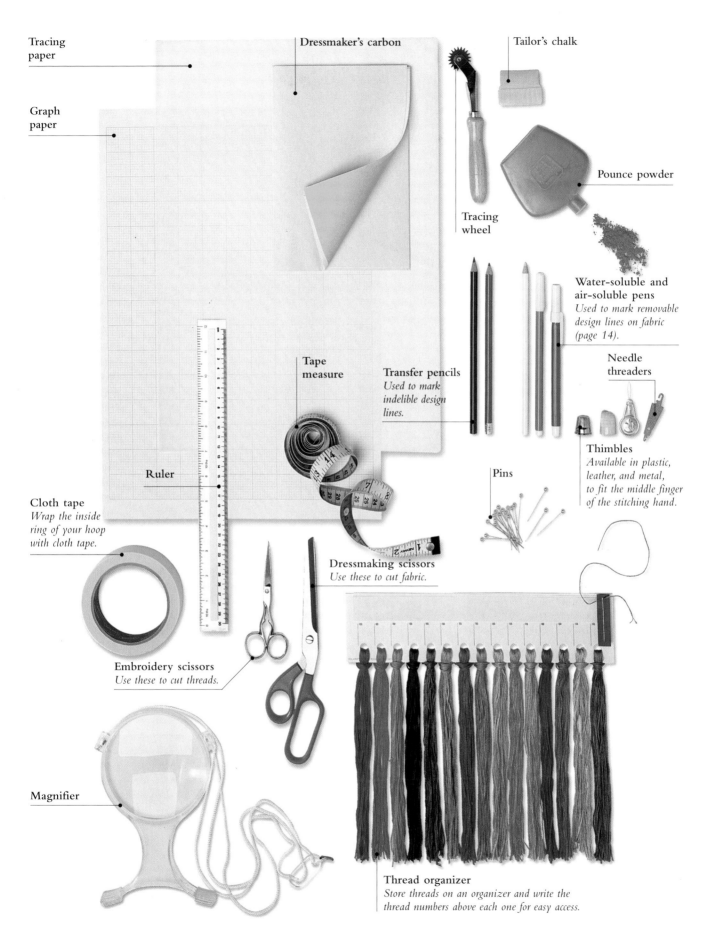

Tracing paper

Graph paper

Dressmaker's carbon

Tailor's chalk

Tracing wheel

Pounce powder

Water-soluble and air-soluble pens
Used to mark removable design lines on fabric (page 14).

Needle threaders

Tape measure

Transfer pencils
Used to mark indelible design lines.

Thimbles
Available in plastic, leather, and metal, to fit the middle finger of the stitching hand.

Pins

Ruler

Cloth tape
Wrap the inside ring of your hoop with cloth tape.

Dressmaking scissors
Use these to cut fabric.

Embroidery scissors
Use these to cut threads.

Magnifier

Thread organizer
Store threads on an organizer and write the thread numbers above each one for easy access.

Design Sources

A keen eye for detail and a little imagination can help you transform patterns
from everyday objects to creative designs on fabric.

ALTHOUGH DRAWING IS a useful skill, designing is far more dependent on the ability to look. The detail in everyday objects can be the basis of creative designs on fabric.

Historically, inspiration has been drawn from nature, religion, and social circumstance. Today, it is as valid to be inspired by commercial art, postcards, and magazines as by nature. The aim is to express a personal view.

Recording Ideas

The would-be designer should carry a notebook and a selection of crayons or coloured pencils at all times. When something catches your eye, record it in your notebook using coloured marks and descriptive words. The overall aim is to remember the original idea so you can use it later in embroidery.

Creating a Pattern From a Motif

For a first attempt at designing, study a style that appeals to you and create a new interpretation, using motifs from wallpaper, a fabric, or the motifs in this book (pages 16–17, 116–119, 132–5, 147, 160–161, 171–3). Note how certain shapes and lines embody the style of a particular period: Art Deco, for example, is characterized by clean curves and by sharp geometrics. Art Nouveau features long, swirling lines and extravagant floral shapes, whereas Celtic style embodies elaborate crosses, knots, and border designs.

The exercise below shows you how to create a simple pattern for embroidery from one motif. This technique is just a starting point – you could enlarge or reduce a similar design on a photocopier; you could also cut it out, reverse it, and draw around the outline to give a mirror image.

Creating a pattern from a motif
1 *Trace a simple motif. This one is taken from a William Morris fabric (left).*

2 *Duplicate the leaf and place the images side by side to create a repeating border pattern.*

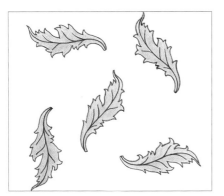

3 *Place the motifs randomly and at varied angles on a plain background. This gives a sense of movement.*

4 *Position motifs to create a mirror image, or repeat and turn 180° (right). This could frame a monogram.*

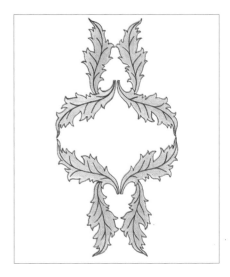

12

Stitching a Motif

Having determined the basic design, it is time to choose fabric, thread, and stitches. First, choose a stitch suitable for outlining. This could be stem stitch, backstitch or perhaps chain stitch (see basic stitches and the stitch library, pages 20–109). You may prefer to couch the outline with a heavy or goldwork thread (page 128). A scattering of knots, dots, or seeds within the outline highlights certain areas, leaving fabric to show through. The leaf could be filled in with satin stitch (page 32), or an alternative, to create varied textures. Experimentation will throw up interesting possibilities, but think always of the ultimate aim – whether your work is to be a delicate or bold piece, and what it is to be used for.

Using Colour

In practice, with all the wonderful shades of embroidery threads available, choosing colours can be difficult. Rely on your observations: look closely at flowers and leaves, and notice how the colours change. Match threads to the colours you see. Your eye will soon discover that white is never white, and black is never black; they are both made from a rich variation of hues. Colours that initially seem clear and sharp are often several values duller or lighter than they appear. Look through half-closed eyes to blur your vision slightly and give a truer image of your end result.

Outlining a motif

1 *Outlining with a lightweight thread can give an elegantly simple line.*

Using a textured filling

2 *This heavier outline contrasts with a seeded filling which lightens the motif.*

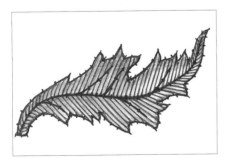

Using a couched outline

3 *This couched outline gives the leaf edge a thorny texture.*

Colour Wheel

A colour wheel explains the relationship between colours. You can use it to work out which colours will go well together.

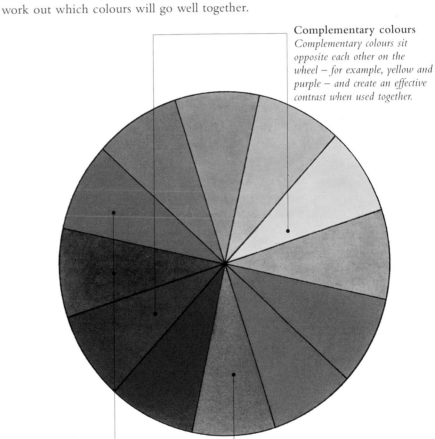

Complementary colours
Complementary colours sit opposite each other on the wheel – for example, yellow and purple – and create an effective contrast when used together.

Analogous colours
These sit side by side on the wheel, and usually include only one primary. Analogous colours harmonize well together.

Colour values
Colours range in value from light to dark. Graduate them for shading effects.

Transferring Motifs

There are many traditional and modern transfer methods, from pounce powder and dressmaker's carbon to disappearing ink. Use the method that best suits your fabric and design.

THERE ARE SEVERAL standard methods of transferring a design onto fabric. The choice depends on the original source of the design. Always test the transfer first.

Hot-iron Transfers

Commercial designs can be bought already printed on transfer paper. To use a transfer, place it in position face down on the right side of your fabric. Press down with a hot iron and hold for a count of ten. Keep the iron still, or the design will blur. The iron temperature should be set to suit the fabric. Lift the iron and carefully remove the paper from the fabric. The design will appear (in reverse) on the fabric.

Hot-iron transfers are indelible and won't wash out, so take great care when using this method.

Photocopy Transfers

Both black-and-white and also colour photocopied designs can be transferred directly to the fabric. Dampen the right sides of the photocopy and the fabric using a mixture of one cup water, one cup white spirit and a few drops of liquid detergent. Place the fabric right side up on a felt pad or piece of thick fabric and lay the dampened photocopy face down on it. Press with a hot iron (set for cotton). Note that this method will not work on synthetic fabrics.

Soluble Pens

Soluble pens are useful transfer tools as they are easy to use and make strong, visible marks. However, although the ink will disappear from most fabrics, do test these pens on fabric scraps first, because soluble pens can mark some types of fabric permanently.

Water-soluble pen This is a very popular method of transferring designs, as all the pen marks disappear when sponged with water. Trace or draw the design on paper using a bold felt-tipped pen. Lay the paper drawing under the fabric and then place paper and fabric on top of a lightbox. If you do not have a lightbox, tape them to a windowpane so that daylight shines through and illuminates the design. Draw over the design on the fabric using the water-soluble pen.

Complete your embroidery, then carefully remove any visible design lines by gently dabbing the fabric with a piece of damp sponge. The same technique, using a graphite pencil, will not harm your fabric, but again, do check that graphite marks will disappear from your fabric by testing sample scraps before you begin your project.

Air-soluble pen This pen works in a similar way to the water-soluble pen, but the image disappears by itself an hour or so after being drawn, so it is ideal when using fabric or threads that are not colourfast. Proceed as for the water-soluble pen. It is also important to remember to redraw your design lines, if necessary, before they disappear!

Tacking

Tacking involves working loose running stitches over fabric and tracing or tissue paper to mark design lines. The paper is removed to leave the tacking lines, which are removed as each area is stitched. This technique will not damage your fabric in any way. Tacking is also used to mark the centre lines on fabric.

Hot-iron transfers

1 *Trace the design onto tracing paper using an ordinary pencil. Turn the paper over and draw over the design on the reverse, using a transfer pencil as shown.*

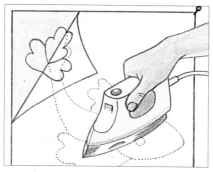

2 *Place paper, transfer-pencil side down, on the right side of the fabric and press, holding the iron down for a count of ten and keeping it perfectly still so the motif does not blur (see hot-iron transfers, above).*

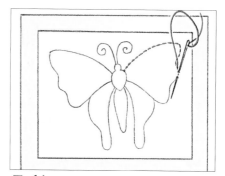

Tacking

Trace the design onto tissue or tracing paper. Pin face up on right side of fabric. Using a contrasting thread, tack over all the design lines. Remove paper.

Dressmaker's Carbon

This method requires a tracing wheel (page 11), which can be purchased from most needlework stores. You can also use a knitting needle (see below) instead of a tracing wheel to transfer more detailed parts of the design.

Pounce Powder

The pounce powder technique is a traditional transfer method used in tailoring. Old-fashioned pounce powder (sometimes known as inking powder) or powdered white chalk can be bought from artist supply stores. Use a pin, stiletto or unthreaded sewing machine to make the pinholes through tracing paper (see below), then brush powder over the holes to transfer the outline of the design onto your fabric.

Enlarging and Reducing Designs

Photocopying is usually the simplest method of enlarging and reducing your designs. Most photocopiers give you a number of size differentials to choose from, plus the option of adjusting the lightness or darkness of the final image.

However, you can use the traditional method which is illustrated below. This is relatively simple to achieve and is particularly useful if you do not have access to a photocopier – you need only a pencil and tracing paper that is divided into squares in order to transfer your chosen image.

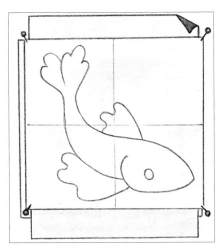

Pouncing

1 *Trace design and pin or tack paper, face up, on fabric on a fabric pad. With a pin or stiletto, pierce design lines through paper.*

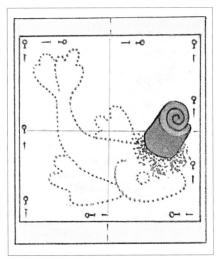

2 *Using a small make-up brush or a rolled scrap of felt, carefully rub a small quantity of the pounce powder over the pricked holes made in Step 1.*

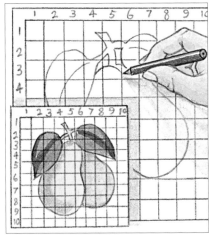

3 *Remove the paper and any excess pounce powder. To create a more lasting image, connect the dots using a pencil or a water-soluble pen.*

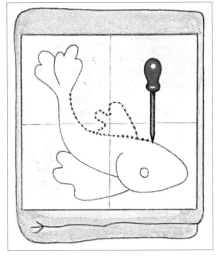

Dressmaker's carbon

1 *Draw or trace the design on paper. Take the carbon paper and lay it face down on fabric, with the paper over it, face up.*

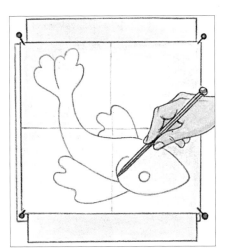

2 *Run the tracing wheel over and along the lines of the design, thus making a carbon copy on the fabric. Use a knitting needle for more control over detailed areas.*

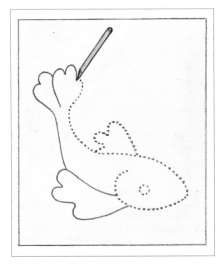

Enlarging a design

Trace the design onto squared paper. Then redraw the image to a larger or smaller scale, square by square.

TRACE-OFF MOTIFS *appear throughout this book, and all are annotated with stitch suggestions. Use these motifs to practise new stitches or create your own designs.*

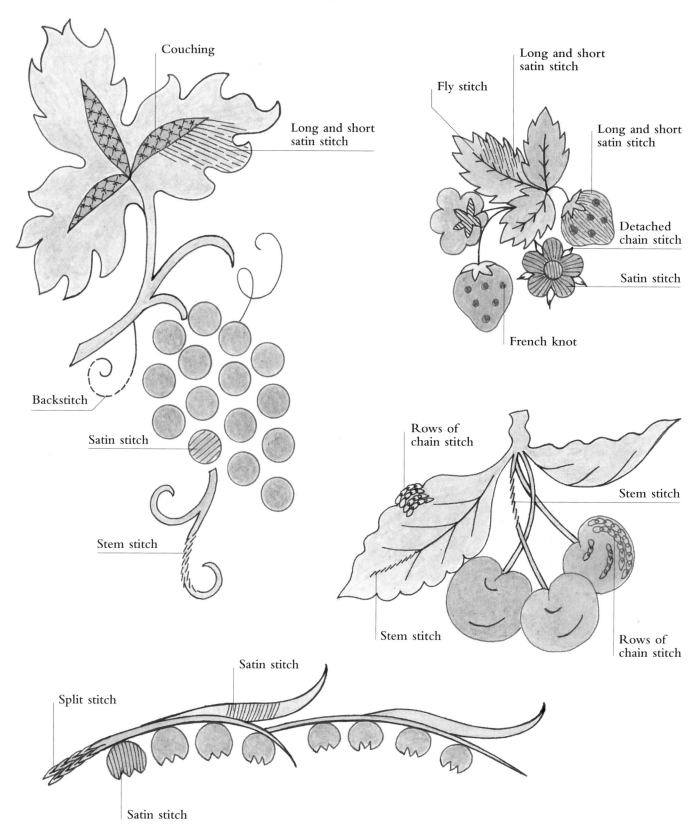

Couching

Long and short satin stitch

Backstitch

Satin stitch

Stem stitch

Fly stitch

Long and short satin stitch

Long and short satin stitch

Detached chain stitch

Satin stitch

French knot

Rows of chain stitch

Stem stitch

Stem stitch

Rows of chain stitch

Satin stitch

Split stitch

Satin stitch

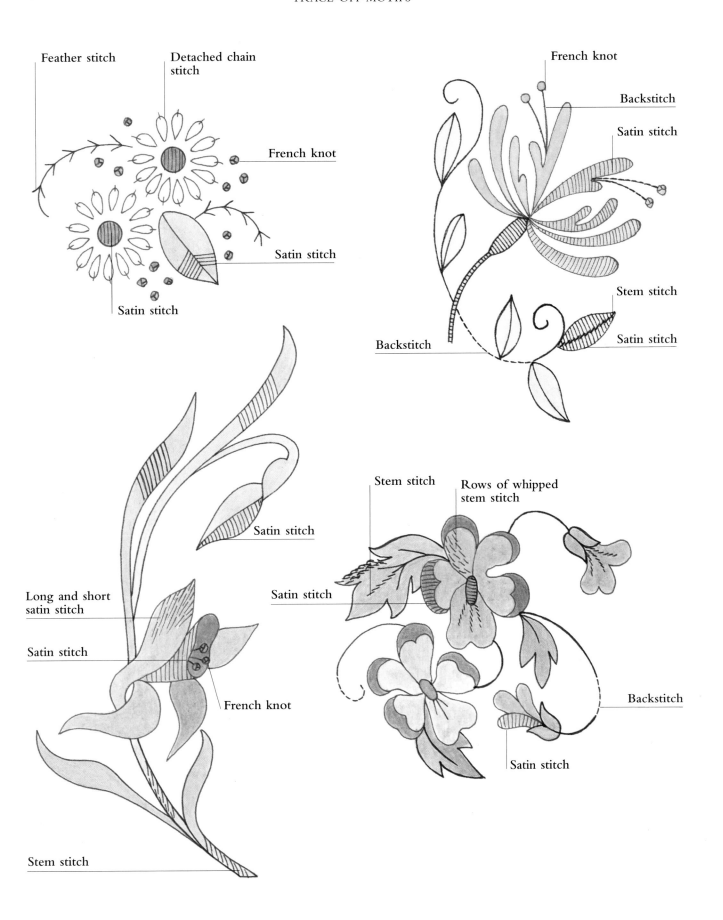

Feather stitch

Detached chain stitch

French knot

Satin stitch

Satin stitch

French knot

Backstitch

Satin stitch

Stem stitch

Satin stitch

Backstitch

Satin stitch

Long and short satin stitch

Satin stitch

French knot

Stem stitch

Stem stitch

Rows of whipped stem stitch

Satin stitch

Backstitch

Satin stitch

Getting Started

Mastering these basic embroidery techniques will help you save time, get your project off to a good start, and give a really professional finish – on both sides of the fabric.

Preparing the Fabric

If you are embroidering an item of clothing, it is a good idea to wash, dry, and press the item before beginning. Specialist embroidery fabrics do not require prewashing, but should be pressed. To prevent fraying, secure the edges of the fabric with a row of zigzag stitches, or cut close to the edge using pinking shears. For embroidery canvas or heavy fabrics, bind the edges with cloth tape or hem the edges (page 180).
Finding the centre of the fabric For regular-shaped fabric, simply fold the fabric twice from edge to edge and mark the middle point.
Drawing guidelines on fabric While you are practising, draw guidelines on fabric first. Use a ruler with a graphite pencil or air- or water-soluble pen to plot the guidelines. Soluble pens are good for project work, since some stitches will not cover graphite guidelines. You can also mark fabric with lines of tacking.

Using Hoops

Place the smaller ring underneath the centre of the fabric. Slightly open the screw on the larger ring and push down over the fabric so that the piece is caught firmly between the large and small ring. Pull the fabric edges to make sure it is taut, and tighten the screw to hold the fabric securely in position. It is always best to remove the hoop after each stitching session because it can distort the fabric.

Making a Thread Organizer

Before beginning a project, it is a good idea to make a thread organizer. Cut a strip of medium-weight acid-free cardboard measuring approximately 3 x 4 in (7.5 x 10 cm) and, using a hole punch, punch one hole for each colour

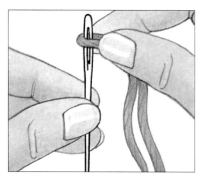

Threading a needle
1 *Double the thread a short distance from the end, then fold it around the needle eye as shown.*

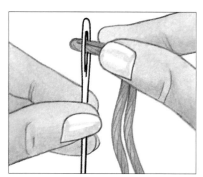

2 *Push the folded thread through the needle eye as shown. Hold the needle steady as you do this.*

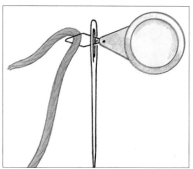

Using a needle threader
1 *Push wire loop through needle eye; push thread through wire loop.*

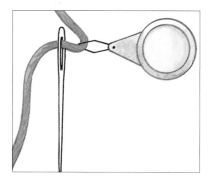

2 *Carefully pull the wire loop with inserted thread back through the needle eye, as shown above.*

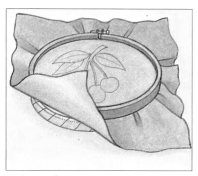

Using a hoop
1 *Bind smaller ring with cloth tape. Place under fabric. Place larger ring over fabric, centring the image.*

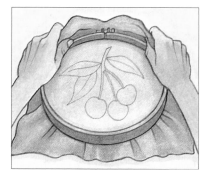

2 *Push down on the larger ring. Pull edges to adjust fabric until taut, and tighten screw on outer ring.*

down one long side. Cut the thread into 12 or 20 in (30.5 or 51 cm) lengths and loop it through the holes. Write the corresponding DMC colour number next to each shade of thread.

To prevent part skeins and leftover ends from becoming tangled, wrap them around acid-free cardboard or plastic bobbins, and label them with a colour number. Store neatly in a clear plastic box or a file-card holder. Unsealed clear plastic bags are also useful for storing families of coloured threads. If you build up a large collection, it might be worth investing in a storage box with small drawers such as the ones designed for screws and nails.

Stitching Position

While stitching, comfort should be the main priority, so there are several points to consider. First, make sure that your back is adequately supported and, if necessary, place a cushion in the small of your back. Position your work to give maximum access and to avoid repetitive strain. In addition, if a stitch is awkward to execute, try turning the fabric around so that you are approaching it from a different direction.

Change your working position regularly, take regular breaks every ten or fifteen minutes, and never strain your eyes by working in poor light. A daylight bulb magnifying lamp is also a sound investment for the avid stitcher.

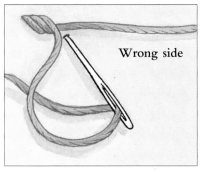

Overstitching

Pull threaded needle through the fabric from the back to the front, leaving a tail at the back 1½ in (4 cm) long. Begin stitching, holding this thread at the back of the work so it is secured by stitching. Trim off excess thread.

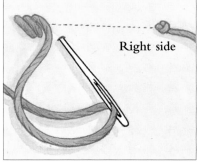

Using knots

Make a knot at end of thread and go down on front of fabric. (Working left to right, position knot 1½ in/4 cm to right of first stitch.) Work stitches over thread at back. When secure, cut off the knot and pull tail to back.

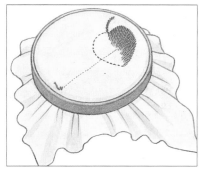

"Away" waste knot

Make a knot at end of thread and go down to back of fabric so knot is on top, as shown, 6 in (15 cm) away from area of work. To finish, clip knot and weave tail into back of work.

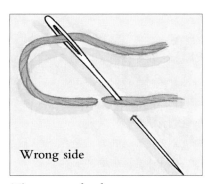

Tie-on method

Working from the back, take a tiny stitch and leave a short tail. Make a tiny cross stitch to pierce the tail. Test the tie-on. This method is useful for crewelwork (page 112) and where the cross will be covered with stitches.

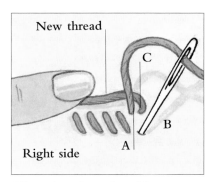

Changing threads mid-row

To change threads mid-row, come up at A. Thread new thread in new needle and come up at C. Hold thread as shown, go down at B with old thread and fasten off. Continue with new thread.

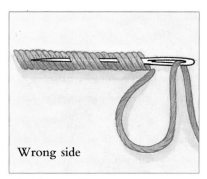

Finishing off

To finish a length of thread, take needle and thread through to the back of fabric and weave it in and out of three or four adjacent stitches. Pull the thread through the stitches gently.

Basic Stitches

The 10 stitches that are demonstrated in this chapter form the basis of all embroidery stitches. Once you have mastered them, you can progress to the stitches in the stitch library.

Most basic stitches are simple to work, and many are ideal for strengthening edges, filling motif shapes, working curves, and adding texture, as shown in the stitched example overleaf. These stitches are used to create the projects that follow this section.

Basic Stitches

Basic Stitches Sampler

The stitches that are demonstrated here form the basis of the stitches in all the stitch families. Striking effects can be achieved by varying the sizes, angles, and colours of the stitches – herringbone stitch, for example, is shown in open and closed diamond shapes. The green inner borders are made from single-wrap French knots and the red outer border from chain stitch. All the reds are worked in DMC cotton perlé and all the greens in six-strand, stranded cotton.

1 Blanket stitch *page 25*
2 Running stitch *page 28*
3 Buttonhole stitch *page 25*
4 Backstitch *page 30*
5 Cross stitch *page 29*
6 French knot *page 33*
7 Feather stitch *page 27*
8 Satin stitch *page 32*
9 Stem stitch *page 31*
10 Chain stitch *page 24*
11 Herringbone stitch
    page 26

LEARNING TO DO these ten simple stitches properly is the only hard work embroidery requires. Just like driving a car, once you master them, they become second nature. In this section you will find information that forms the backbone of all embroidery. Stitching techniques and methods have developed over the centuries and have resulted in an extensive library of stitch variations, but all of these variations rely on your ability to produce the following ten little gems.

Many traditional techniques centre on the use of just one basic stitch. Look at the glorious chain-stitched fabrics of India or Persia, or the precise cross-stitch samplers of the 1800s; the skill needed to create these pieces was the mastery of a single basic stitch. Peasant cultures, in particular, discovered a favourite stitch and produced all their decorative items with it. Chinese embroideries owe their glory to the fine execution of satin stitch. Learn how to work these stitches properly and mastering the variations will prove to be a very simple matter.

The "Perfect" Stitch

Historically, the principal difference between good and bad embroidery was defined by the art of creating a perfectly neat, even stitch. Modern embroiderers have shifted the emphasis to the impact of an overall design, with more emphasis on colour and texture than on the precision of the stitch itself. Stitches are now used more as painting tools than for their own sake, but any artist will tell you that the validity of their modern abstract composition has its roots in a thorough knowledge and understanding of the basic principles of technique.

Once you have learned to do these stitches properly, you will be able to use them appropriately and with ease in any piece of work, freestyle or traditional. You can then look at the more advanced variations and choose your stitches with full knowledge of their potential within the composition you wish to create.

Hints and Tips

When practising the stitches in this section, it is important to understand the qualities that will help to make each stitch regular.

Herringbone stitch, backstitch, blanket stitch, and running stitch For these stitches, success relies strongly on even spacing between each stitch and in uniform sizing of each element within the stitch. In particular, herringbone stitch should be worked so that each stroke of thread is precisely slanted; work within parallel guidelines to achieve straight rows. Begin by practising this stitch on an evenweave fabric and then progress to plain weave.

Stem stitch Here you are trying to create what the eye sees as a continuous line of stitches, which can be achieved by carefully inserting and positioning the needle so that the beginning and end of each stitch is barely visible.

French knots A perfect French knot should sit on the fabric like a bead; it should not flop around exposing strands of thread at its root.

Chain stitch and feather stitch Chain stitches and feather stitches should be equal in size, and it is also important to keep an even tension so that the loops have a consistent openness or roundness.

Cross stitch When working cross stitch, make sure that all the stitches cross in the same direction. Again, it is important to keep the stitches uniform.

Satin stitch Good satin stitch relies on a number of basic principles. You must take care to keep an even edge around your stitches by placing the needle precisely and you must also make sure that the stitches are placed flush to each other and that the threads remain completely flat and untwisted.

Basic Techniques

Here are two simple techniques to help you master the stitches in this section.

The "stab" method

1 *The stab method helps give your stitching an even tension. Hold hoop firmly and use stabbing motion to prick fabric surface with needle.*

2 *Bring the needle to the back of the fabric, pulling thread through gently. Then repeat the stabbing motion to come up on the right side of your work as shown above.*

Working looped stitches

Use your non-stitching thumb to hold and guide the thread around the needle as you work. This will help prevent the thread tangling or knotting.

Chain Stitch

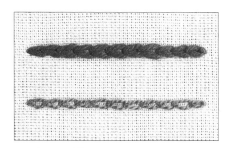

Work as a filling stitch with heavy thread such as matt cotton (top) or aim for an open effect with cotton perlé (bottom).

CHAIN STITCH IS one of the most widely used of the basic stitches and is equally popular with both contemporary and traditional embroiderers. A member of the looped stitch family (page 86), chain stitch is also known as *tambour stitch* and *point de chainette*. There are fine historic examples from the East and the West, although the technique and tools used to achieve it vary considerably.

This simple line stitch originated in India and Persia, where it is worked at great speed with a fine hook called an *ari*. Western cultures favour the use of the tambour hook or the needle and thread, although from the right side of the fabric, these techniques look identical. Interestingly, chain stitch was one of only two stitches produced by the earliest sewing machines.

Uses

Chain stitch is commonly used as an outline stitch or worked in close rows as a filling. In all cases you should aim for an even row of equally sized stitches. When worked with a tambour hook (page 185), chain stitch forms a basis for beadwork (page 156).

Variations

As a contemporary embroidery stitch, chain stitch offers many variations (see the looped stitch family, page 86). *Detached chain stitch* (see variation below) is a most useful variation of basic chain stitch. It is worked exactly like basic chain except that each stitch is finished individually and secured to the fabric with a small straight stitch at the top of the loop. When worked in circles, detached chain stitch is more popularly known as daisy or lazy daisy stitch.

Threads and Fabrics

Chain stitch is suitable for a multitude of DMC threads, from the finest silks to the heaviest cottons, and is very effective on plain weave fabrics. When used as a filling stitch, delicate shading effects can be achieved by gradating colours within the unbroken chain. Fine outlines can also be created, and you will certainly find that curved shapes can be intricately followed. Experiment with lengths of chain worked in single strands of thread.

Technique

Before beginning to work with chain stitch, you may want to define the stitching area by drawing guidelines (page 18). Then choose your thread and plan the size of your stitches accordingly. Work your design outlines first, and stitch in smooth even rows.

See Also:
Embroidery threads *page 8*
Pochette bag *page 34*
Knotted stitch family *pages 72–85*
Looped stitch family *pages 86–99*
Paisley shawl *page 98*
Laced stitch family *pages 100–109*
Beads and Embellishments *pages 156–165*
Monogramming *pages 166–177*

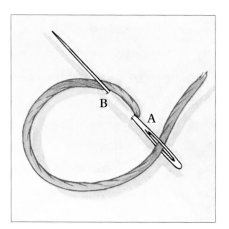

1 *Come up at A. Go down to left of A, coming up at B. Loop thread under needle point from right to left.*

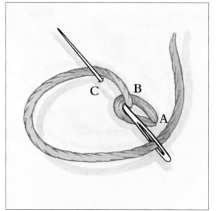

2 *Pull thread through. Go down to left of B, inserting through loop, and come up at C. Loop thread as in Step 1.*

Detached chain stitch
Work a detached stitch by repeating Step 1. Pull through and make a small stitch to anchor loop. Work five detached stitches in a circle to create a lazy daisy stitch.

Buttonhole and Blanket Stitch

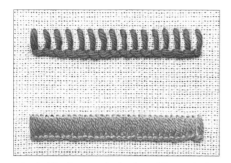

Both blanket stitch (top) and buttonhole stitch (bottom) can be worked with fine or heavy threads.

BUTTONHOLE AND blanket stitches belong to the extensive family of looped stitches (page 86). Buttonhole stitches are placed very close together to form a tight line. Blanket stitches are worked the same way, except space is left between each vertical stitch. While this is the strict definition, the difference has become almost academic, and you will often find blanket stitch referred to as buttonhole and vice versa.

Uses

Buttonhole stitch was developed for practical as well as for decorative uses. Primarily a border stitch worked in a neat and even line, it is perfect for finishing off and giving strength to raw edges. As its name suggests, buttonhole stitch is used extensively in the trades of tailoring and dressmaking.

Other Uses

One of the most popular decorative applications for buttonhole stitch is on cutwork. This technique involves edging a design with a tightly placed border of stitches and cutting away unwanted areas of fabric between these borders with a pair of sharp-pointed scissors to create an attractive openwork effect.

A plain border can also be spiced up by arranging blanket stitches into groups of twos or threes, and you could also gradate the lengths of each group of verticals to form pyramids or stepped effects. Although blanket stitch is usually worked in straight rows, it can also look very effective when stitched in full and half circles. In this way you can create spider web effects and circular motifs as a basis for floral designs.

Variations

Buttonhole stitch is also a very useful filling stitch. Encroaching buttonhole stitch (page 60) gives depth and texture to a motif.

Buttonhole needle lace Buttonhole stitch is popularly used in crewel work to create a needle lace effect. To achieve this look, work a foundation row of stitches. On the row beneath, do not take the needle through the fabric. Instead, use the bottom loops of the first row to anchor the stitches of the second row in place.

Threads and Fabrics

Any DMC thread or fabric can be used to work this stitch. When making your selection, consider how your thread and fabric could complement each other, either as a match or a contrast.

Technique

To work an attractive buttonhole stitch, always keep the tops of the stitches level. Before beginning, draw guidelines on your fabric (page 18). If you want to space the stitches or gradate their length, then take care to ensure that the spaces and lengths remain even and consistent within the design.

See Also:
Embroidery threads *page 8*
Cutwork butterfly tablecloth *page 40*
Satin stitch family *pages 56–63*
Knotted stitch family *pages 72–85*
Looped stitch family *pages 86–99*
Crewelwork *pages 112–127*

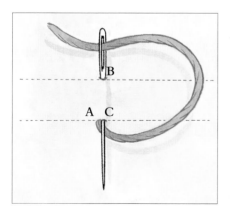

1 *Come up at A, go down at B, come up at C, just to immediate right of A. Carry thread under needle point from left to right. Pull thread through.*

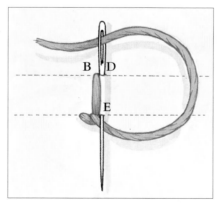

2 *Go down at D (just to immediate right of B). Come up at E, keeping thread under needle point.*

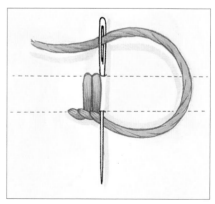

3 *Continue in this way along row, keeping all stitches even and close together as shown.*

Herringbone Stitch

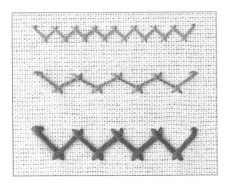

Vary threads and angle of stitch for contrasting effects. Stranded cotton (top), cotton perlé (centre), and matt cotton (bottom) have been used here.

Herringbone stitch has many pseudonyms. *Mossoul stitch, Persian stitch, Russian stitch, Russian cross stitch, plaited stitch, catch stitch,* and *witch stitch* all describe one ancient, basic design that has decorated garments and furnishings throughout the world for many centuries. This popular stitch is commonly associated with embroidery from the Greek islands, and it is also widely used in India. Herringbone stitch is a member of the cross stitch family (page 64).

Uses

Herringbone can be used as a border and as a filling stitch. You can create effective patterns by varying the position of each row of stitches. For example, the stitches can touch top to bottom, forming a row of diamond shapes. Alternatively, they can be interlocked to create a lattice effect. You can also adjust the angle of the slanting stitches to give a lighter or heavier overall effect. It is important, however, to keep the rows of stitches uniform.

Variations

Generally used for working borders, basic herringbone stitch has a number of variations. Tied herringbone (page 105), for example, is a composite stitch which is popularly used for more intricate decoration.

Closed herringbone stitch This filling stitch is probably the most useful variation of basic herringbone. Closed herringbone is worked the same way as basic herringbone, except no space is left between the individual stitches, so that the back of your work consists of two parallel rows of backstitch.

Threads and Fabrics

Herringbone is a versatile stitch that can be worked in many different DMC threads, and it is particularly effective when stitched in matt cottons using a bold combination of colours. It is possible to decorate surfaces quite extravagantly with this stitch, and it is surprisingly economical on thread.

Like many other stitches in the cross stitch family (page 64), herringbone stitch is relatively easy to stitch when worked on an evenweave fabric, simply because it is possible to plot the distance between strokes by counting the holes in the fabric. When working on plain weave fabric, drawn guidelines are recommended (page 18).

Technique

Herringbone stitch is worked from left to right. When it is executed correctly, you will see that the back of your work appears as two parallel rows of running stitch. Some stitchers prefer to draw parallel guidelines on their fabric before they begin, to help keep their stitching neat and even.

See Also:
Embroidery threads *page 8*
Basic techniques *page 23*
Cross stitch *page 29*
Fish motif towel *page 38*
Cross stitch family *page 64–71*
Laced stitch family *pages 100–109*

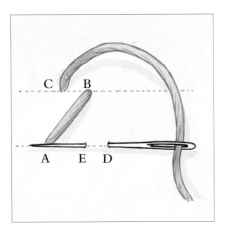

1 *Come up at A, go down at B, come up at C. Cross down and insert at D, coming up at E. Threads will cross at top.*

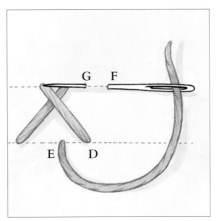

2 *Cross up and insert at F, then come up at G. Pull through. Threads will cross at bottom.*

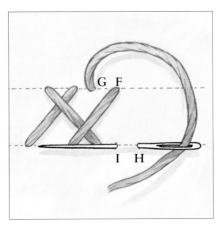

3 *Cross down and insert at H, coming up at I. Continue along row by repeating Steps 1 and 2.*

Feather Stitch

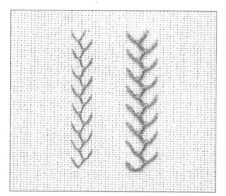

Used for edging and following curves, feather stitch is worked here in stranded cotton (left) and in cotton perlé (right).

FEATHER STITCH BELONGS in the looped stitch family and creates a light feathery line that alternates delicately from side to side. It is also known as *plumage stitch* and *briar stitch*.

Uses

Feather stitch is a popular decorative stitch on traditional English smocks. It is similar to blanket stitch, but the main difference is that the arm of each stitch is placed at an angle instead of being upright. In basic feather stitch this arm alternates from right to left.

Used as a filling stitch, feather stitch is effective for filling large areas of a motif, such as leaf shapes. Work the stitch in a straight line, extending the loops so that they represent leaf veins. Alternatively, feather stitch can be worked in a single curved line to resemble a fern leaf, which makes it particularly useful for ribbon embroidery (page 142). It is also an excellent stitch to use for covering raw selvedges, as it creates a decorative hem or border as an attractive contrast to a plain background.

Feather stitch can also be used to join two pieces of fabric. On crazy quilts, it is used to cover and decorate seams. Colourful threads enhance the design of the patchwork.

Variations

There are a number of useful and more elaborate variations of feather stitch. These include double feather stitch, closed feather stitch, and feathered chain stitch, which are fully described in the stitch library (pages 95, 96). Closed feather stitch can be used as a couching stitch (page 136) and is very effective when worked over several brightly coloured strands of thread, laid on the fabric in parallel lines.

Threads and Fabrics

Choose your threads to complement the weight and texture of your background fabric; any fabric is suitable for this stitch. You can produce fine spidery columns using single strands of DMC cotton, which is useful for creating delicate branches of feathery foliage. The natural wave in this stitch will add a softness to your design. Heavier cottons give a bolder effect.

Technique

To master this stitch, begin by practising it in a column, working from the top to the bottom. Begin by drawing four parallel guidelines on your fabric (page 18), and position your stitches so that they are an equal distance away from the centre line. Always make sure that you insert your needle at a downward angle, pointing towards the centre.

Once you have mastered the basic technique, you will find that feather stitch works well on curves too.

| **See Also:** |
| Embroidery threads *page 8* |
| Basic techniques *page 23* |
| Fish motif towel *page 38* |
| Looped stitch family *pages 86–99* |
| Paisley shawl *page 98* |
| Couching and goldwork *pages 128–141* |
| Ribbon embroidery *pages 142–155* |

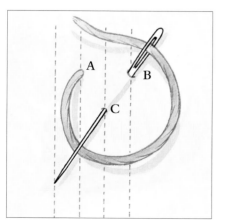

1 *Come up at A, go down at B, and come up at C. Carry thread under needle point from left to right.*

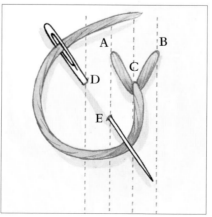

2 *Take needle to left of C, go down at D, and come up at E. Carry thread under needle point from right to left.*

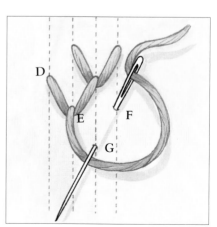

3 *Continue in this way, going down at F, coming up at G. Carry thread under needle point from left to right.*

Running Stitch

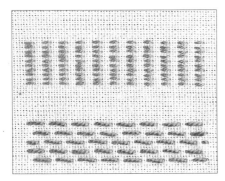

Work this simple stitch in columns (stranded cotton, top) or stagger the rows (cotton perlé, bottom) to add pattern and texture to a design.

RUNNING STITCH takes its name from the action of running the needle and thread in and out of the fabric to create a simple and versatile line stitch. Often confused with darning stitch, running stitch has spaces between each stitch that are equal to the length of the stitches. In darning stitch it is usual to pick up only a few threads of the fabric between each stitch. Running stitch is a member of the straight stitch family (page 46).

Uses

Running stitch is used as a soft motif outline and as a regular filling stitch and forms the basis for quilted designs. It is also used as a foundation stitch for stitches such as St. George's cross (page 65) and the composite whipped running stitch (page 101).

Variations

Darning stitch (page 49) was very fashionable in the 18th century, when stitchers used it to create complete samplers. Many fine examples which show complex fillings and pattern arrangements can be found in museums throughout the world.

Pattern darning is made up of an arrangement of stitches worked in horizontal rows to create geometric patterns. This is achieved by staggering the positions of the individual stitches from row to row. Pattern darning is useful for filling in the background to a main design; gradate the lengths of the stitches for more elaborate effects. To create your own designs, try plotting simple patterns on graph paper.

Damask darning works on the same principle. Rows of stitches are staggered horizontally, vertically, and diagonally to create a pattern.

Threads and Fabrics

The DMC threads you choose add another dimension to your design, as the simplicity of running stitch invites variations of colour and texture. As always, consider your background fabric as you select colours and threads. Running stitch can be worked on both plain weave and evenweave fabrics.

Technique

Running stitch is worked from right to left. When working running stitch, your major consideration should be rhythm, because the rows of stitches are created by repeatedly weaving your needle in and out of the fabric.

Keep your lines of stitching straight and work your stitches evenly. Take only two or three stitches at a time to avoid distorting the weave of the fabric and tangling the thread. When working with delicate or heavy fabrics, you may want to use a stab stitch method as an alternative (page 23).

See Also:
Embroidery threads *page 8*
Basic techniques *page 23*
Pochette bag *page 34*
Straight stitch family *pages 46–55*
Cross stitch family *page 64–71*
Laced stitch family *pages 100–109*
Monogramming *pages 166–177*

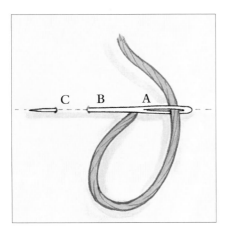

1 *Come up at A, go down at B, then come up at C. Do not pull thread through fabric.*

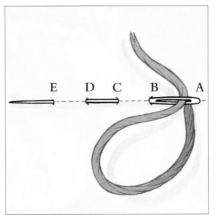

2 *Go down at D, come up at E. Pull thread through gently, so fabric does not pucker.*

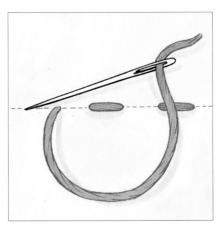

3 *Continue following design line as shown by repeating Steps 1 and 2. Keep stitches even.*

Cross Stitch

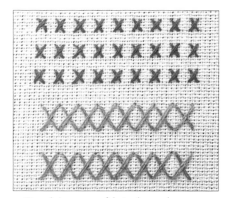

On plain weave fabric shown here, use guidelines for evenly spaced stitches and pull thread through gently, particularly with linked crosses (bottom).

THIS FAVOURITE OF all the embroidery stitches has been known for centuries all over the world. Also known as *sampler stitch*, *Berlin stitch*, and *point de marque*, cross stitch has its own family of stitches (page 64). It is used traditionally in the Greek islands, Scandinavia, central and eastern Europe, and India. In contemporary freestyle embroidery, imaginative examples of cross stitch can be found worked to any scale and at any angle.

Uses

This simple, effective stitch is used to form striking geometric designs. It can, however, be worked finely to create delicate figurative images. Although it is more widely worked as a counted thread technique, it is a useful filling or line stitch on plain weave fabric.

Variations

There are a number of variations on basic cross stitch, and these can be found within the cross stitch family (page 64). They include long-armed cross stitch (page 66) which you can work on a large scale, and two-sided cross stitch (page 68) which is reversible and therefore useful when both sides of an edge will show – on a handkerchief or scarf, for example.

Threads and Fabrics

Cross stitch can be worked in any DMC thread, but for the neatest results you should choose a thread with a smooth texture such as stranded cotton, to enhance the crispness of the stitches. Cross stitch is most often worked on evenweave fabrics on which the threads between the stitches can be counted, thus ensuring neat, regular rows. Evenweave fabrics can be bought in specific counts (threads per inch), and the thickness of your thread should be dictated by the count of your fabric (the higher the count, the finer the thread). Aida fabric has a clear grid of holes and is perfect for beginners or for practising the stitch. Cross stitch can also be worked on plain weave fabric, provided you draw guidelines to make sure your stitches are evenly sized.

Technique

Cross stitches can be worked one at a time (see below) or the first half of several stitches can be worked in a row and then crossed on the return journey (see Steps 1 and 2). Your choice will depend on the complexity of the design. The main rule is to keep all the top stitches crossed in the same direction, so that the surface of your work has an even, regular appearance. If you are working with plain weave fabric, it is important to draw guidelines before you begin (page 18).

See Also:
Embroidery threads *page 8*
Embroidery fabrics *page 10*
Working with a hoop *page 18*
Teddy bear bib *page 36*
Cross stitch family *pages 64–71*
Geometric place mat *page 70*
Monogramming *pages 166–177*

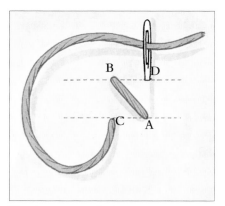

Single cross stitch
Come up at A, down at B, up at C, down at D. The stitch can be reversed so that top half slants from lower right to upper left.

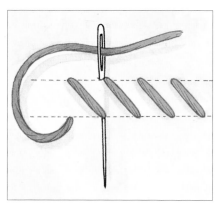

1 *To work a row, make even, equally spaced diagonal stitches, working from bottom to top. Then go down at top left of previous stitch to work back across row.*

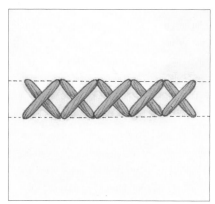

2 *Continue in same manner, slanting stitches in opposite direction to form line of crosses.*

Backstitch

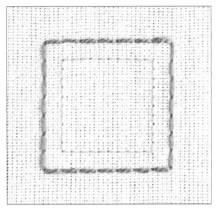

This outline stitch creates bold contours when worked with thread such as cotton perlé (outer), or use delicate flower thread (inner) to suggest form.

BACKSTITCH CLOSELY resembles a row of machine stitching and can be used when a well-defined outline is required. The appearance you are aiming for is a row of small, evenly sized stitches that imitate a drawn line.

A member of the straight stitch family (page 46), backstitch is also known as *stitching* and *point de sable* and is a close relation of Holbein (double running) stitch (page 48), which is used in blackwork and Assisi work.

Backstitch is used in canvaswork, freestyle embroidery, and counted cross stitch to outline shapes, define coloured areas, and represent detail, and it is often worked on a background of needlepoint to create added surface decoration.

Uses

Backstitch is an ideal drawing tool. It can be worked over a densely stitched background to follow a motif shape and is popularly used to edge satin motifs where a gentle gradation is required. Backstitch will follow curved lines with ease and can be used to create circles and spirals within a design.

Variations

Backstitch forms the basis of a number of composite stitches, such as threaded backstitch and Pekinese stitch (page 103), which are both described in the laced stitch family.

You can also experiment by creating your own composite stitches: start by stitching two or three parallel rows of backstitch and then experiment by weaving or looping contrasting threads in and out in various directions. You can use this stitch to outline more intricate stitches such as herringbone (page 26) and to create neat bands and borders.

Backstitch trellis Because of its simplicity, backstitch can be arranged to create a very simple filling that resembles a trellis. You can stitch this with diagonal lines in both directions or, if you prefer, using horizontal and vertical lines. To create a trellis, work several parallel rows of stitches equal distances apart and then work rows in the opposite direction, so that each stitch forms one complete side of a diamond or square.

Threads and Fabrics

Backstitch can be worked in any DMC thread. Choose the thread according to the weight of the background fabric, which can be plain weave or evenweave. Beginners might prefer to work on an evenweave fabric, because the even count of the fabric will help to keep all the stitches equally sized.

Technique

This simple stitch is very suitable for beginners' practice. Work it in straight lines and then curves to improve your technique. Always work from right to left and keep your stitching even.

See Also:
Embroidery threads *page 8*
Embroidery fabrics *page 10*
Teddy bear bib *page 36*
Straight stitch family *pages 46–55*
Parrot cushion *page 52*
Laced stitch family *pages 100–109*
Monogramming *pages 166–177*

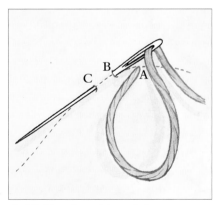

1 *Working from right to left, come up at A, go down at B, then come up at C. Pull thread through.*

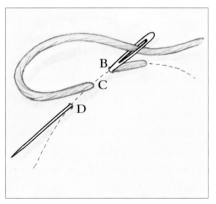

2 *Go down again at B to make a backstitch, then come up at D, ready for the next stitch.*

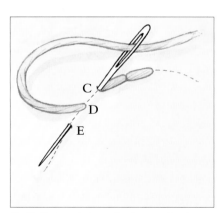

3 *Pull thread through, then go down at C and come up at E. Repeat as above to work a backstitched line.*

Stem Stitch

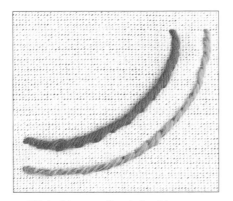

Work this versatile stitch with a matt cotton (outer) for a heavy cord effect. Use a brighter cotton perlé (inner) for textured fillings and elegant outlines.

A POPULAR OUTLINE stitch and part of the straight stitch family (page 46), stem stitch is one of the oldest embroidery stitches, dating from ancient Egypt and Peru.

Stem stitch has neatly overlapping lines that give a smooth, slightly raised finish. Also known as *crewel stitch*, *stalk stitch*, and *South Kensington stitch*, stem stitch is simple and pleasing to work.

Uses

As its name suggests, stem stitch is commonly used to represent the stems of flowers. However, this versatile stitch has many alternative uses. It is ideal for following curves and working intricate linear details, and its subtle texture means that it can be successfully used as a filling stitch within a motif.

Variations

To create a more pronounced line, basic stem stitch can be whipped with another thread (see whipped stem stitch, page 102). The second thread could be a different colour or texture, and you can try using metallic threads.

You can also create a laid band of stem stitch by working a vertical column of horizontal threads and whipping closely packed rows of stem stitch over these threads. In this instance, work the stem stitch from bottom to top and do not let your needle enter the fabric – use the horizontal base stitches as an anchor.
Stem filling stitch In addition to its linear qualities, stem filling stitch is also a good stitch for filling irregular-shaped motifs. Make sure that each stitch is of an equal size, except the first and last stitches in the row, which can be tailored to fit the motif. Work the stitches in tightly packed rows in a uniform direction for a textured effect.

Threads and Fabrics

In theory, you can use any DMC thread to create stem stitch, but if you require texture for filling, it would be wise to experiment with different thicknesses and weights of thread. DMC cotton perlé, for example, will easily cover the surface of the fabric, and crewel wool will provide you with depth and texture. Interesting shading effects can also be achieved with rows of stem stitches in gradating or contrasting colours.

Stem stitch can be worked on any plain weave fabric, and it can also be worked on tightly woven evenweaves.

Technique

To work stem stitch correctly, always keep your working thread below your needle. If you keep the thread above the needle, you will not be working the stitch correctly. Check that the reverse of your fabric shows a neat row of backstitches; this means that your stitching is accurate. Work with a forward and backward motion and keep all the stitches evenly and equally sized.

See Also:
Embroidery threads *page 8*
Embroidery fabrics *page 10*
Working with a hoop *page 18*
Cyclamen picture *page 42*
Straight stitch family *pages 46–55*
Seashell tablecloth *page 62*
Laced stitch family *pages 100–109*

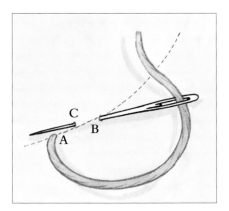

1 *Come up at A, go down at B, come up at C above working thread. Pull thread through.*

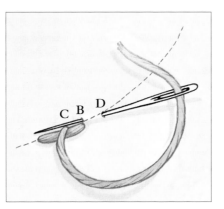

2 *Keeping working thread under needle, go down at D and come up at B to complete second stitch.*

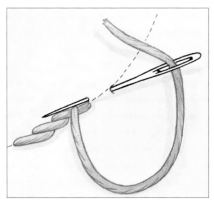

3 *Repeat Step 2 to continue stitching along row as shown, keeping stitches evenly sized.*

Satin Stitch

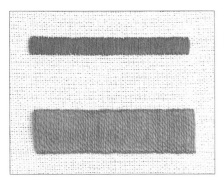

Keep threads parallel and thread tension even for a smooth, silky finish. Using a thicker thread will cover the fabric more quickly.

SATIN STITCH IS the basic stitch of a number of specialist embroidery techniques and has its own stitch family (page 56). It is perhaps best seen in Chinese and Japanese embroidery, where flowers spring from silken robes in stunning combinations of smooth textures and jewel-bright colourings. Also known as *damask stitch*, satin stitch is quite easy to work and is extremely pleasing to the eye.

Uses

Satin stitch is a filling stitch used to create a smooth surface decoration. It is made up of simple straight stitches laid close together in parallel lines to create a solid filling. This stitch is widely used to fill motifs of all shapes, and it is well represented in crewelwork (page 112). It is also particularly useful for monograms (page 166).

Variations

There is a whole family of variations within the satin stitch family (page 56) that will help you to create raised areas of stitching and delicate shading. Light and shadow play a large part in the beauty of this stitch, so do bear this in mind when planning the angles within your motifs. Avoid creating long stitches, as they can become loose and untidy – it is better to split your motif into smaller areas. To fill a large motif, you can use long and short stitch (page 59) as an alternative.

Another useful variation is raised satin stitch (page 57). This is worked over a stitched or padded base and gives your image a three-dimensional effect, making good use of light and shadow. This stitch was extensively used in decorative stumpwork, an embroidery technique that was extremely popular in Europe in the 17th century.

Threads and Fabrics

For the best effects, choose your DMC threads carefully. You are aiming to achieve a smooth, silky finish, so use a lustrous thread that will cover the fabric well. DMC stranded cotton, cotton perlé, and silk threads are excellent options. This stitch can be worked on any plain weave or evenweave fabric, so your main consideration should be practicality.

Technique

Satin stitch is quite simple to execute, but for the best results, stretch your fabric over a frame. The stitches should be placed next to each other to prevent the background fabric showing through.

When filling a motif, begin at its narrowest point and work from the bottom to the top. Take special care to keep the edges smooth. The threads can be placed in any direction but should lie parallel to one another within a motif. It helps to outline your motif with backstitch (page 30) before you work the satin stitch. Place the stitches just over the backstitch line to make sure of an even edge. Draw guidelines on your background fabric before you begin (page 18).

See Also:
Embroidery threads *page 8*
Working with a hoop *page 18*
Cyclamen picture *page 42*
Satin stitch family *page 56–63*
Seashell tablecloth *page 62*
Laced stitch family *pages 100–109*
Crewelwork *pages 112–127*
Monogramming *pages 166–177*

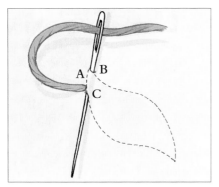

1 *Come up at A, go down at B, and come up at C. Pull thread through gently, ready for next stitch.*

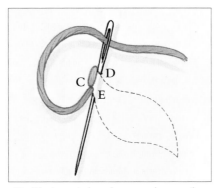

2 *Placing stitches close together, go down at D and come up at E. Follow exact guidelines of motif for even edge.*

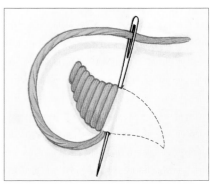

3 *Continue to fill motif in this manner, keeping an even tension so that the surface remains smooth.*

French Knot

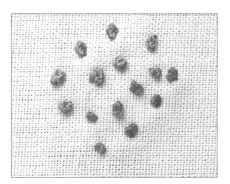

These bead-like stitches are worked here in cotton perlé using two and three wraps of thread.

THIS POPULAR, compact raised stitch resembles a bead lying on its side. Also known as *French dot, knotted stitch, twisted knot stitch,* and *wound stitch,* French knot is the most commonly used stitch in the knotted stitch family (page 72).

French knots are extremely versatile. They can be used individually or in a row where a soft edge is required. You can achieve stunning results by grouping them close together to create a densely covered area. They also look very effective when worked in small groups to form a flower centre.

Uses

Used primarily for surface decoration and to create texture and soft outlines, French knots are also a useful shading tool. Try working individual stitches in a variety of different colours and threads to emphasize shadow and light.

Variations

Long-tailed French knot Also known as *long tack knot stitch* and *Italian knot stitch,* this useful variation is worked in much the same way as a basic French knot. Instead of inserting the needle back at your starting point, place it a short distance away, then push the wrapped threads down the needle to form a knot and insert the needle in the fabric to form a tail.

Colonial knot The colonial knot is more stable than the French knot, and is therefore a better stitch to use when working with heavier threads.

Hold the needle to the right of and under the working thread. Then slip the thread around the needle from right to left to form a figure-eight shape, so that the needle goes through both loops. Go down through fabric close to your starting point, holding working thread as you pull through to form the knot.

Threads and Fabrics

Wool, matt-finish, and high-sheen threads can all be used to great effect. In particular, experiment with DMC cotton perlé and your finished results will resemble little pearls of colour on the surface of the fabric. These stitches can be worked on a small scale using a single strand, but patience is needed to finish a complete composition. French knots can be worked on any fabric, but on loose-woven fabric work over a thread or intersection or the knot will pull through to the back of the fabric.

Technique

Achieving the perfect French knot requires some practice, and it helps to stretch your fabric over a frame or hoop so that both your hands are free.

You can wrap the thread around the needle in a clockwise or a counter-clockwise direction, as long as you are consistent. You can increase the knot size by using more strands of thread in the needle, using a heavier thread (see *colonial knot*), or increasing the number of wraps. Take extra care with multiple wraps, because the thread is more likely to tangle. Some stitchers prefer to wrap the thread around the needle only once.

See Also:
Embroidery threads *page 8*
Working with a hoop *page 18*
Cutwork butterfly tablecloth *page 40*
Knotted stitch family *pages 72–85*
Valentine blanket *page 82*

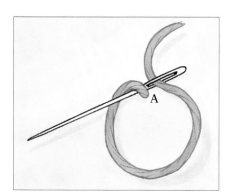

1 *Come up at A and wrap thread around needle once in counter-clockwise direction.*

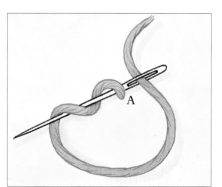

2 *Wrap thread around needle a second time in same direction, keeping needle away from fabric.*

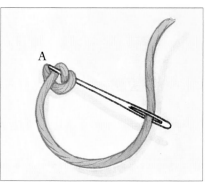

3 *Push wraps together and slide to end of needle. Go down close to starting point, pulling thread through to form knot.*

Pochette Bag

This practical bag uses just four variations of basic chain stitch. Stitch in rows to create a patterned fabric, then fold and sew to complete.

Size

7¼ x 4⅛ in (18.5 x 10.5 cm)

Materials and Equipment

7 in (18 cm) square black felt
7½ in (19 cm) square black felt
7½ in (19 cm) square fusible webbing
½ in (1 cm) round wooden bead
Medium-sized crewel needle
Black sewing thread
Tailor's chalk
Metal ruler

Thread

DMC stranded cotton:

■	310, 1 skein	▨	90, 1 skein
▨	3731, 2 skeins	■	3804, 3 skeins
▨	223, 3 skeins	▨	3350, 2 skeins

Preparation

1 *First position the 7 in (18 cm) square of felt on a flat surface with a corner at the centre top. With tailor's chalk draw a line down the centre from top to bottom.*

Stitching

2 *Using six strands of fuchsia thread (3804), work a single row of large heavy chain stitches over the chalked line.*

3 *Mark off 24 evenly spaced vertical lines on either side of the central row of chain stitch and stitch over them, working from top to bottom and following the stitch and colour chart. When two colours are listed together, use the first for the foundation row and the second for the lacing. For feathered chain, alternate colours 3731 and 3350. Use six strands of thread throughout, except for the backstitch on backstitched chain, where you should use two strands of thread.*

4 *Repeat Step 3 to work the right-hand side of the felt, again working out from the central row of heavy chain stitches. When complete, your embroidered piece should be symmetrical.*

Stitch and Colour Chart

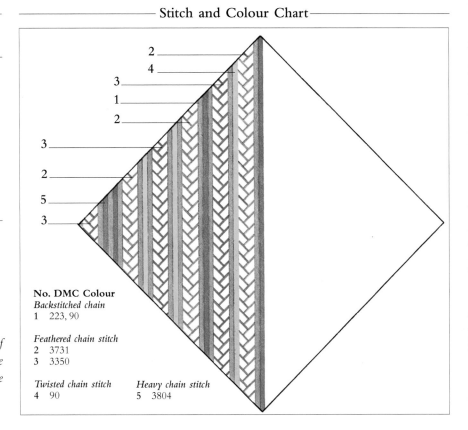

No. DMC Colour
Backstitched chain
1   223, 90

Feathered chain stitch
2   3731
3   3350

Twisted chain stitch   *Heavy chain stitch*
4   90   5   3804

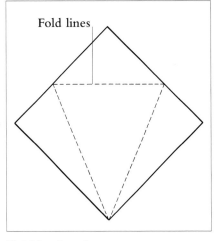

Fold lines

Finishing Step 5

Finishing

5 *Place face down with fusible webbing on top, then the 7½ in (19 cm) square of black felt. Press to fuse in place. Trim larger felt square to match. With plain felt uppermost, fold sides to centre (see left). Pin and slipstitch front seam with sewing thread.*

6 *Make a plait using fifteen, six-strand 20 in (51 cm) lengths of leftover cotton, including the black cotton (310). Bind with fuchsia, 1½ in (4 cm) from the ends. Open out the end threads to form tassels. Make a second plait using fifteen 28 in (71 cm) lengths. Twist the two plaits together, and place each end of the short plait level with top corner of bag. A short section of the long plait will hang free.*

7 *Stitch both plaits to top of bag with black sewing thread. Work buttonhole stitch over two lengths of six-strand fuchsia and use for button loop on centre point of flap. Cover bead in two strands of fuchsia by repeatedly sewing through central hole and over bead. Stitch bead to front of bag, aligning with loop.*

Teddy Bear Bib

Use crossed stitches and simple backstitch outlines in fresh primary colours to create this appealing design that children will love.

Size

Motif: 7½ x 7 in (19 x 18 cm)

Materials and Equipment

12 x 14 in (30.5 x 35.5 cm) white
   27-count evenweave fabric
12 x 14 in (30.5 x 35.5 cm) white cotton
2¼ yd (2 m) red bias binding
Red sewing thread
Ready-made bib
Medium-sized tapestry needle
Stretcher, scroll, or slate frame

Thread

DMC coton à broder, 1 skein:

■	666	▨	436
■	336	■	898
▨	444	☐	White (blanc)
■	911		

Preparation

1 Trace design; enlarge to 153 per cent. Transfer to fabric (page 14).

Stitching

2 Fill in the trousers with navy cross stitch in blocks of four stitches, leaving four threads of fabric between each hole. Position the blocks alternately on each row to form a checked pattern.

3 Outline the trousers and braces with navy backstitch (336). Work a row of navy chain stitch in the centre of each strap. Outline the shirt in red backstitch (666); fill with vertical rows of red insertion stitch.

4 Backstitch the vertical stripes between the insertion stitches, working two navy outer rows and the centre row in white between the stripes. Work the paws and feet in brown vertical straight stitches (898); surround with sand backstitch (436).

5 Outline the head and ears in sand backstitch, then fill the centre of the head and the outer ears with backstitch. Outline

Stitch and Colour Chart

No. DMC Colour			
Zigzag stitch	*Blocks of 4 cross*	*Insertion stitch*	*Backstitch*
1 336	*stitches*	8 666	11 336
	5 666		12 911
Star filling stitch	6 336	*Chain stitch*	13 444
2 911		9 336	14 666
3 444	*Leaf stitch*		15 436
	7 911	*Straight stitch*	16 898
Ermine stitch		10 898	17 White
4 444			

the eyes in backstitch. Fill pupils, inner ears, and nose in straight stitch.

6 Outline the bricks with backstitch and fill the panels with star filling stitch. Work the balloons in the same way, using the filling stitches indicated on the stitch and colour chart.

Finishing

7 Trim the fabric, using the ready-made bib as a pattern. Back it with white cotton, and then finish the edges with bias binding, leaving 15 in (38 cm) for the ties. Alternatively, you may prefer to stitch the embroidery separately, and then appliqué it (page 170) onto a ready-made bib.

Fish Motif Towel

This repeating border pattern uses feather stitch to create the rippling water around the swimming fish, while the feather stitch fins give texture to their bodies.

Size

Panel: 5½ x 18½ in (14 x 47 cm)

Materials and Equipment

1 hand towel (ours measures 19 x 40 in/
    48.5 x 101 cm)
9½ x 22 in (24 x 56 cm) 22-count
    cream evenweave fabric
9½ x 22 in (24 x 56 cm) wooden frame
No. 24 tapestry needle (for border)
No. 7 crewel needle
Staple gun or drawing pins
Tracing paper
Pencil

Thread

DMC stranded cotton, 1 skein:

☐ 746		☐ 747	
☐ 725		☐ 3766	
☐ 782		☐ 517	

Stitch and Colour Chart

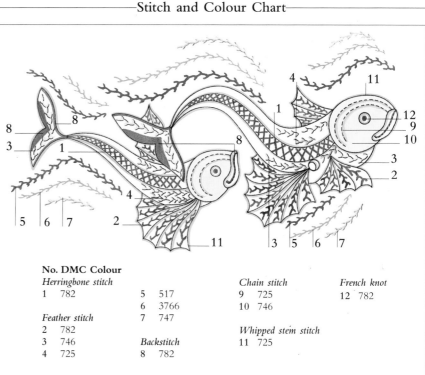

No. DMC Colour

Herringbone stitch			
1	782	5	517
		6	3766
Feather stitch		7	747
2	782		
3	746	*Backstitch*	
4	725	8	782

Chain stitch		*French knot*	
9	725	12	782
10	746		
Whipped stem stitch			
11	725		

Preparation

1 Stretch fabric over frame using staples or drawing pins to secure it. (Cover the heads with masking tape so threads do not snag on them.) Trace outline from the chart and enlarge to 210 per cent. Tack into position on fabric. Work over outlines in running stitch, then tear away tracing paper.

Stitching

2 Use two strands of thread throughout. Work whipped stem stitch in yellow (725) for the solid outlines of each fish. Work a row of bronze herringbone stitch (782) to form the fish's spine. Fill the fins with a row of bronze feather stitch, graduating the sizes of these stitches to fit. Work small single rows of yellow feather stitch (725) and cream (746) for the scales.

3 Work three rows of backstitch in bronze thread inside the central V shape of the fish's tail. Still using bronze thread, work one row of backstitch inside the V shape at the base of the tail. Then fill the remaining area of the tail with a single row of feather stitch

in cream, as indicated on the stitch and colour chart shown above.

4 To work the head, begin by working a row of yellow chain stitch (725) over each of the dotted lines on the head (see the stitch and colour chart above). Then fill the rest of the head with rows of cream-coloured chain stitch (746), with two more rows above the yellow chain-stitch row. Then define the fish's mouth with a single row of backstitch in bronze (782) over the dotted line in the mouth. To create the eye, work a single large French knot, again using the bronze thread.

5 Complete the main design by working rows of feather stitch over the wavy lines to represent the water. Use three shades of turquoise thread: the darkest shade (517) for the area closest to the outline of the fish, then a row of medium turquoise (3766) followed by a row of pale turquoise (747).

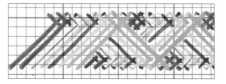

Chart for herringbone border

6 Leaving five holes of fabric free at the top and bottom of the design, work the border in herringbone stitch as shown above, placing each row over and just to the right of preceding row. From left, stitch rows 1 and 2 in 517; row 3, 746; row 4, 725; row 5, 782; row 6, 747; rows 7 and 8, 3766. Each hole in the fabric is used twice.

Finishing

7 Remove from frame. Turn under top and bottom edges so one line of holes is visible; press. Using the row of stitches as a guide, stitch by hand or machine along this row through the border and towel. Trim side edges, turn under, press, and stitch in place.

Cutwork Butterfly Tablecloth

Cutting away fabric around stitched outlines gives this delicate stencilled effect known as cutwork. First, work foundation rows of running stitch to help secure cut edges.

Size

Cloth: 45 in (114.5 cm) square
Motif: 8 in (20.5 cm) square

Materials and Equipment

45 in (114.5 cm) square closely
 woven white tablecloth
Medium-sized crewel needle
Embroidery scissors
Tracing paper, pencil
Masking tape, water-soluble pen

Thread

DMC stranded cotton, 1 skein:

- 3805
- 725
- 208
- 3790
- Blanc
  B5200, 2 skeins

Colour Chart

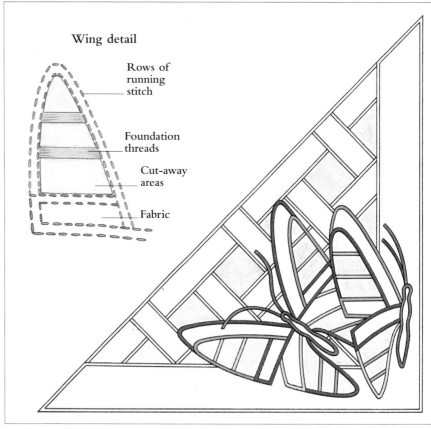

Wing detail

Rows of running stitch

Foundation threads

Cut-away areas

Fabric

Preparation

1 *Trace design from colour chart, and enlarge to 150 per cent. Place tracing under a corner of the back of the cloth, 2 in (5 cm) in from hemmed edge. Tape into position. Using a lightbox or natural light source, draw the design onto fabric using a water-soluble pen. Remove tracing. Repeat for all four corners.*

Stitching

2 *Using one single strand of embroidery thread in colour indicated on the chart, outline design with small running stitches, placing each line of stitching just inside drawn line. (These lines of stitching help to secure cut edges and form guidelines for buttonhole stitch. Shaded areas will be cut away later.)*

3 *Where lines of stitching fall on cut-away areas, omit running stitch and work foundation threads for cutwork bars (see wing detail above). Using two strands of thread in appropriate colour, secure thread at one end of bar, and then stitch eight parallel foundation threads over fabric, leaving threads free over fabric surface. Fasten off. Repeat as necessary.*

4 *For drawn lines over white background, outline with small running stitches.*

5 *Using two strands of embroidery thread, start to cover foundation lines with buttonhole stitch. Position stitches so "purl" edge of stitch falls around outer edge of a shape or against a cut-away area. Make stitches equal length to completely cover the two lines of running stitch. Position stitches close together so the fabric does not show through. Where there is a cutwork bar, work buttonhole around laid threads only, leaving background fabric free behind the stitching.*

Cutting and Finishing

6 *When complete, carefully trim away the fabric (the shaded areas on the chart), taking great care not to damage stitching. Press finished work over a damp cloth on the wrong side.*

Stitch detail

Cyclamen Picture

Long and short stitches create the painterly quality of this design. Two shades of colour are sometimes used in the same needle to give a subtle, graduated effect.

Size

Framed picture: 9 x 11 in
(23 x 28 cm)
Panel: 4¼ x 6 in (11 x 15 cm)

Materials and Equipment

10 x 12 in (25.5 x 30.5 cm) medium-
weight fabric in cream
Fine crewel needle
Embroidery hoop
Tracing paper, pencil

Thread

DMC stranded cotton, 1 skein:

▨ 3688	▨ 3346
▨ 3689	▨ 3345
▨ 3687	▨ 433
▨ 3347	

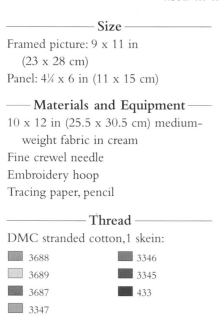

Preparation

1 *Trace the design (the design shown right is actual size) and transfer to the centre of the fabric. Mount fabric in hoop.*

Stitching

2 *Use two strands of cotton throughout. For stem stitch (11 on chart) two colours are listed together; here, work with one strand of each colour in the needle. Where two colours are listed together for stitches other than stem stitch, work two separate rows of stitches in colour indicated.*

3 *Work the flower heads in long and short stitch in a variety of pink threads (see the stitch and colour chart, right). Begin by working the buttonhole circle at the bottom of each flower head, and then work each petal, stitching upwards from the circle. Keep the edges of each petal gently graduated and well defined.*

4 *Work the leaves in graduating colours, using long and short stitch. Keep the definition between each coloured band loose for subtle gradation. Work from the bottom*

Stitch and Colour Chart

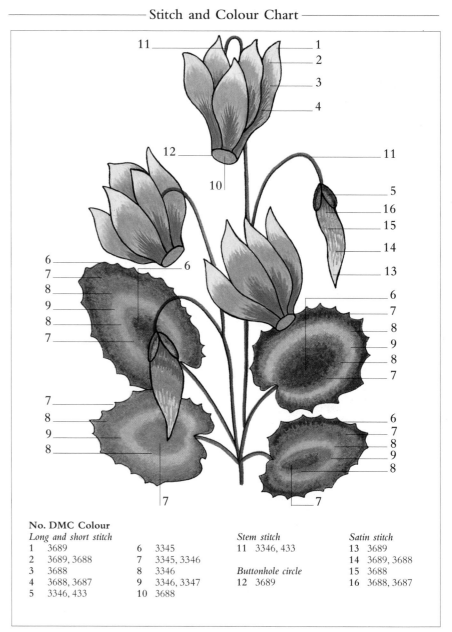

No.	DMC Colour		
Long and short stitch			
1	3689	6	3345
2	3689, 3688	7	3345, 3346
3	3688	8	3346
4	3688, 3687	9	3346, 3347
5	3346, 433	10	3688

Stem stitch		*Satin stitch*	
11	3346, 433	13	3689
		14	3689, 3688
Buttonhole circle		15	3688
12	3689	16	3688, 3687

centre of each leaf and span the stitches outwards. For the bud, work diagonal bars of satin stitch in shades of pink, and at 13 and 14 on the chart work two rows of satin stitch. The angle of the stitches should slope down from left to right.

5 *For the stems, work two rows of stem stitch in medium green (3346) and*

brown (433). Where a stem crosses a leaf, work it over the top of the long and short stitch so that it is pronounced.

Finishing

6 *Block the finished embroidery carefully (page 181). Then mount your work on an acid-free board (page 181) and frame as you desire.*

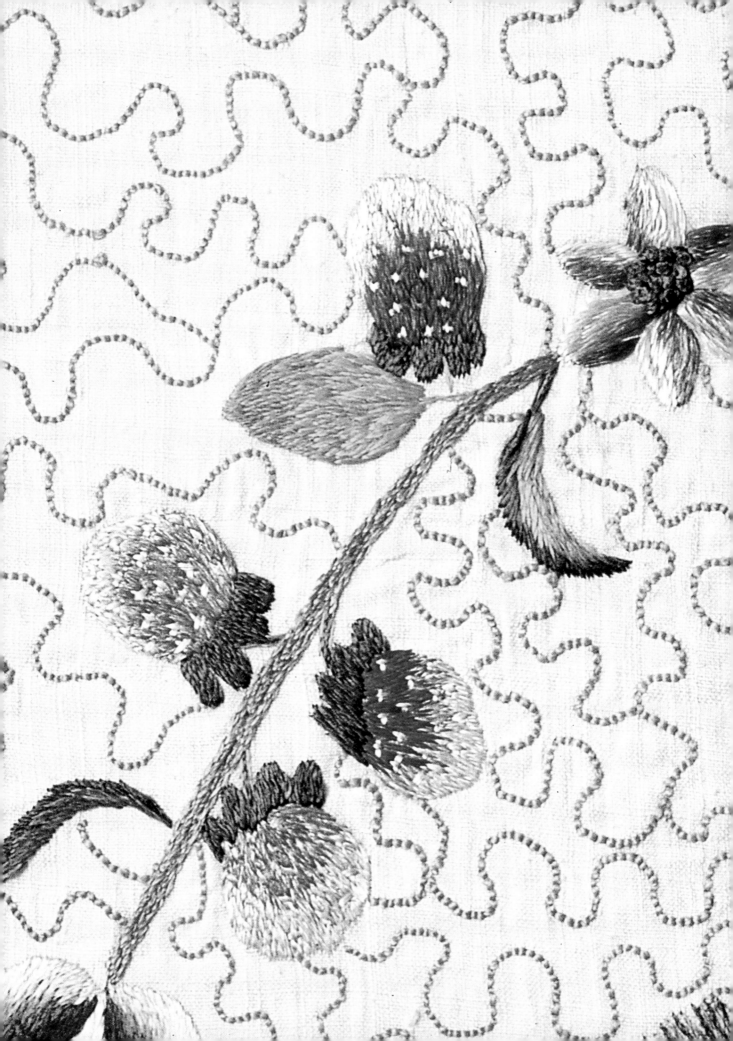

Stitch Library

The stitches illustrated in this section
are divided into six "families" – straight,
satin, cross, knotted, laced, and looped
– each with its own characteristics and
uses. The stitches are arranged in order of
increasing difficulty.

There is a project for each stitch family
to demonstrate the stitches, showing
the wonderful range of versatile effects
that can be created.

Straight Stitch Family

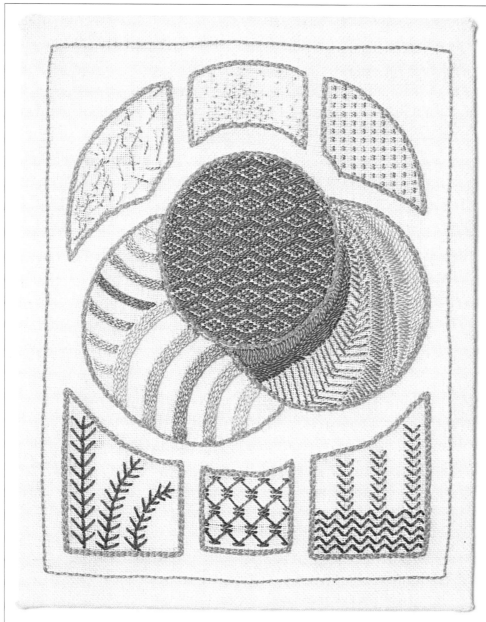

Straight Stitch Family Sampler

There are 10 straight stitches to learn in this family, and all are demonstrated here to show the range of textures and patterns you can achieve. Arrowhead stitch, for example, gives a sharp, geometric effect when stitched in columns but can create a gentle wave effect when worked in a block. The inner and outer orange borders use double running stitch (page 48). All the stitches are executed in DMC cotton perlé on an evenweave fabric.

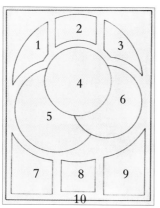

1 Straight stitch *page 47*
2 Seed stitch *page 50*
3 Dot stitch *page 51*
4 Darning stitch (pattern darning) *page 49*
5 Split stitch *page 48*
6 Open fishbone stitch *page 51* (see also fishbone stitch, *page 60*)
7 Fern stitch *page 49*
8 Chevron stitch *page 50*
9 Arrowhead stitch *page 49*
10 Double running stitch (inner and outer orange borders) *page 48*

STRAIGHT STITCHES are the oldest, the most basic, and also the most versatile of all the embroidery stitches. Stem stitch, for example, can be traced back to 900 B.C., when it was used extensively in Egyptian and Peruvian embroidery. Split stitch was very popular in the Middle Ages for depicting figurative images, and in the 18th century, the humble darning stitch was as popular as cross stitch is today. Samplers were created using clever variations of stitch length, direction, and colour designed to catch the light and make subtle patterns on the fabric.

Straight stitches can be used for both filling and outlining. In contemporary embroidery, straight stitch is often used as a highlighting tool, stitched randomly across a dense background to depict the movement of rain or grass. It can also be used to give a bold stroke of colour or contrasting texture.

Threads and Fabrics

Your choice of threads depends on the design. If you need to create a number of smooth, even outlines, for example, you could try working with DMC stranded cotton or flower threads to give a soft and even finish.

Straight stitches work well on both plain weave and evenweave fabrics.

If you are a beginner, you may find it easier to work with an evenweave fabric, since you are able to count the threads of the fabric in order to map out your stitching. Plain weave fabric, however, is a much more flexible medium, because its finer weave is more suitable for working fine detail, such as figurative images or intricate curves.

Techniques

Straight stitches are perfect for the novice embroiderer because they form the basis of many more complicated embroidery stitches. Try placing equal sized stitches equal distances apart, or work stitches such as stem stitch (page 31) in spirals and circles to see if you can create a smooth, unblemished line.

Basic straight stitch (below) can be worked at any angle, as in sunray motifs, for example, or you can work the stitches closely together to form satin stitch (page 32).

Try using split stitch (page 48) to outline delicate work, or fern stitch (page 49) for long-stemmed, fragile leaf shapes. Open fishbone stitch (page 51) is an alternative for leaf shapes.

You could also experiment with arrowhead and chevron stitches (pages 49, 50) for borders, or work them in even rows as filling stitches. Chevron stitch is also used to create diamond or honeycomb patterns in smocking. Dot stitch (page 51) comprises two tiny adjacent straight stitches and, when completed, resembles a coffee bean. Scatter stitches randomly over a plain background, or work them in clusters to highlight the edge of your design.

Seed stitch (page 50) can be used as a light filling within an enclosed outline. Double running (or Holbein) stitch (page 48) can look particularly effective when it is worked alongside darning stitch (page 49), especially when double running stitch is used as a border with darning stitch worked as a filling stitch (or pattern darning), as in the sampler shown opposite.

When you have mastered the stitches in this family, turn to the laced stitch family (page 100) to whip and weave threads of different colours and textures through your existing stitches.

See Also:
Running stitch *page 28*
Backstitch *page 30*
Stem stitch *page 31*
Parrot cushion *page 52*
Laced stitch family *pages 100–109*
Couching and goldwork *pages 128–141*
Monogramming *pages 166–177*

Straight Stitch
Stroke Stitch

This most basic of all embroidery stitches can be worked to any length, at any angle, and with any thread.

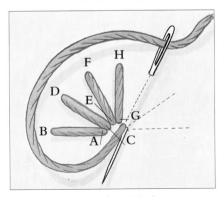

1 *To create a straight-stitch fan, come up at A, go down at B, up at C. Repeat, going down at D, up at E, down at F, up at G, and down at H.*

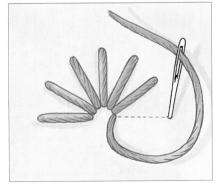

2 *Continue working in this way until you have worked a half-circle of evenly spaced stitches. Tie off thread on back of work.*

Double Running Stitch

Holbein Stitch, Chiara Stitch, Two-sided Line Stitch, Two-sided Stroke Stitch

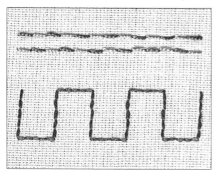

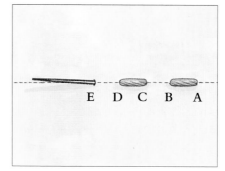

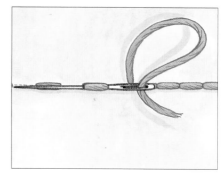

This stitch consists of one row of evenly spaced running stitches, with a second pass used to fill the spaces. Draw guidelines to help keep your stitches regular.

1 *Come up at A, go down at B, up at C, down at D, and up at E. Continue along row, keeping space between stitches same length as stitches.*

2 *For return journey, turn fabric 180° if desired. Repeat Step 1, but fill in spaces between existing stitches, keeping thread tension even.*

Split Stitch

Kensington Outline Stitch

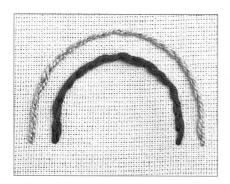

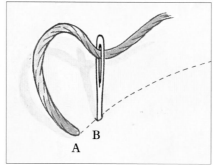

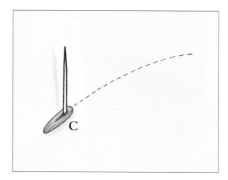

Split stitch is similar to stem stitch, but here the needle splits the thread of the previous stitch to create a neat line.

1 *Come up at A and go down at B, forming a straight stitch on outline of motif. Pull thread through.*

2 *Come up at C (just short of half-way between A and B), piercing thread of previous stitch as shown.*

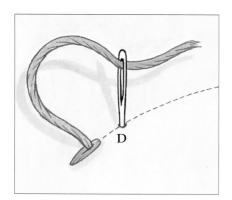

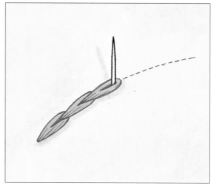

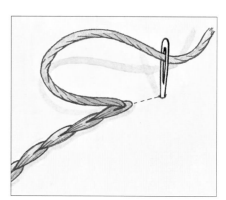

3 *Pull thread through and go down at D to form next stitch, following outline of motif.*

4 *Repeat Steps 2 and 3, continuing to pierce last stitch worked. Pull thread through gently; do not break thread fibres.*

5 *When row is complete, work a final straight stitch, taking thread to back of fabric, and tie off.*

Darning Stitch
Tacking Stitch, Damask Stitch

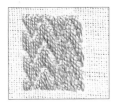
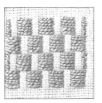
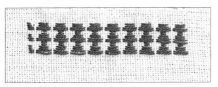

This long running stitch can be used as a decorative filling stitch by working rows of alternately spaced stitches close together to form geometric, regular, or more randomly spaced patterns.

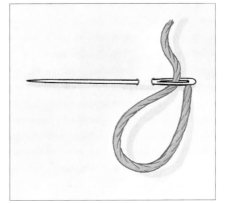

1 *First thread needle in and out of fabric to create single row of horizontal straight stitches. Work from right to left, and keep stitching even.*

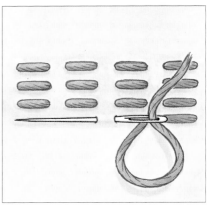

2 *To make evenly sized and spaced rows as shown, continue working back and forth along area to be filled, until pattern is completed.*

Arrowhead Stitch

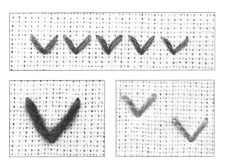

Two straight stitches lying at an angle to each other form the arrowhead shape of this stitch, usually worked in pairs, placed horizontally or vertically.

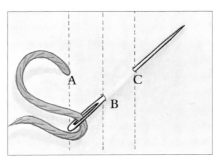

1 *Come up at A, go down at B (the central point between the two stitches), and come up at C on the right-hand guideline. Pull thread through.*

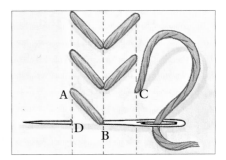

2 *Go back down at B, then take needle across horizontally and directly below A, ready to begin next stitch at D. Repeat from Step 1 as desired.*

Fern Stitch

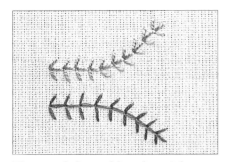

Three angled, equal length straight stitches meet at a central base point. Groups of stitches are worked top to bottom to form a fern-leaf shape. Draw guidelines before you begin.

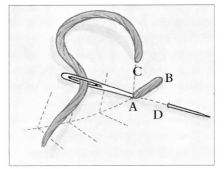

1 *Come up at A on central stem of design. Go down at B, then come up at C, go back down at A, and come up at D as shown.*

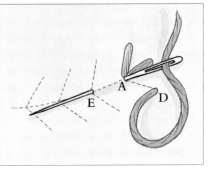

2 *Go down at A again and up at E on centre guideline, ready for next group of stitches. Repeat from B in Step 1.*

Chevron Stitch

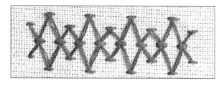

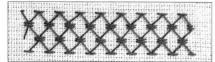

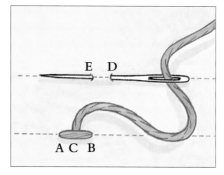

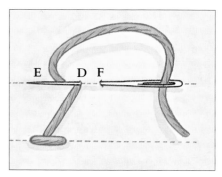

This stitch is made up of two diagonal lines worked in opposite directions and joined across top and bottom with small horizontal straight stitches. Draw guidelines before beginning.

1 *Come up at A, go down at B, come up at C (centre of horizontal stitch just made). Do not split thread. Go down at D, come up at E.*

2 *Go down at F and come up at D (centred between E and F), ready to begin next stitch.*

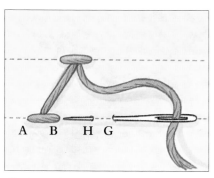

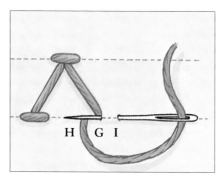

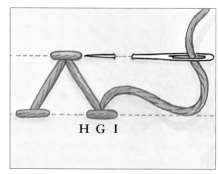

3 *Cross down and insert at G, and then come up at H as shown. (Length of stitch should be same as A–B.) Pull thread through.*

4 *Go down at I and come up at G (centre of bottom horizontal stitch), and pull thread through. You have now completed a single chevron stitch.*

5 *To work a row, repeat from Step 1 to end of row. To finish, take thread under at I (end of Step 4) and tie off on back of fabric.*

Seed Stitch
Speckling Stitch, Seeding Stitch

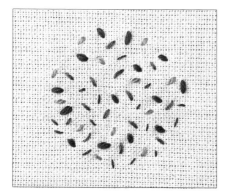

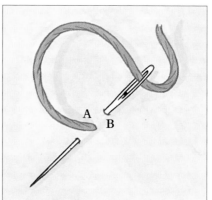

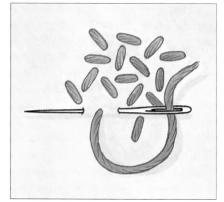

This is a filling stitch consisting of tiny straight stitches, usually of even length, placed randomly at contrasting angles.

1 *Come up at A and go down at B. Come up again where you want next stitch to start.*

2 *Work stitches at random angles, as shown here, to fill in design shape or background area.*

Dot Stitch
Rice Grain Stitch

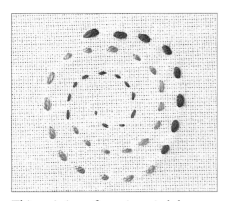

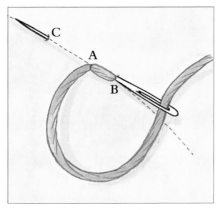

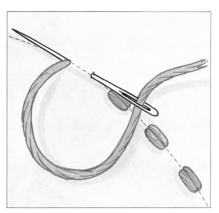

This variation of running stitch has a slightly raised finish. It is created by working two backstitches side by side, with each stitch sharing the same entrance and exit holes.

1 *Come up at A and go down at B. Come up again at A and down again at B, then come up at C.*

2 *Work in an evenly spaced line to create a dotted-line effect, or place dots at random.*

Open Fishbone Stitch

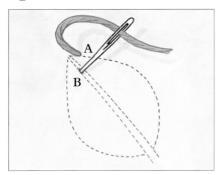

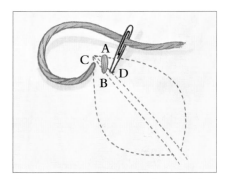

This straight stitch pattern is worked diagonally and in alternate directions. Stitches are spaced slightly apart, so background fabric shows through. Draw guidelines before beginning.

1 *First come up at A and go down at B, to make a small sloping diagonal stitch. Pull thread through.*

2 *Come up at C (opposite but slightly below A), and then go down at D. Follow central guidelines precisely.*

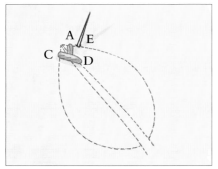

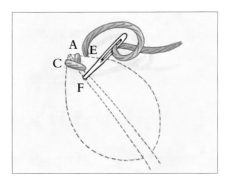

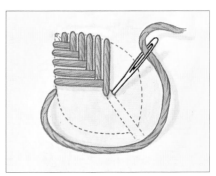

3 *Come up at E, close to A. Remember to place stitches exactly on motif outline for even edges.*

4 *Go down at F so that stitch lies parallel to A–B, allowing some background fabric to show through.*

5 *Work alternate sides to build shape. Stitches should cross each other evenly to give consistent ridge, or leaf vein.*

Parrot Cushion

This project uses simple sewing techniques and basic embroidery stitches to create and enhance the design. The parrot motif can also be used as a decorative panel for a box top or a bag.

16 x 16 in (40.5 x 40.5 cm) square

Materials and Equipment

20 x 60 in (51 x 152.5 cm) wide navy cotton fabric
12 in (30.5 cm) square of felt in red, yellow, orange, blue, and green
Scrap of brown felt
12 in (30.5 cm) square fusible webbing
Matching sewing thread
Crewel needle (suitable for weight of the fabric)
16 in (40.5 cm) square cushion pad
Pinking shears

Thread

DMC stranded cotton, 1 skein:

■	817	■	798
▢	973	■	702
■	971	■	838

(Or colours to match the felt squares)

Preparation

1 From the navy fabric, cut a 20 in (51 cm) square for the cushion front and mark the centre lines in both directions with a line of tacking. Then enlarge the cutting pattern to 205 per cent.

2 Trace each section of the parrot onto the paper side of the fusible webbing, leaving a narrow margin between each piece. (As the cutting pattern is marked on the paper side of the fusible webbing, it is a mirror image of the final design.) Label each pattern piece with the relevant colour, following the cutting pattern (right). Then cut out the individual pattern pieces.

3 Pin each pattern piece to the relevant felt colour and cut out, following cutting pattern above. For the dotted lines on the pattern, cut with pinking shears; cut the solid lines with scissors. When cutting around zigzag lines, add a ¼ in (6 mm) seam

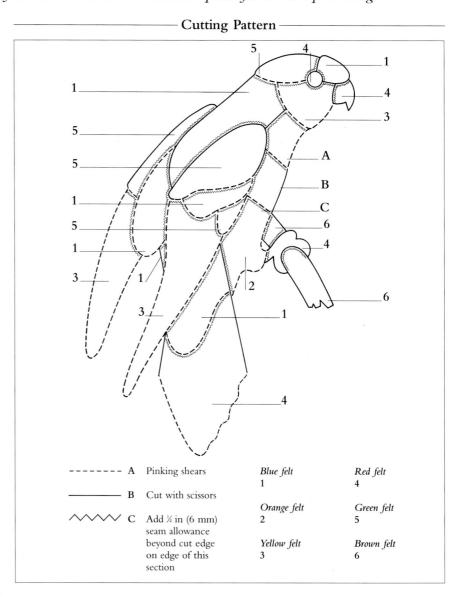

- - - - - A	Pinking shears	*Blue felt* 1	*Red felt* 4
———— B	Cut with scissors		
⋀⋁⋀⋁ C	Add ¼ in (6 mm) seam allowance beyond cut edge on edge of this section	*Orange felt* 2	*Green felt* 5
		Yellow felt 3	*Brown felt* 6

allowance: these edges will be slipped under cut edges of the adjacent section.

4 Peel the paper from the back of each piece of webbing and assemble the parrot centrally on the right side of the front panel of the cushion. Match the centre lines on the chart (overleaf) to the centre lines marked on the cushion front in Step 1.

5 Check that all seam allowances have been slipped under the relevant adjacent

edges. Cover with a cloth and press to fuse in place. Let the fabric cool.

Stitching

6 Using two strands of embroidery thread in a colour to match the felt shape, attach the beak, branch, and claw with backstitch worked close to the felt edge. Stitch dividing lines on the beak and claw as marked. Attach all other straight edges with blanket stitch and all pinked edges with backstitch, echoing the pinking with a line of zigzag stitches.

Stitch and Colour Chart

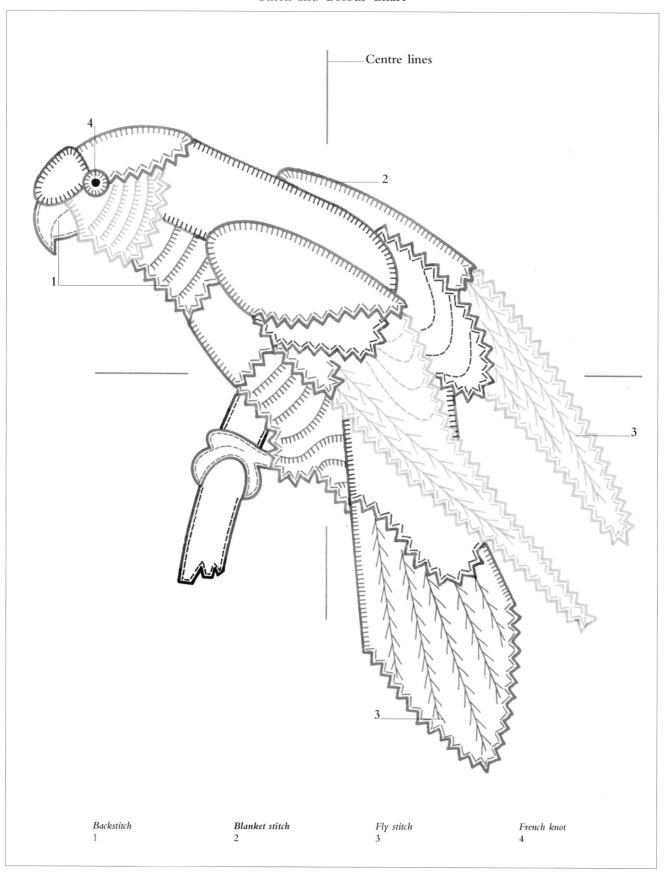

Centre lines

4

2

1

3

3

Backstitch	Blanket stitch	Fly stitch	French knot
1	2	3	4

7 Now work the detail embroidery. Still using two strands of thread and working in a colour that matches the felt, work lines of blanket stitch across the yellow and orange face, throat, and leg sections, placing the straight edges of the stitches as shown.

8 Work the five rows of stitching on the red tail section in fly stitch, starting each line at the lowest end of the tail.

9 Backstitch the upper four lines on the yellow front wing section and fly stitch the remaining two lines, again starting at the lowest end of the wing.

10 Work the three lines of stitching on the yellow back wing section in fly stitch, starting at the end of the wing. Work the three lines on the blue back-wing section in backstitch.

11 Using brown thread, work a large French knot in the centre of the red eye. When the embroidery is complete, press the work carefully.

Finishing

12 After the parrot is stitched, trim the cushion front panel to form a 17 in (43 cm) square. Remove the tacking threads marking the centre lines. From the remaining navy fabric, cut two 12 x 17 in (30.5 x 43 cm) pieces for the cushion back. Following the cutting pattern for the border feathers above, enlarge to 168 per cent, then cut out the pattern piece for the corner and side feathers. Cut the solid lines with scissors and the dotted lines with pinking shears. From the remaining felt, cut out four corner feathers from red, clipping into the dot at the corner, and 36 side feathers in the following colours: 4 red, 8 orange, 8 yellow, 8 green, and 8 blue.

13 Along one long edge of each cushion back piece, fold ⅛ in (3 mm) to the wrong side, turn under the raw edge, and stitch in place. Press. Then overlap the two finished edges of the cushion back pieces to form a 17 in (43 cm) square and tack them together along the edges.

Cutting Pattern for Border Feathers

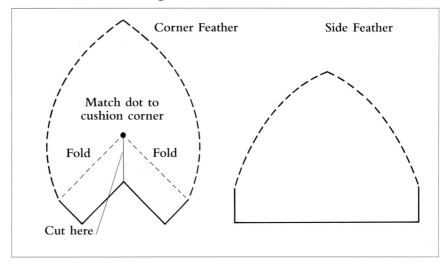

Corner Feather   Side Feather

Match dot to cushion corner

Fold   Fold

Cut here

Detail of Border Feathers

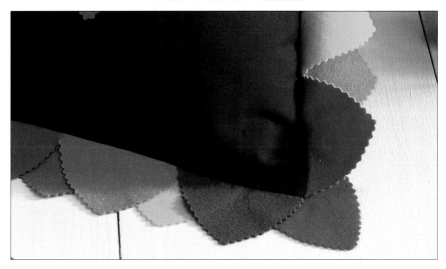

14 Lay the cushion front right side up. Place five side feathers along each side of the cushion, matching the straight edges of the feathers with the cut edges of the fabric. Use the following sequence of colours, working from left to right along each side: green, orange, red, yellow, and blue. Tack them in place.

15 Open the cut in the corner feather shapes and fold back the edges (see the diagram above). Place these feathers over the other feathers at the cushion corners, matching the folded edges of the corner feathers to the corner edges of the cushion. Pin these corner feathers in place. They will be tacked in place with the set of feathers in Step 16.

16 Now lay another set of feathers over the first set, placing them midway between the first set of feathers, positioning the first and last feathers about ½ in (1.3 cm) in from the corners. Use the following colour sequence, working from left to right along each side: yellow, blue, green, and then orange. Tack this set of feathers in place.

17 Match the cushion back and front, right sides together and enclosing the feathers. Then stitch the front to the back, taking a ½ in (1.3 cm) seam. Pivot the corner stitching accurately. Finish all raw edges to complete. Turn the cushion right side out, press carefully over a towel or thick cloth, and then insert the cushion pad.

Satin Stitch Family

Satin Stitch Family Sample

This sample shows the different textures and gradations of colour you can achieve using the stitches in this family. Satin stitches are ideal for filling and raising areas of a motif; raised satin stitch and fishbone stitch are popularly used for creating three-dimensional effects.

The stitches are worked in DMC cotton perlé to emphasize the play of light and shadow on the lustrous sheen of the thread.

1 Basket filling stitch *page 58*
2 Raised satin stitch *page 57*
3 Raised fishbone stitch *page 61*
4 Fishbone stitch *page 60*
5 Encroaching buttonhole stitch *page 60*
6 Flat stitch *page 59*
7 Encroaching satin stitch *page 58*
8 Romanian stitch *page 61*
9 Long and short satin stitch *page 59*

SATIN STITCHES are used primarily as filling stitches to create a raised solid area in a design. Because they maximize light and shadow, these stitches often give a lustrous sheen.

Several stitches in this family are commonly used for shading. Long and short satin stitch (page 59) is the most popular of the shading stitches; it is made up of one row of long and short stitches, followed by rows of long stitches. It is often used to fill irregular shapes and is effective on circular motifs where the shading spans out from a central point. In basic satin stitch (page 32), shading is created with definite bands of colour. However, encroaching satin stitch and encroaching buttonhole stitch (pages 58, 60) form overlapping rows of stitches, allowing for gradation of colour within a single section of motif.

Threads and Fabrics

Lustrous threads such as DMC stranded cotton and cotton perlé maximize light and shadow, but crewel yarn and other threads can also be used. Plain weave and evenweave fabrics are both suitable, although plain weaves tend to be more popular.

Techniques

Satin stitches call for smooth surfaces and even edges. Although these stitches are quite simple, success certainly depends upon the careful positioning of each individual stitch. When you are filling a motif, you should pay special attention to graduating the edges gently, as jagged edges can spoil the smooth look you are trying to achieve.

It sometimes helps to define the edge of the motif, so experiment with different outlines; try using stitches such as stem stitch (page 31) or split stitch (page 48). The texture of linear stitches such as these highlights the solidity and smoothness of the satin stitches.

Three-dimensional effects Raised satin stitch (see below) is used to create a padded effect. Work a bottom layer of stitches in satin stitch (page 32), and then work over these base stitches in the opposite direction. Or outline first with backstitch (page 30), then fill a motif with darning stitch (page 49) and work satin stitch over the top. By raising the motif in this way, you are maximizing the sheen of the thread by using light and shadow to its fullest effect.

A useful alternative is encroaching buttonhole stitch (page 60). Each row is laid over the ridge of the row above to build texture and lift the motif from the surface of the fabric.

Leaf shapes Four stitches in this family are particularly useful for creating leaf shapes. Fishbone stitch (page 60) is worked with diagonal stitches placed flush to each other to fill the motif; flat stitch is created by crossing the threads slightly, so you can use it to raise the centre of the leaf (or the centre of any motif, such as a column – see page 59); and a truly three-dimensional effect can be created with raised fishbone (page 61) by overlaying diagonal stitches in criss-cross fashion. To create the central vein of a leaf, use Romanian stitch (page 61), which gives a cord-like texture.

When filling leaf motifs, work from base to tip or tip to base – whichever direction you feel is most comfortable.

Block effects Basket filling stitch (page 58) consists of a series of small stitched blocks worked evenly in rows and relies on exploiting the effects of light and shadow. To execute basket filling stitch, work alternate horizontal and vertical blocks of stitches side by side.

> **See Also:**
> Using a hoop *page 18*
> Basic satin stitch *page 32*
> Cyclamen picture *page 42*
> Seashell tablecloth *page 62*
> Crewelwork *pages 112–127*
> Monogramming *pages 166–177*

Raised Satin Stitch
Padded Satin Stitch

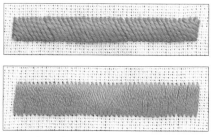

Lay a foundation of basic satin stitch (page 32), and then work over the top of it in the opposite direction. Draw the shape of your motif on the fabric as a guideline before beginning.

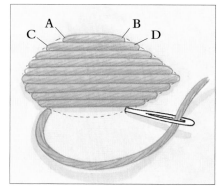

1 *Come up at A, go down at B, up at C, and down at D. Continue to fill motif with basic satin stitch. Secure thread.*

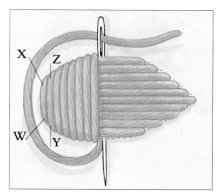

2 *Come up at W, go down at X, up at Y, and down at Z. Continue until base stitches are completely covered.*

Encroaching Satin Stitch

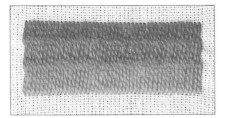

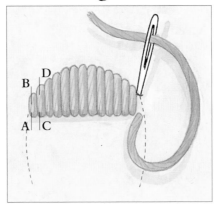

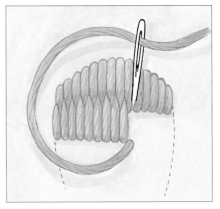

Horizontal bars of satin stitch are worked evenly, with each row encroaching very slightly into the one above to provide subtle shading effects.

1 *Working from left to right, come up at A, go down at B (at edge of motif), up at C, and down at D. Continue to complete row 1.*

2 *To work similar band of stitches, insert needle between and just above base of two corresponding stitches on previous row. Keep stitches even.*

Basket Filling Stitch
Basket Satin Stitch

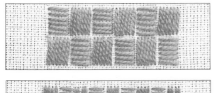

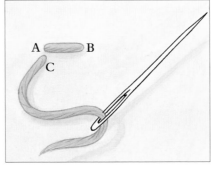

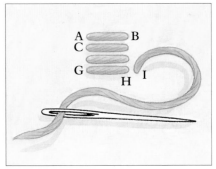

Four horizontal and four vertical straight stitches, all of equal length, are worked in adjacent blocks. This stitch works best on evenweave fabrics.

1 *Come up at A, go down at B, and up at C as shown to work block of horizontal straight stitches.*

2 *Complete four stitches, coming up at G and going down at H. Come up at I, ready to work next block.*

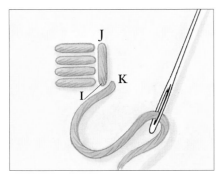

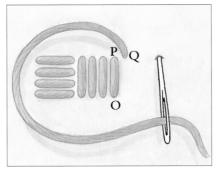

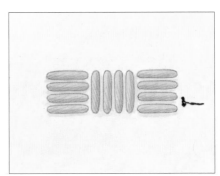

3 *Repeat block, placing stitches vertically: go down at J, up at K, and so on. Keep stitches evenly spaced.*

4 *Complete four vertical stitches, coming up at O and going down at P. Come up at Q as shown.*

5 *Repeat block of horizontal stitches. Make sure that stitches are of equal length to keep block shapes regular.*

Flat Stitch

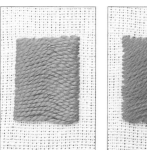

Similar to fishbone stitch (page 60), here slightly slanted stitches cross to form a wide central wedge. Draw guidelines before you begin.

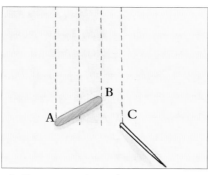

1 Come up at A, go down at B, and come up at C, working accurately to guidelines as shown.

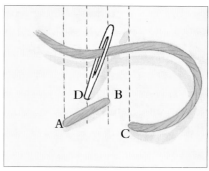

2 Cross over stitch A–B and go down at D. Pull thread through. Let the motif shape determine slant of stitches.

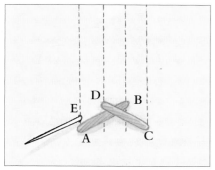

3 Come up at E, just above A, following outline of motif. Pull thread through, ready for next stitch.

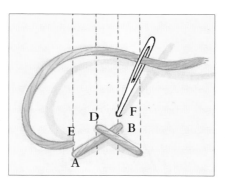

4 Cross over and go down at F. You can pack stitches tightly or allow fabric to show, depending on desired effect.

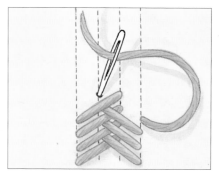

5 Continue in this way until outline is completely filled. To create dense texture, pack stitches tightly together.

Long and Short Satin Stitch

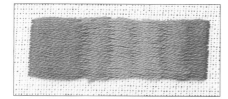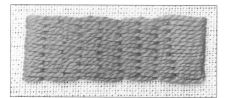

This stitch consists of a first row of long and short vertical stitches followed by rows of long stitches. By subtle changes of colour on each row, soft shading effects can be achieved.

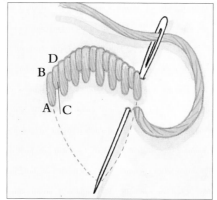

1 Come up at A, go down at B, up at C, and down at D. Continue alternating long and short stitches across row from left to right. Secure thread.

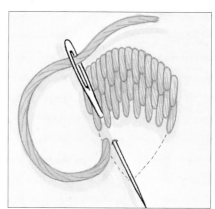

2 Repeat, this time working long stitches only across row to fill motif. The last row will require some short stitches.

Encroaching Buttonhole Stitch

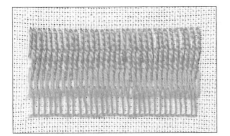

A slightly raised effect is created by positioning rows of basic buttonhole stitch (page 25) over the ridge of buttonhole stitches on previous row.

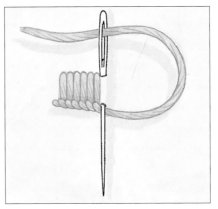

1 First work a single row of basic buttonhole stitch (page 25) as shown. Secure thread on back of fabric.

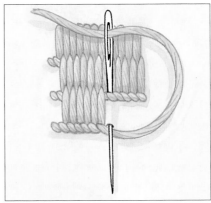

2 On next row go down above ridge, working between stitches of previous row. For shading effect, vary thread colour.

Fishbone Stitch

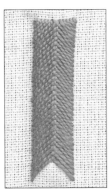

Straight stitches are worked diagonally, crossing over slightly on a central line to form a thin spine. Draw guidelines before beginning.

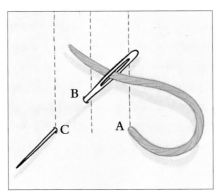

1 Bring needle up at A and go down at B, slightly to left of centre guideline. Come up at C.

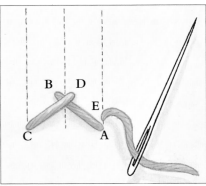

2 Go down at D, slightly to right of centre guideline, crossing over stitch A–B and coming up at E.

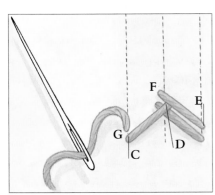

3 Go down at F, slightly to left of centre guideline, and come up at G. Pull thread through.

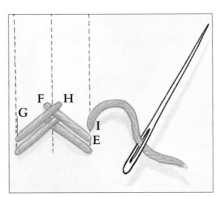

4 Go down at H, crossing over stitch E–F, and then come up at I. Pull thread through.

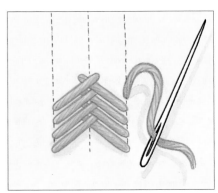

5 Continue in this way, overlapping stitches close to central guideline, until column is complete.

Raised Fishbone Stitch

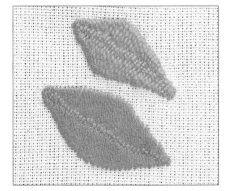

This stitch is created by criss-crossing the thread from one side of the motif to the other. Draw guidelines before beginning.

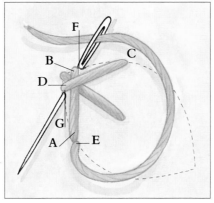

1 Make a vertical stitch from centre of motif to tip. Then come up at A, down at B, up at C, down at D, up at E, down at F, and up at G.

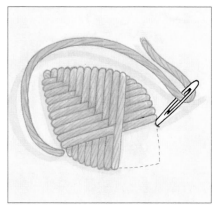

2 Continue placing each stitch flush to the one above and following outline until motif is filled. Take care to gently graduate the motif outline.

Romanian Stitch

Oriental Stitch, Antique Stitch, Indian Filling Stitch, Janina Stitch

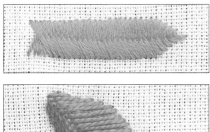

Stitches are tied down at the centre to form a raised seam. Draw guidelines and keep needle above working thread.

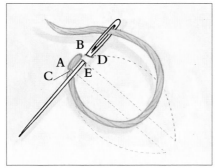

1 Come up at A and go down at B to form horizontal stitch. Come up at C, go down at D, and come up at E above working thread.

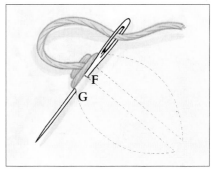

2 Go down at F, crossing second horizontal stitch. Come up at G, following motif outline.

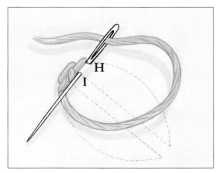

3 Cross over and go down at H, bringing needle up at I above working thread as shown.

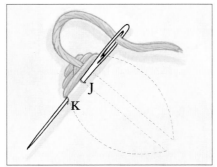

4 Go down at J, crossing over horizontal stitch, and come up at K, ready to begin next stitch.

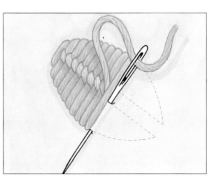

5 Continue in this way. Keep raised seam straight and even by following motif outlines as accurately as possible.

Seashell Tablecloth

*This bright design uses the fresh colours of sea and sand. Stem stitch,
backstitch, and satin stitch are used to outline and fill the central shells.*

Size

Finished cloth: 34 in (86.5 cm) square
Motif: 7½ in (19 cm) square

Materials and Equipment

36 in (91.5 cm) square closely woven
    white fabric (or shop-bought cloth)
Medium-sized crewel needle
12 in (30.5 cm) embroidery hoop
Tracing paper
Water-soluble pen
Pencil

Thread

DMC stranded cotton, 1 skein:

▢	745	▦	958
▢	744	▦	959
▢	743	▦	964
▢	742	▦	976
▢	741	▦	991

Preparation

1 *Make a 1 in (2.5 cm) hem on fabric
edges. Trace design, enlarge to 173 per
cent; transfer to cloth (page 14). Mount fabric
in hoop, place tracing over centre, and tack
along design lines. Tear away paper.*

Stitch and Colour Chart

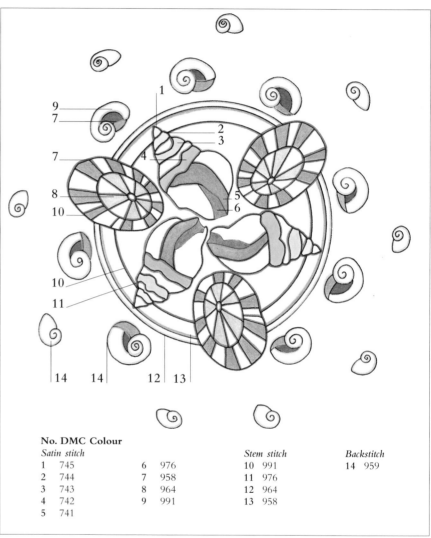

No. DMC Colour

Satin stitch				Stem stitch		Backstitch	
1	745	6	976	10	991	14	959
2	744	7	958	11	976		
3	743	8	964	12	964		
4	742	9	991	13	958		
5	741						

Stitch direction chart

Stitching

2 *Use single strands of thread throughout,
except for the winkles (the smallest shells
outside the central circles), which are outlined*
with two strands. Follow the stitch and colour
chart above; for satin stitch, refer also to the
stitch direction chart (left).

3 *Outline the whelks (large pointed shells)
from the base in rust stem stitch (976).
Satin stitch areas 1, 2, 3, 4, 5, and 6 (see
chart) working over the stem stitch.*

4 *Outline the limpets (large round shells)
in darkest turquoise stem stitch (991),
then fill with satin stitch, using the colours
indicated on the chart.*

5 *Backstitch outlines for the winkles in two
strands of medium turquoise (959). Then
work the two satin-stitch blocks on each of the
larger winkles, following the colour chart.*

6 *Outline the three central circles in stem
stitch, using the colours indicated on the
stitch and colour chart.*

Finishing

7 *When the embroidery is complete, place
damp cloth over wrong side of piece and
press carefully.*

Cross Stitch Family

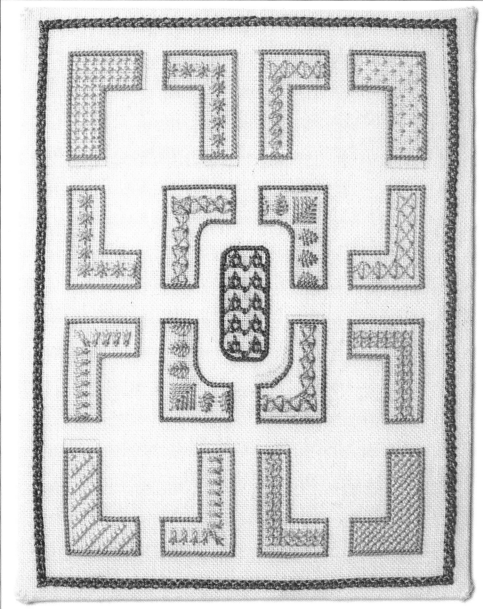

Cross Stitch Family Sampler

The nine stitches in this family are perfect for creating simple borders and also as filling stitches, such as the delicate arrangement of crosses used in star filling and ermine stitches. You can achieve striking effects by varying the space between each stitch. St. George's cross stitches can be scattered individually or packed tightly together as a filling stitch. Montenegrin and two-sided insertion stitches can be used to form intricate lattice patterns.

COUNTED CROSS STITCH is now enjoying a strong revival; these attractive stitches worked on evenweave fabric are very simple to create and give pleasing results.

There are, however, many stitches within this particular family that also lend themselves to modern freestyle embroidery. Modern embroiderers do tend to use cross stitches freely. St. George's cross stitch and long-armed cross stitch (pages 65, 66), for example, can be worked to a very large scale, whereas leaf stitch (page 69), which was extremely popular in the designs of the 1930s and 1940s, has found a new lease of life in pretty floral designs.

Cross stitches are used extensively in samplers, which will provide you with good examples of the effects you can achieve. Some of these stitches make perfect filling stitches, while others can be used for edgings and for sprinkling over plain backgrounds to add texture.

Two-sided cross stitch (page 68) gives the super-neat among us the chance to make the back of the work look as presentable as the front, while ermine stitch (page 67), with its delicate fleur-de-lis appearance, can be worked to great effect scattered on a background. It is traditionally used in blackwork.

When deciding where to use cross stitches, you might also like to consider the symbolism of the cross. In addition to its many saintly associations, the St. George's cross was once also used as a symbol of the sky and the pagan weather gods. It also denotes passion and faith.

Threads and Fabrics

The stitches in this family can be worked in a variety of mediums and on plain or evenweave fabrics. Choose DMC threads that reflect the weight of your motif. You could, for example, work with anything from metallic to cotton threads or heavy yarns, depending on the boldness of your overall design.

You will find that a number of these stitches, such as star filling stitch (page 66) are used primarily in needlepoint but a freestyle application, using a variety of DMC threads, will give you interesting and sometimes surprising results.

Never be limited by what appears to be a formal or rigid construction of stitches, such as the simple shape of the cross. Stitches are merely tools, and you can experiment with them in any way that suits your personal style.

Techniques

The most basic rule of cross stitch is that all your top stitches should cross in the same direction (see basic stitches, page 20). This is obviously important when you are creating rows of stitches for a border or some other formal design. The exception in the stitches that follow is two-sided cross stitch (page 68). In this stitch the first cross in a row is crossed in the opposite direction to that of the other crosses.

To make the most of the crisp geometry of the cross, take particular care when spacing your stitches. Draw guidelines on plain weave fabric to ensure that your stitches are placed evenly together, and watch carefully for any twisted or split threads that might disturb the overall symmetry you are trying to achieve.

By arranging the stitches cleverly you can also create interesting arrangements of angles, which can be used to create stand-alone motifs or as filling stitches within a design. Work blocks of stitches in a variety of colours.

As an alternative, you can also try experimenting with overlapping rows of differently coloured cross stitches. This will create a series of dense shaded areas within your design.

See Also:
Basic cross stitch *page 29*
Teddy bear bib *page 36*
Geometric place mat *page 70*
Crewelwork *pages 112–127*
Cottage garden picture *page 152*

St. George's Cross Stitch

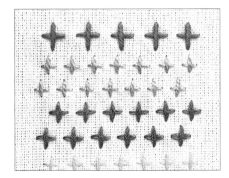

This delicate cross stitch is placed upright on the fabric to form a plus sign. It can be stitched in even rows or scattered randomly.

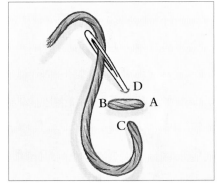

1 To work a single cross, come up at A, go down at B, come up at C, and go down at D as shown.

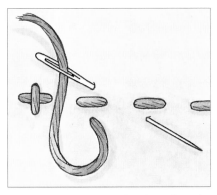

2 To create a row, work a line of evenly spaced horizontal stitches. Then cross each with a same-sized vertical stitch.

Long-armed Cross Stitch
Long-legged Cross Stitch, Plaited Slav Stitch, Twist Stitch

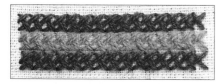

For even results, the long diagonal base stitch should be twice the length of the stitch that crosses it. Work from left to right, and draw guidelines before you begin stitching.

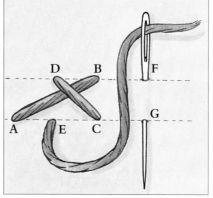

1 *Work a long diagonal stitch from A to B, and then come up at C. Slant over to D and come up at E. Go down at F, and come up at G.*

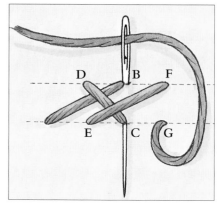

2 *Cross back to B and come up at C, ready to work next stitch. Continue across row, spacing stitches evenly and following guidelines.*

Star Filling Stitch

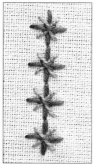

This stitch consists of a St. George's cross stitch (page 65) topped with a diagonal cross stitch of equal size and a small cross stitch worked in the centre.

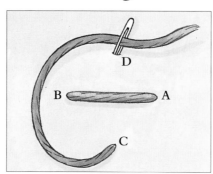

1 *Work a single St. George's cross stitch (page 65), stitching from A to B, then from C to D as shown.*

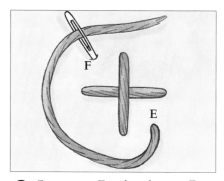

2 *Come up at E and go down at F, working a diagonal stitch of equal length across middle of first cross.*

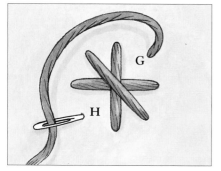

3 *Come up at G and then go down at H to complete second cross, again keeping stitch equal in length.*

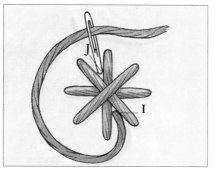

4 *To begin first half of the small inner cross, come up at I and then go down at J as shown.*

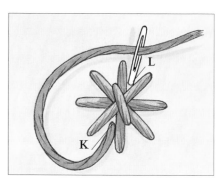

5 *Come up at K and go down at L to complete small cross, keeping K–L the same length as I–J.*

Ermine Stitch

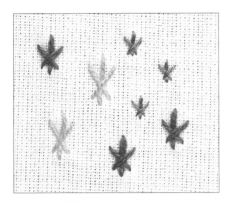

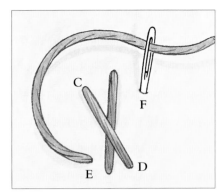

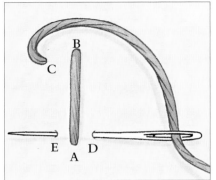

Used for fillings, this is a straight vertical stitch with an elongated cross placed just above the base. Space evenly for a dotted effect, or work in rows for a dense texture.

1 *Come up at A and go down at B to create a vertical stitch. Come up at C, cross over to D, and come up at E.*

2 *Go down at F to complete elongated cross, keeping E–F the same length as C–D, as shown.*

Zigzag Stitch

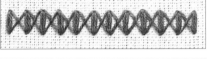

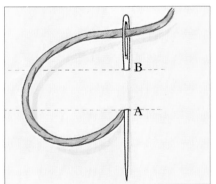

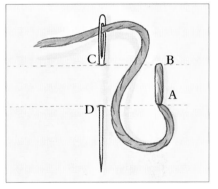

Popular for edgings and fillings, this stitch is made up of alternate upright and diagonal stitches worked in two journeys. Draw guidelines before beginning, and work row one from right to left.

1 *Come up at A, go down at B, then come back up at A as shown. Pull thread through.*

2 *Go down at C to make diagonal stitch, then come up at D directly below C.*

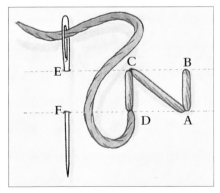

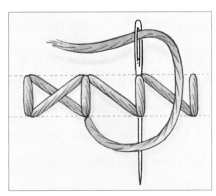

3 *Repeat Steps 1 and 2, keeping thread tension even and working precisely on guidelines for even effect.*

4 *Continue in this way along row, following guidelines and forming zigzag pattern as shown.*

5 *To work return row, slope diagonal stitches in opposite direction, keeping vertical stitches on back.*

Montenegrin Cross Stitch

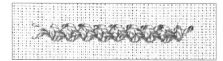

This stitch resembles long-armed cross stitch (page 66), but it has vertical stitches added. It has the advantage of being reversible.

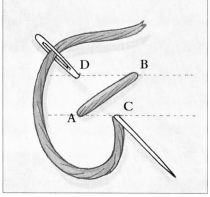

1 *Come up at A and go down at B. Come up at C and cross over to D. Come up at C again.*

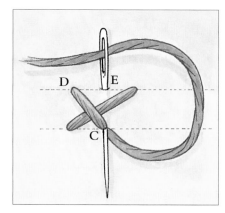

2 *Go down at E to make vertical stitch on front and on back. Come back up at C, ready to begin next stitch.*

Two-sided Cross Stitch

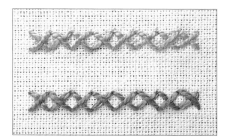

This basic cross stitch variation gives the same stitch on both sides of the fabric. Before beginning, secure thread on right-hand side, leaving a long loose end. When complete, unfasten beginning thread end, thread it into a needle, and fasten securely. This keeps the back of the work neat.

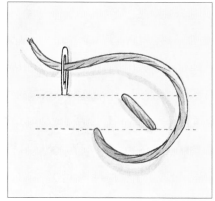

1 *Working from right to left, make a foundation row of diagonal stitches. Work from bottom to top, and leave evenly sized spaces between each stitch.*

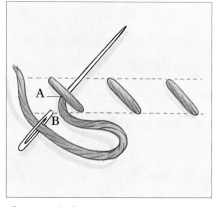

2 *At end of row come up at A, under last diagonal stitch. Then go down at B and come up to right of A (under diagonal stitch) to form half-stitch.*

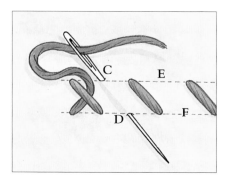

3 *Go down at C (forming two half-stitches) and come up at D. Pull thread through. Work back across row to complete cross stitches, going down at E and coming up at F.*

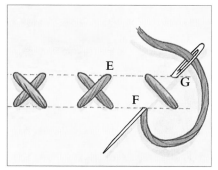

4 *Complete final stitch by going down at G. Come back up at F and work back across row, filling in spaces between crosses with diagonal stitches, working from bottom to top.*

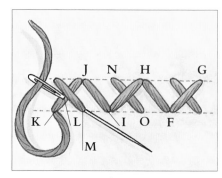

5 *At end of row come up at K and go down at L in centre of half-stitch made in Step 2. Come up at M and work across row, going down at N and up at O to complete the stitches.*

Leaf Stitch
Fir Stitch

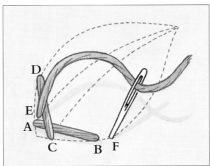

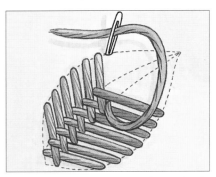

The area where threads cross creates a central vein. The length of diagonal stitches is gently graduated, which distinguishes it from open fishbone stitch, worked at a more acute angle.

1 *Come up at A, go down at B, and come up at C. Go down at D to form central cross, and come up at E, directly in line with A. Go down at F.*

2 *Continue in this way to form a bank of stitches crossed in the centre. Graduate stitch length, and be sure that the spaces between each stitch are even.*

Two-sided Insertion Stitch

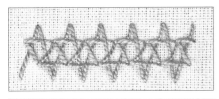

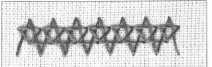

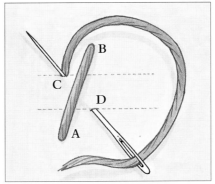

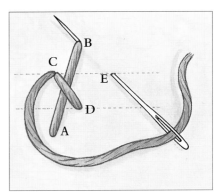

Resembling a row of elongated star shapes, this stitch is generally used for decorative borders rather than joining two pieces of fabric. Back of stitch forms lattice pattern, so it is reversible.

1 *Come up at A and go down at B to form a long diagonal stitch. Come up at C, cross over to go down at D, and then come up again at C.*

2 *Go down at E and come up at B, making a horizontal stitch as shown. Stitch exactly on the guidelines.*

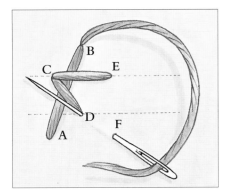

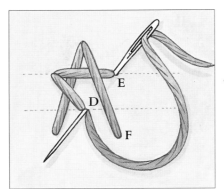

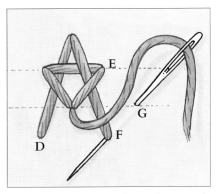

3 *Go down at F and come up at D. Make sure that stitch B–F is the same length as stitch A–B.*

4 *Go down at E again to form a triangle, and come up again at D to complete inner triangle.*

5 *Go down at G, making a horizontal stitch. Come up at F, ready to begin next star.*

Geometric Place Mat

*Six stitches from the cross stitch family are used here to create textured,
geometric shapes that form this stylized design.*

Size

12 x 9¾ in (30.5 x 25 cm)

Materials and Equipment

20 x 24 in (51 x 61 cm) 28-count
white evenweave fabric
Medium-sized crewel needle
White sewing thread
Contrasting sewing thread

Thread

DMC cotton perlé No. 5, 1 skein:

 666   797

444   699

Preparation

1 Press the fabric before you begin. With a contrasting sewing thread, tack a cross to mark the centre of the fabric. (Refer to the centre mark on the stitch and colour chart, right.) One square on the chart represents two threads of fabric.

Stitching

2 Using backstitch, outline the circle in yellow (444) and the triangle in green (699). In cross stitch, and working over two threads, outline the rectangle in blue (797). Fill in the yellow circle with loosely spaced leaf stitches.

3 Now work the lines of varied cross stitches. Each line is worked within the outline on the chart; it is four threads wide and all stitches are square. They should be worked over four threads in both directions, except the zigzag stitch, where the crosses are 4 threads high and 6 threads wide.

4 Starting from the top of the design, work the first block of horizontal lines as follows (see the stitch and colour chart): top line, zigzag cross stitch in red (666); next, long-armed cross stitch in blue (797), then zigzag cross stitch in yellow (444). Finally, work St. George's cross stitch in red thread, and then cross stitch, also in red thread.

Stitch and Colour Chart

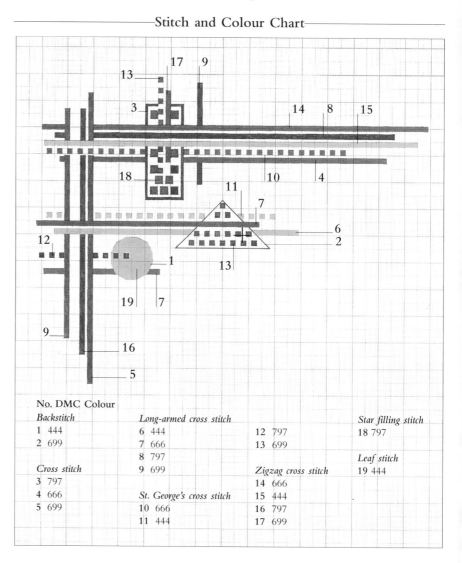

No.	DMC	Colour
Backstitch		
1	444	
2	699	
Cross stitch		
3	797	
4	666	
5	699	

Long-armed cross stitch	
6	444
7	666
8	797
9	699
St. George's cross stitch	
10	666
11	444

12	797
13	699
Zigzag cross stitch	
14	666
15	444
16	797
17	699

Star filling stitch	
18	797
Leaf stitch	
19	444

5 Then work the next block of horizontal lines. To create the top line, work St. George's cross stitch in yellow (444); follow with long-armed cross stitch in red (666), long-armed cross stitch in yellow, then a line of St. George's cross stitch in blue (797). Finish the horizontals with a line of long-armed cross stitch worked in red.

6 Beginning at the left-hand edge of the design, create the vertical lines of stitches as follows: long-armed cross stitch in green (699); zigzag cross stitch in blue (797); cross stitch in green (699); St. George's cross stitch

in green; zigzag stitch in green; and finally, long-armed cross stitch in green.

7 Fill in the triangle shape using rows of green St. George's cross stitch. Then fill in the rectangle shape with star filling stitch in blue (797), positioning the stitches evenly.

Finishing

8 Block the piece (page 181). Trim fabric to a rectangle, 10¼ x 13 in (27.5 x 33 cm). Make a ½ in (1.3 cm) hem along all edges and mitre corners. If needed, press on the wrong side over a damp cloth.

Knotted Stitch Family

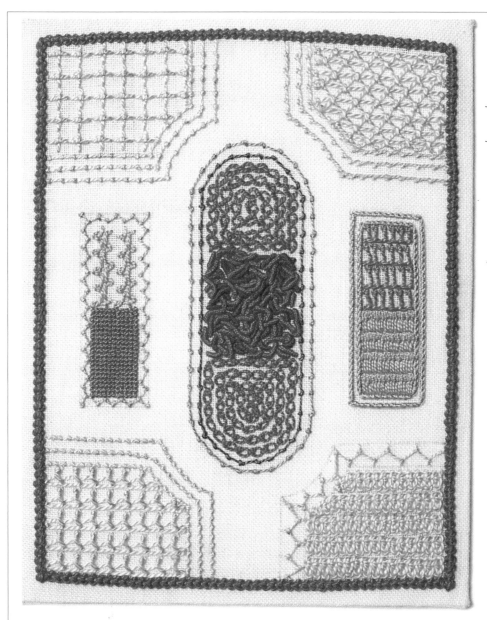

Knotted Stitch Family Sampler

The 19 stitches in this family make attractive border and filling stitches. Four-legged knots are placed together to form a lattice panel; crested chain stitch creates a more decorative grid, and diamond stitch is worked to form a network of triangles.

The central bullion stitches are raised from the fabric surface to give movement and texture, hence its alternative name of **worm stitch**. *Pearl stitch and Armenian edging have a beadlike quality, ideal for border work, and double knot stitch is worked closely to produce a dense plait, with which the sampler is framed.*

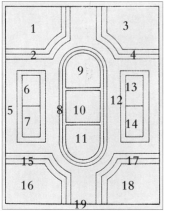

1 Four-legged knot *(page 73)*

2 Coral stitch *(page 74)*

3 Diamond stitch *(page 78)*

4 Scroll stitch *(page 76)*

5 Zigzag coral stitch *(page 74)*

6 Spanish knotted feather stitch *(page 81)*

7 Chinese knot *(page 74)*

8 Armenian edging *(page 77)*

9 Knotted chain stitch *(page 78)*

10 Bullion stitch *(page 75)*

11 Knotted cable stitch *(page 79)*

12 Portuguese knotted stem stitch *(page 77)*

13 Knotted buttonhole stitch *(page 81)*

14 Tailor's buttonhole stitch *(page 81)*

15 Pearl stitch *(page 75)*

16 Crested chain stitch *(page 80)*

17 Knotted insertion stitch *(page 79)*

18 Rosette chain stitch *(page 80)*

19 Double knot stitch *(page 76)*

THE KNOTTED stitches illustrated within this section all consist of stitches that incorporate a number of knots in the sewing process. For this reason, the knotted stitch family includes stitches that form individual knots and those that use the knot as part of other line or filling techniques.

Tailor's buttonhole stitch and knotted buttonhole stitch (page 81), for example, make excellent border stitches and are particularly useful for special techniques such as cutwork. Worked in even rows, these stitches provide a lovely smooth finish to fabric edges. Other stitches, particularly ones such as Chinese knot and bullion stitch (pages 74, 75), have stronger identities in their own right.

Chinese knot, as its name suggests, was widely used in traditional Chinese embroidery, with the individual knots being worked on a very small scale and clustered together to form subtly shaded areas on the fabric.

Bullion stitch – although a little tricky to work – has a broad range of applications, particularly within floral designs. When worked in small circles and clusters, bullion stitch can be used to create rose motifs, with a multitude of delicately shaded petals.

Coral stitch and zigzag coral stitch (page 74) are widely used. These simple stitches form a delicately knotted line, reminiscent of a string of pearls or a flower centre.

Threads and Fabrics

Experiment with different types of DMC fabrics and threads to discover the potential textures of knotted stitches.

Silk threads will highlight a plain background, while cotton perlé will give your knots a textured sheen. Arranging knotted stitches in clusters of soft embroidery cotton will create a three-dimensional effect within your design.

Knotted stitches can be worked on plain and evenweave fabrics. However, individual knots need to be worked over a thread or intersection, or the knot will pull through to the back of the fabric.

Techniques

Knotted stitches are extremely versatile, and you can use them to create endless varieties of texture and effect, from areas of delicate shading to completely impressionistic compositions.

Practise creating evenly sized knots. Most knotted stitches require you to wrap the thread several times around the needle, and you will need to control these wraps with your non-working hand as you ease the needle through to complete the stitch.

When working individual knots, aim to produce a neat form and regular shape. Think of the knots as beads that sit evenly on top of your fabric. The simplest way to achieve perfectly shaped stitches is to work on a frame with the fabric stretched taut (page 10).

A row of detached knots positioned evenly around your motif produces an interesting highlight to your design; detached knots also serve to break and soften the edge of an image.

Think also about the degree of contrast between flat and raised stitches within your composition. Whether you are using your knots to fill a motif or to outline a border, the raised stitches will reflect the light and add substance to your design.

If you find that these stitches are difficult to work at first, do persevere. The finished results are certainly well worth the effort.

See Also:
Chain stitch *page 24*
Buttonhole and blanket stitch *page 25*
French knot *page 33*
Pochette bag *page 34*
Valentine blanket *page 82*
Paisley shawl *page 98*
Crewelwork *pages 112–127*

Four-legged Knot

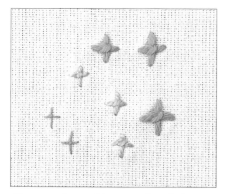

Commonly used in crewelwork (page 112), this stitch comprises an upright cross with a knot in the centre. It can be used as a filling stitch or scattered to accent a strong motif.

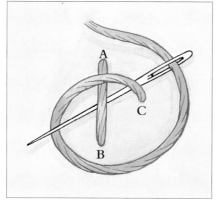

1 *Come up at A, go down at B. Come up at C, lay thread across vertical stitch. Slide needle right to left, under working thread and stitch and over working thread.*

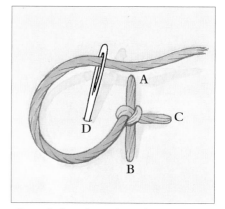

2 *Pull through gently to form knot. It should be in the centre of vertical thread base. Then go down at D as shown to complete the cross.*

Coral Stitch

Beaded Stitch, German Knot, Knotted Stitch, Snail Trail

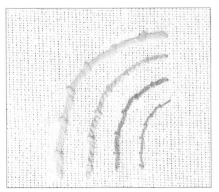

Worked from right to left, this is a straight stitch with a knot at the end, good for textured or curved outlines. To use as a filling stitch, stagger position of knots from row to row.

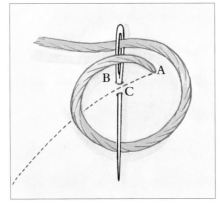

1 *Come up at A and loop thread over needle as shown. Go down at B (under thread) and up at C (over thread). Pull thread through to form knot.*

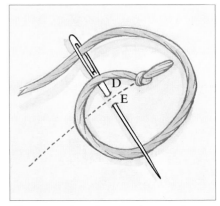

2 *Repeat Step 1, going down at D (under thread) and up at E (over thread) as shown, then pull thread through to form second knot.*

Zigzag Coral Stitch

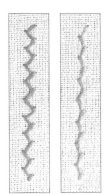

This stitch is worked in a similar way to coral stitch, with base stitches forming a zigzag pattern. Draw guidelines if you are working a straight band.

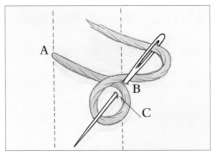

1 *Come up at A, go down at B above thread. Come up at C, taking thread over, then under, needle. Pull to form knot.*

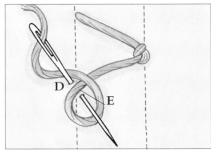

2 *Make a loop with the thread, then go down at D above loop and come up at E through loop. Pull to form knot.*

Chinese Knot

Peking Knot, Forbidden Knot, Blind Knot

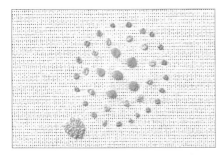

This is a close relative of the French knot (page 33), but it produces a firmer, rounder shape.

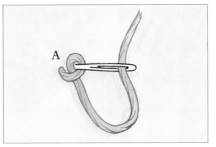

1 *Come up at A. Make small loop as shown. Insert needle into fabric through centre of loop and pull to form knot.*

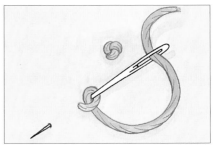

2 *Come up in position for next stitch and repeat. Secure knots with small stitch on back of fabric.*

Bullion Stitch

Coil Stitch, Worm Stitch, Porto Rico Rose, Post Stitch, Grub Knot

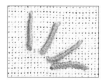

In this detached knot, the thread is coiled around itself to give a corded effect. The stitch can either lie flat or curve up from the fabric to add texture and dimension.

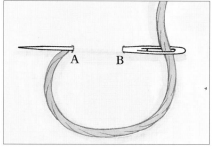

1 Come up at A, go down at B, and back up at A, as though forming backstitch. Do not pull needle through.

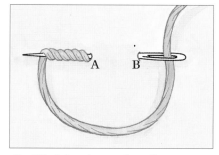

2 Wind thread around needle point until a length equal to or greater than the distance between A and B is covered.

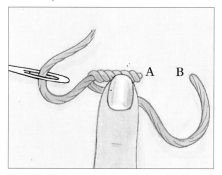

3 Hold down coiled threads with finger and pull needle gently through. Be careful not to distort coil by pulling thread too hard.

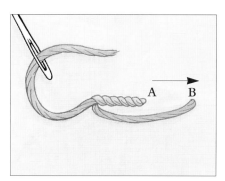

4 Stitch now resembles a coiled cord. Bring needle to right to move coil in place between A and B. Pull extra thread through coil to take up slack.

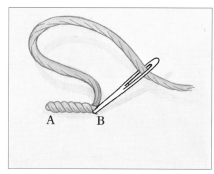

5 Go down at B again to anchor stitch in place. If coil is longer than A–B, coil will be raised on fabric surface, giving three-dimensional effect.

Pearl Stitch

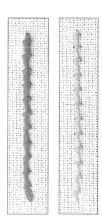

This knotted straight stitch is used mainly for outlining. It creates a raised beaded line and can be worked in fine or heavy threads. The distance between knots will depend on length of vertical stitches.

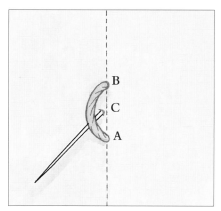

1 Come up at A, go down at B, and up at C. Pull thread through, leaving stitch A–B loose and keeping working thread above needle.

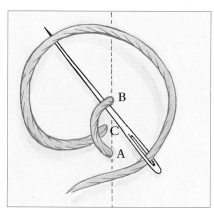

2 Make loop as shown. Slide right to left through stitch A–B and under loop just made, without picking up fabric. Pull to form knot. Repeat from B in Step 1.

Double Knot Stitch

Palestrina Stitch, Tied Coral Stitch, Old English Knot Stitch, Smyrna Stitch

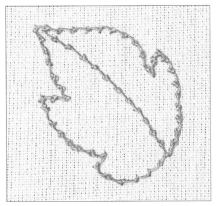

Used extensively in Italian embroidery, the knots give a beaded appearance. To emphasize this, choose a thread such as cotton perlé.

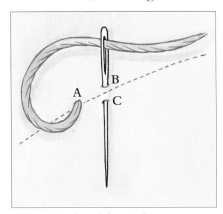

1 *Working from left to right, come up at A, go down at B, and come up at C to form horizontal stitch.*

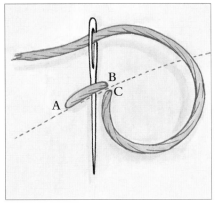

2 *Slide needle through stitch from top without picking up background fabric. You have now formed a wrap.*

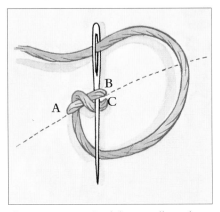

3 *Repeat Step 2, sliding needle under stitch and then over first wrap and working thread as shown.*

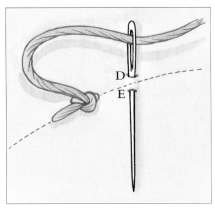

4 *Pull gently to form knot on fabric surface. Then go down at D and come up at E to begin next stitch.*

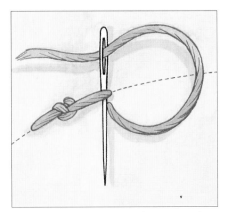

5 *Repeat Steps 2–4 and continue along design line as shown, keeping all knots evenly spaced.*

Scroll Stitch

Single Knotted Line Stitch

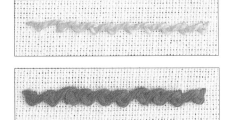

Consisting of a simple line of knots, this flowing, wavelike stitch is worked from left to right and is particularly useful for outlines.

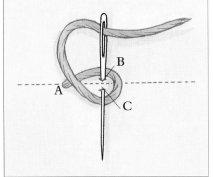

1 *Come up at A, go down at B, and up at C. Loop thread behind top of needle and under needle point.*

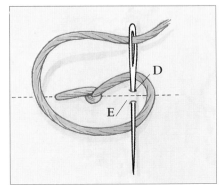

2 *Pull needle through to form knot. For next stitch, go down at D and up at E, looping thread as shown. Repeat.*

Portuguese Knotted Stem Stitch

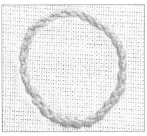

In this stitch the knots are formed by two whipping stitches. Used for straight and curved raised lines, it gives a knotted rope effect.

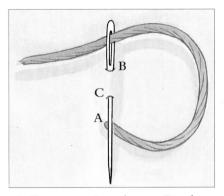

1 *Come up at A, go down at B to form vertical stitch. Come up at C (halfway between A and B) to left of vertical stitch.*

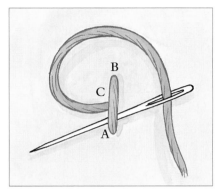

2 *Take thread around stitch from left to right, then slide needle from right to left under stitch but not through fabric.*

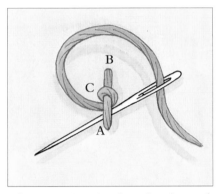

3 *Repeat Step 2, taking thread around and under stitch as before, and pull thread through. You have now wrapped the stitch twice.*

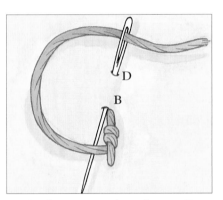

4 *To form next stitch, go down at D and then come up at B, keeping thread over needle as shown. Pull thread through gently.*

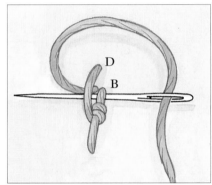

5 *Now slide needle under top half of original vertical stitch and under loop of second stitch. Repeat to form second wrap. Repeat Steps 4–5 as required.*

Armenian Edging

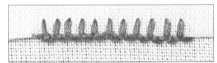

Use Armenian edging as a decoration for a hemmed edge. Work from left to right, and keep the stitches small and evenly spaced.

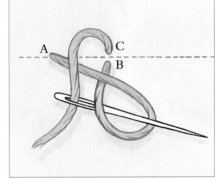

1 *Come up at A, form a loop as shown, and go down at B, coming up at C. Pass needle through loop from left to right.*

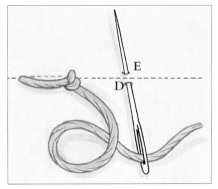

2 *Pull tightly to form knot. For next stitch, form loop and go down at D, up at E. Pull through. Then pass needle through loop from left to right as before.*

Diamond Stitch

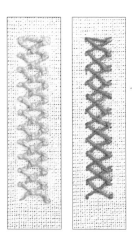

This popular border stitch looks similar to a trellis and is worked from top to bottom. Draw two parallel guidelines before you begin.

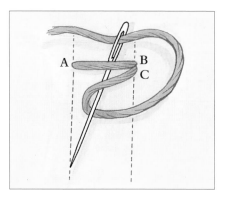

1 Come up at A, down at B, and up at C. Pass needle under stitch A–B, then carry working thread over needle from right to left and loop under needle point. Do not pick up background fabric.

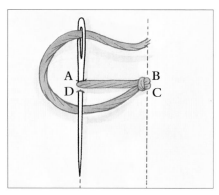

2 Pull to form knot close to B and C. Go down at A and up at D, with needle under stitch A–B and over working thread. Pull loosely to form knot close to A and D, leaving pulled thread slack.

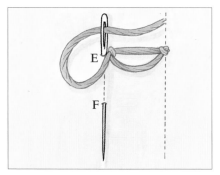

3 Go down at E (just below first knot A–D) and then come up on guideline at F as shown. Pull thread through.

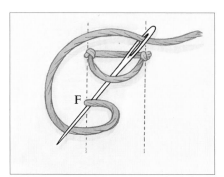

4 Slide needle from top to bottom under slack thread and loop it under, then over, working thread as shown. Pull to form knot centred on slack thread.

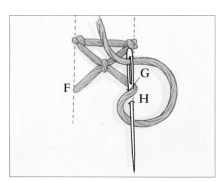

5 Go down at G over working thread and come up at H. Loop thread from left to right under needle point. Pull to form knot. Repeat Steps 3–5 as desired.

Knotted Chain Stitch
Link Stitch

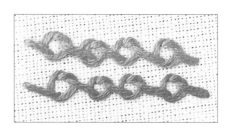

This stitch is made from a chain of knots linked together with a straight stitch. Most often used to create a decorative line, it is worked from right to left. Work each stitch loosely.

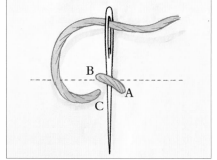

1 Come up at A, go down at B, and come up at C to form small stitch. Slide needle from top to bottom under this stitch to form loop. Do not pick up background fabric.

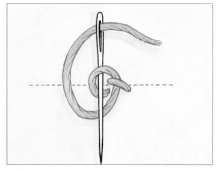

2 Take thread around left side of loop and insert needle through loop from top to bottom, under top thread and over two bottom threads. Pull gently to leave loop to left. Continue from B in Step 1.

Knotted Cable Stitch
Knotted Cable Chain Stitch

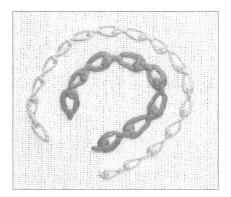

This decorative line stitch is a combination of chain stitch (page 24) and coral stitch (page 74). Draw a guideline before you begin.

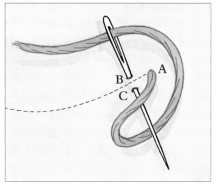

1 *Come up at A, go down at B, and up at C. Carry thread over needle and then back under needle point as shown. Pull thread to form knot.*

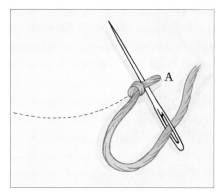

2 *Slide needle under the stitch between A and the knot just worked, bottom to top, as shown. Do not pierce background fabric.*

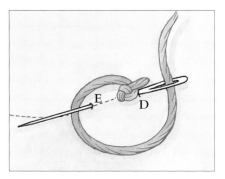

3 *Pull thread through. Go down at D behind knot, then come up at E. Keep working thread under needle point. Pull through to make chain stitch.*

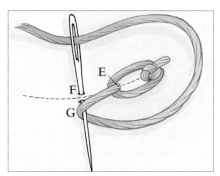

4 *Go down at F, come up at G, and take working thread over needle and under needle point as shown. Pull through to form knot.*

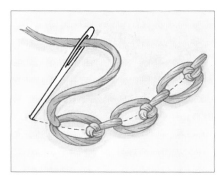

5 *Repeat Steps 2–4 to continue working along design line, completing row of linked chain and coral stitches with a small straight stitch.*

Knotted Insertion Stitch
Knotted Faggot Stitch

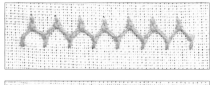

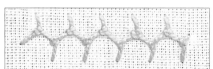

This decorative band is commonly used to join two pieces of fabric. The space between dotted lines represents the open area between two pieces of fabric. Ensure that the fabric edges are hemmed before beginning (page 180).

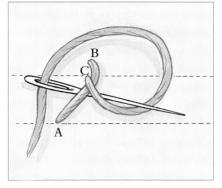

1 *Come up at A, down at B, up at C. Lay thread over slanting stitch left to right. Slide needle under stitch, then under and over working thread. Pull through.*

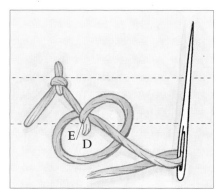

2 *Go down at D, come up at E and pull through. Make loop. Slide left to right behind both threads and out through loop to form knot. Repeat from B in Step 1.*

Rosette Chain Stitch
Bead Edging Stitch

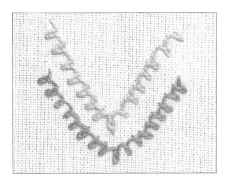

Useful for bordering delicate work, this twisted chain resembles braid. When worked in cotton perlé, it creates a raised effect. Work from right to left.

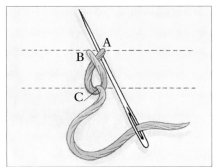

1 *Come up at A. Make loop and go down at B. Come up at C through loop, and pull through. Slide needle under stitch close to A as shown. Pull through.*

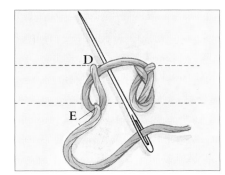

2 *Make loop and go down at D. Come up at E through loop; slide needle under slack thread close to D. Pull to form second knot. Repeat Step 2 as desired.*

Crested Chain Stitch
Spanish Coral Stitch

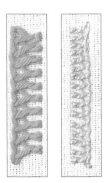

This stitch combines chain stitch (page 24) and coral stitch (page 74). Use for bands and borders and for outlining curved motifs. Work top to bottom, and draw parallel guidelines.

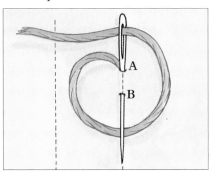

1 *Come up at A. Go down just to the right of A and come up at B, looping thread under needle point from left to right. Pull to form knot.*

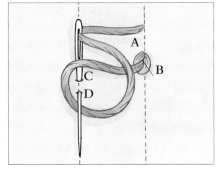

2 *Go down at C, behind working thread, and come up at D. Loop thread under needle point from left to right. Pull to form second knot.*

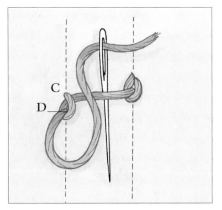

3 *Slide needle from top to bottom under horizontal stitch between knots. Do not pick up background fabric.*

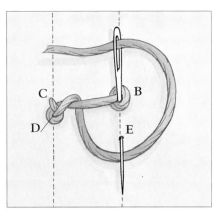

4 *Go down at B through knot. Then come up at E, with working thread under needle point. Pull through to create a slanting stitch.*

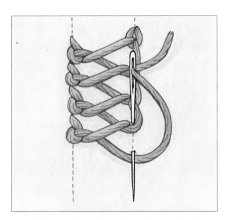

5 *Repeat from Step 2, using a slanting stitch as the anchor point for each new stitch as shown.*

Spanish Knotted Feather Stitch
Twisted Zigzag Chain Stitch

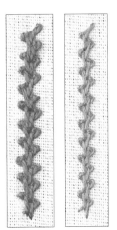

Worked from top to bottom, this stitch creates a braidlike band. Knotted, twisted loops are worked alternately to left and right of a centre line. Mark three parallel guidelines on fabric first.

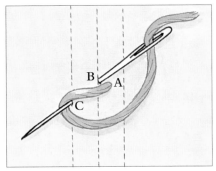

1 *Come up at A, down at B, and up at C. Take working thread over needle from A and then under needle point from left to right. Pull to make crossed loop.*

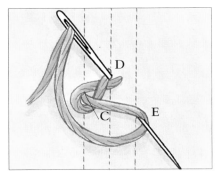

2 *Go down at D and come up at E, taking working thread over needle as shown and then back under needle. Pull to make second crossed loop.*

Tailor's Buttonhole Stitch

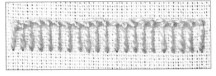

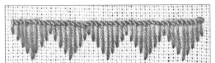

This durable version of buttonhole stitch (page 25) features a knotted edge, useful for heavy-weight fabrics. Place stitches close together and work from left to right.

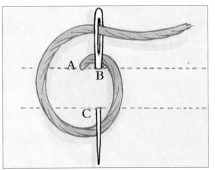

1 *Come up at A. With needle over working thread, go down at B and come up directly below at C. Pull thread to form knot at top.*

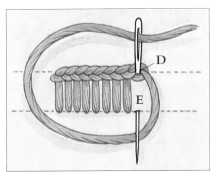

2 *Go down through knot at D and come up at E over working thread. Pull to form another knot and continue.*

Knotted Buttonhole Stitch

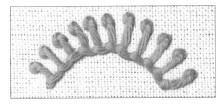

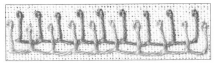

This fancy adaptation of buttonhole stitch (page 25) creates a straight stitch with a knot at the top. It can be worked in an arc or in straight rows.

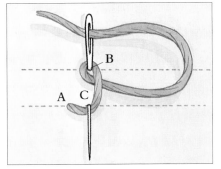

1 *Come up at A, make loop with thread, and hold it in position at top of stitch. Insert needle through loop at B, and come up over working thread at C.*

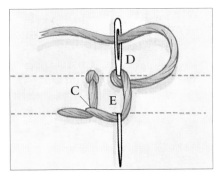

2 *Pull to form knot at top of stitch. Begin next stitch by making loop, then going down at D and up at E.*

Valentine Blanket

This stunning woolwork project uses a decorative heart as its central motif. Knotted stitches are worked with pastel tapisserie wools to give depth and texture to the flower-and-leaf outlines.

Size

Blanket: 42 x 42 in (106.5 x 106.5 cm)
Central heart motif: 10 x 10 in
  (25.5 x 25.5 cm)
Border motif: 1 x 7 in (2.5 x 18 cm)

Materials and Equipment

42 in (106.5 cm) square pure wool
  blanket fabric in cream
Large crewel or chenille needle
Water-soluble pen, sponge
10 in (25.5 cm) square of tracing paper
Scissors for cutting paper
Pencil, ruler
Pins

Thread

DMC tapisserie wools:

☐ Blanc, 2 skeins		▨ 7204, 1 skein	
☐ 7171, 1 skein		▨ 7205, 1 skein	
☐ 7905, 2 skeins		▨ 7221, 1 skein	
▨ 7202, 3 skeins		☐ 7800, 2 skeins	
☐ 7727, 1 skein		▨ 7244, 1 skein	
☐ 7132, 1 skein		▨ 7422, 3 skeins	

Preparation

1 *Begin by placing your blanket fabric on a clean towel and under a damp cloth. Then iron the fabric carefully so that it is completely flat.*

2 *Enlarge heart motif from the template (right) using graph paper, or enlarge to 600 per cent on a photocopier. Cut it out.*

3 *Find the centre of the blanket by folding the blanket fabric lengthwise and then widthwise — the centre is where the folds intersect. Then pin the paper heart over the centre position and draw carefully around it with the water-soluble pen.*

4 *With a ruler, measure 3 in (7.5 cm) in from all edges and mark each corner of the blanket with the water-soluble pen. Draw a straight line on the fabric to join*

Template

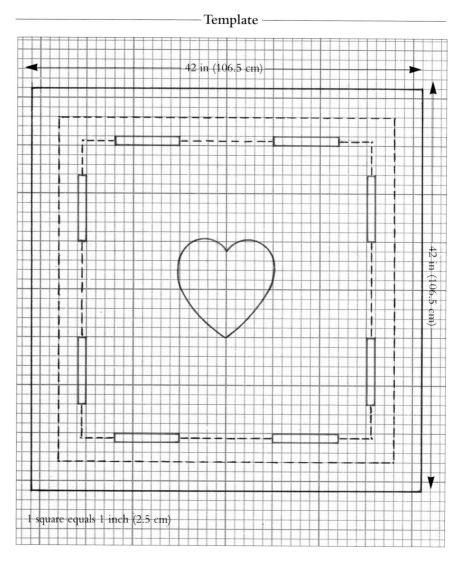

42 in (106.5 cm)

42 in (106.5 cm)

1 square equals 1 inch (2.5 cm)

these corner marks for outer border. Measure another 2¹/₂ in (6.5 cm) from this marked border and then mark each corner in this position. Join the marks to form the inner border on your fabric.*

5 *The border motifs are worked twice on each side of the blanket. These motifs begin 3½ in (9 cm) in from each corner of the inner border (see the template shown above). Each motif measures 7 in (18 cm) in length. Using a water-soluble pen, mark on the blanket fabric the exact positions of the motifs along the inner border.*

Stitching

6 *The stitch and colour chart on the opposite page shows the positions and wool colours to use for each stitch on both the border and heart motif. The motif border is illustrated on the left-hand side of the chart. The stitching on the right-hand side of the heart is an exact mirror image of that on the left-hand side. One full strand of wool yarn is used throughout this design, with the exception of the yellow and pink buttonhole circles, which are all worked using just half the thickness of a normal strand of wool yarn.*

Stitch and Colour Chart

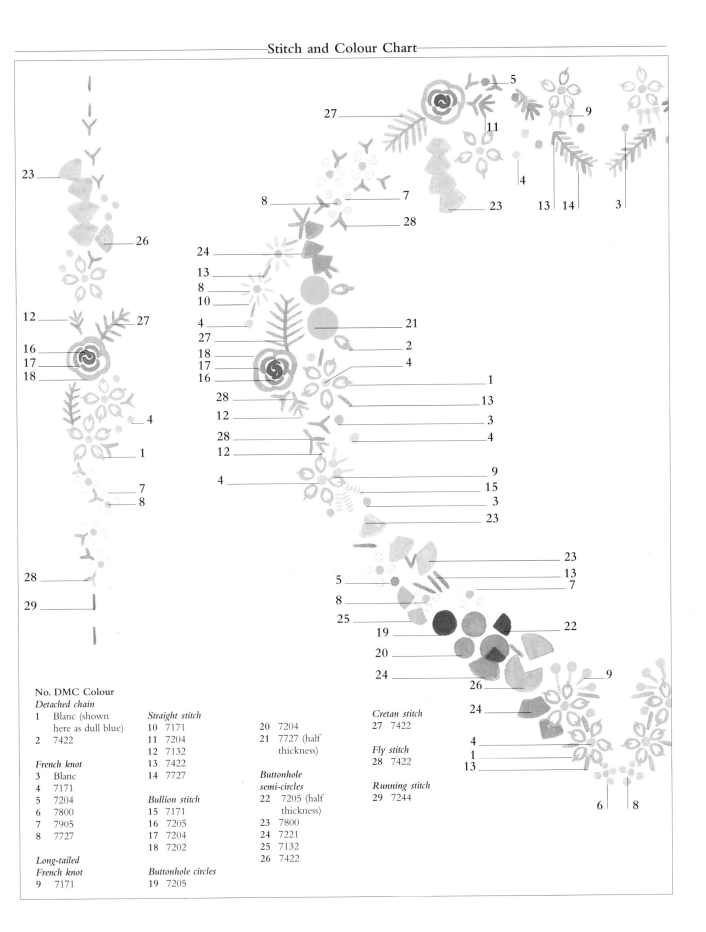

27 _____

5

11

9

4

13 14 3

23

8 _____ 7

28

24 _____

13

8

10

4 _____

27

18

17

16 _____

28

12

28

12

4 _____

21

2

4

1

13

3

4

9

15

3

23

23

13

7

5

8

25 _____

19

20

24

26

24

23

12 _____

27

16 _____
17 _____
18 _____

26 _____

4

1

7
8

28 _____

29 _____

22

9

4

1

13

6   8

No. DMC Colour
Detached chain

| 1 | Blanc (shown here as dull blue) |
| 2 | 7422 |

French knot

3	Blanc
4	7171
5	7204
6	7800
7	7905
8	7727

Long-tailed French knot

| 9 | 7171 |

Straight stitch

10	7171
11	7204
12	7132
13	7422
14	7727

Bullion stitch

15	7171
16	7205
17	7204
18	7202

Buttonhole circles

| 19 | 7205 |

| 20 | 7204 |
| 21 | 7727 (half thickness) |

Buttonhole semi-circles

22	7205 (half thickness)
23	7800
24	7221
25	7132
26	7422

Cretan stitch

| 27 | 7422 |

Fly stitch

| 28 | 7422 |

Running stitch

| 29 | 7244 |

7 To divide the yarn, first cut a 12 in (30.5 cm) length and then carefully untwist the yarn fibres, dividing the length in half as you go. Then hold the divided length of yarn at one end and allow it to untwist fully before you work with it.

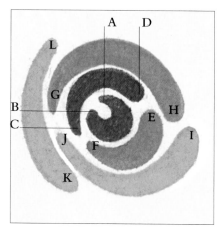

Working a bullion-stitch rose

8 Begin by stitching the bullion roses on the left side of the central heart shape. To create a bullion-stitch rose, first work bullion stitch (page 75) from the centre out, wrapping the yarn eight times around the needle for each stitch. Then follow the letter sequence that is shown above to position the stitches in a circular shape, and use the wool colours 7205, 7204 and 7202 indicated on the stitch and colour chart to graduate the colours of the petals.

9 Work the Cretan-stitch leaves (page 94) in the positions shown on the chart, using colour number 7422.

10 Still working on the left side of the heart design, complete the rest of the flowers, leaves, and buds in the colours and stitches indicated, taking care to follow the heart shape carefully.

11 When the left side is complete, work the right side in a similar way. Each group of flowers sits opposite and is a mirror image of those on the left side.

12 Where the long-tailed French knots are indicated, first work a normal

Detail of Blanket

French knot, wrapping the yarn twice around the needle. Then pull the needle through the wraps in the normal way and insert it back into the fabric a small distance from the knot to form a straight "tail."

13 To create buttonhole-stitch circles and half circles, work each stitch from a common central point, positioning the long strands so that they form a circle. Take care to keep the stitching between the strands even.

14 For the border, follow the motif shown on the left-hand side of the stitch and colour chart. As with the heart motif, start with the bullion-stitch roses and Cretan-stitch leaves, and then complete the remaining flowers, leaves, and buds, keeping

within the guide marks as before. When working the mirror images, make sure that the stem of pale blue flowers always points to the corner of the blanket.

15 When you have completed all the border motifs, join them with a line of evenly spaced running stitches in pale blue tapisserie wool (7800), following the line drawn in Step 5 for the inner border. Finally, work the outer border in running stitch, again following the guideline.

16 Using your needle, pull away five threads at each edge of the blanket to form a narrow fringe. Then use a damp sponge to remove any marks left by the water-soluble pen. With blanket face down on a towel, press gently over a damp cloth.

Looped Stitch Family

Looped Stitch Family Sampler

The 24 stitches in this family make decorative braids and borders as well as versatile filling stitches. Ladder stitch, for example, forms three-dimensional double ridges when worked in column blocks, and heavy chain stitch gives a regular knitted effect. Wheatear stitch creates spiky spirals and is also worked in simple arrow shapes to hold each corner of the broad chain border.

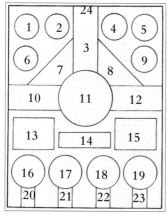

1 Open chain stitch *page 90*
2 Double feather stitch *page 96*
3 Feathered chain stitch *page 95*
4 Crossed buttonhole stitch *page 92*
5 Sword edging stitch *page 93*
6 Cable chain stitch *page 91*
7 Loop stitch *page 87*

8 Closed buttonhole stitch *page 91*
9 Wheatear stitch *page 96*
10 Closed feather stitch *page 96*
11 Petal stitch *page 92*
12 Open Cretan stitch *page 95*
13 Heavy chain stitch *page 90*
14 Plaited braid stitch *page 97*

15 Ladder stitch *page 93*
16 Cretan stitch *page 94*
17 Braid stitch *page 97*
18 Twisted chain stitch *page 89*
19 Chequered chain stitch *page 89*
20 Backstitched chain stitch *page 91*
21 Rope stitch *page 94*
22 Fly stitch *page 88*
23 Zigzag chain stitch *page 89*
24 Broad chain stitch *page 88*

BECAUSE of their simplicity, many of the stitches in this family are prevalent in peasant and ethnic embroidery, where the braids are used to edge garments and the chain stitches worked to fill complete designs. Wheatear stitch (page 96), for example, is used traditionally for surface decoration on English smocks, and Cretan stitch (page 94) has been used for centuries to create decorative clothing. Originating on the Greek island of Crete, this stitch is also found in Persian embroidery.

Although there is little recorded evidence of looped stitches in medieval embroidery, there are examples in Chinese work, where zigzag chain stitch (page 89) is worked on a small scale and incorporated in decorative line work.

These decorative stitches are used to create braid effects, simple flower shapes, and chains of different textures, quickly covering your background fabric.

Within the looped stitch family is a selection of buttonhole stitches that can be used to great effect on edgings. Chain stitch variations work well for both outlining and filling motifs and also provide added texture to a plain chain stitch design. Circles and spirals can be created from many of these stitches – in some cases, they naturally form flower heads and sun or star shapes. In addition

to their simplicity, looped stitches offer a refreshing informality. When worked cleverly, they have the effect of dancing over the surface of the fabric.

The finest examples of this can be found on Elizabethan attire where freestyle foliage and all kinds of motifs drawn from nature are edged and filled with buttonhole stitch variations worked in shades of rich colour.

Threads and Fabrics

Looped stitches work well on both plain and evenweave fabrics. Much of the effect of these stitches depends on which DMC threads you choose. Bold, bright patterns can be achieved with heavy matt cotton thread, and delicate curves with single strands of cotton or silk. However, always take into account the weight of your background fabric and how the different textures will stand together. Beginners may find it easier to practise with cotton perlé, as this holds loops more firmly than softer threads.

Looped stitches are also a popular choice among contemporary crewel embroiderers, as yarns emphasize the soft curves that these stitches create.

Techniques

Quite simply, looped stitches are all worked by looping the thread under or

over the needle before securing it to the fabric. However, the secret of successful looped stitching is to keep all the loops evenly sized. In many instances, you will find it useful to control the loops by holding them down with your non-stitching thumb as you pull the thread through. Drawing guidelines on your fabric will also help to keep your stitches in even lines.

The most difficult stitch to master in this family is plaited braid stitch (page 97). Traditionally used in goldwork (page 128), it forms an embossed and very decorative band. Practise it using a heavy soft cotton thread. You may also find it helpful to pin the thread loops as you work. This keeps the loops open, enabling you to see where next to insert the needle.

Most of the stitches in the looped stitch family can be worked successfully without a frame and benefit from a freestyle approach.

See Also:
Basic stitches *page 20*
Pochette bag *page 34*
Paisley shawl *page 98*
Couching and goldwork *pages 128–141*
Finishing techniques *pages 178–184*

Loop Stitch
Centipede Stitch, Knotted Loop Stitch

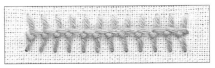

This stitch provides a band of straight stitches with a plaited centre. Try graduating the lengths of the straight stitches for interesting results.

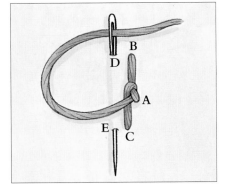

1 *Come up at A, down at B, up at C. Slide right to left under base of stitch A–B, keeping needle over working thread as you come through. Go down at D, up at E.*

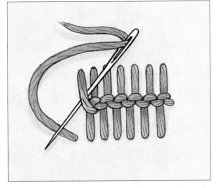

2 *Pull thread through. Slide top of needle under previous stitch from right to left, keeping needle over working thread, and pull through. Repeat from D in Step 1.*

Fly Stitch
Y Stitch, Open Loop Stitch

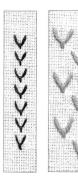 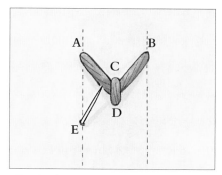

Fly stitch consists of a V-shaped loop, tied down with a vertical straight stitch, which can be varied in length. It works well as scattered, single stitches. To work vertical rows, draw parallel guidelines and place stitches close together.

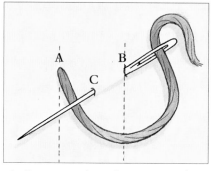

1 *Come up at A, go down at B, and come up at C, keeping needle over working thread.*

2 *Go down at D, forming a small straight stitch to tie down loop. Come up at E to begin next stitch.*

Broad Chain Stitch
Reverse Chain Stitch

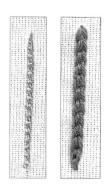

This stitch is very similar to heavy chain stitch (page 90) except that the thread is passed behind one stitch instead of two. Use a firm thread.

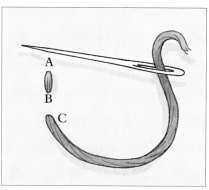 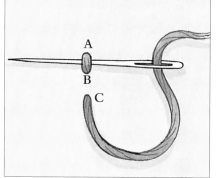

1 *Come up at A and go down at B to make a small straight stitch, then come up at C as shown.*

2 *Slide needle through straight stitch from right to left without picking up background fabric.*

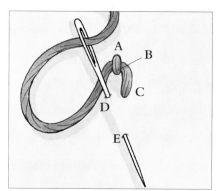 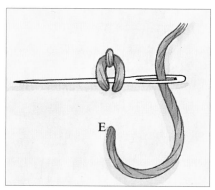 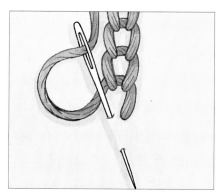

3 *Go down at D, next to C, to complete chain. Come up at E as shown. Pull thread through.*

4 *Slide needle from right to left through chain you have just made. Do not pick up background fabric.*

5 *Repeat from Step 3, sliding needle through previous chain stitch to complete the column of stitches.*

Twisted Chain Stitch

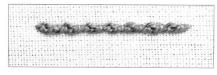

This simple variation on basic chain stitch (page 24) has a textured effect. The stitches can also be worked separately as well as in a row. Hold the chain loop down with your thumb while pulling the working thread through.

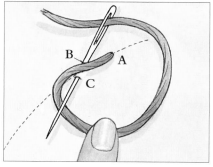

1 Come up at A, go down at B, and up at C, holding thread over and under needle as shown.

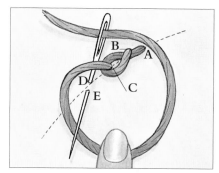

2 Pull thread through to make twisted chain. For next stitch go down at D, up at E. Repeat as desired.

Zigzag Chain Stitch
Vandyke Chain Stitch

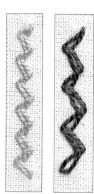

This is used as both a line and filling stitch, and you can work it in a circle to form a flower or star shape. Begin by making a chain loop (page 24).

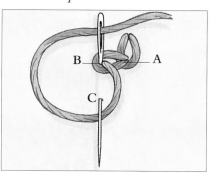

1 Come up at A inside first loop. Make second chain loop at an angle; go down next to A. Come up at B, go down next to B, and come up at C as shown.

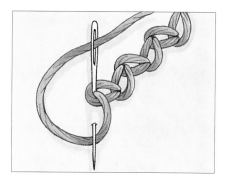

2 Continue to work the stitch, linking each chain loop as shown and alternating angle of loops to create regular zigzag effect.

Chequered Chain Stitch
Magic Chain, Magic Stitch

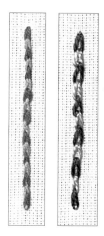

A bi-coloured effect is achieved by using two contrasting thread colours. Alternate the colour by alternating the working thread for each chain loop as shown.

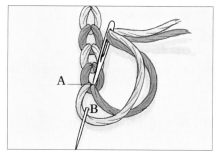

1 Come up at A with both threads, make loop, go down next to A, and come up at B over one thread. Pull both threads through to form loop with first colour.

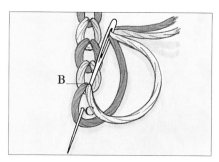

2 Make loop and go down next to B. Come up at C, keeping needle over second thread. Pull through to form loop with second colour. Repeat from Step 1.

Heavy Chain Stitch
Heavy Braid Chain Stitch

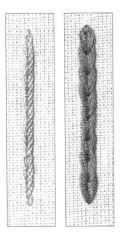

This is a heavy line stitch, which is useful for creating a well-defined outline. Heavy chain stitches can be worked in any direction.

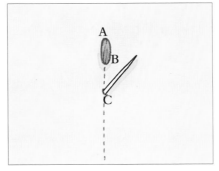

1 Come up at A and go down at B to make a small straight stitch at end of line to be worked. Come up at C.

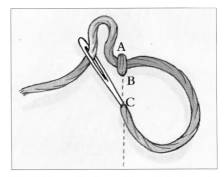

2 Slide needle from right to left through small stitch without picking up background fabric. Go down next to C.

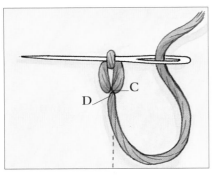

3 Come up at D; slide needle through small stitch again. Go down next to D to make two chains in one stitch.

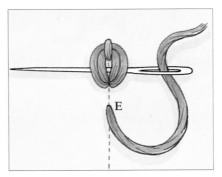

4 Come up at E; slide needle right to left through last two chains; go down next to E. Repeat to make second chain.

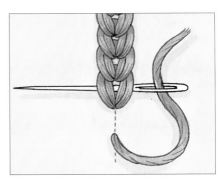

5 Repeat from Step 4, sliding needle through two chains at a time. Keep thread tension even to work loops evenly.

Open Chain Stitch
Ladder Stitch, Roman Chain, Square Chain

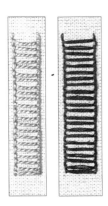

This is worked from top to bottom. Secure the last loop with a straight stitch at each corner. Draw parallel guidelines on your fabric before beginning.

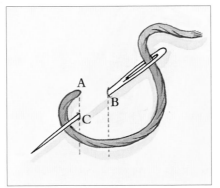

1 Come up at A; go down at B, looping thread under needle; and come up at C as shown.

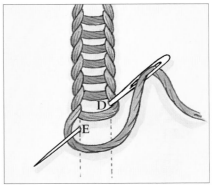

2 Go down at D over previous stitch, coming up at E with thread under needle point. Repeat to create column.

Backstitched Chain Stitch

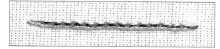

This stitch makes a firm-textured line. Vary the effect by using a contrasting colour or thread type for the backstitch.

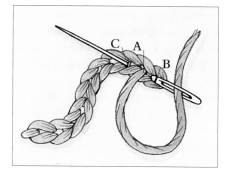

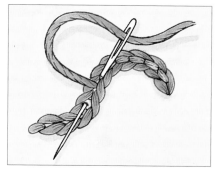

1 *Work a row of chain stitch (page 24). With new thread, come up at A inside second chain. Backstitch into first chain at B, then come up inside third chain at C.*

2 *Continue in this way all along row. Keep backstitches even, and take care not to split thread as you bring needle up through chain.*

Cable Chain Stitch

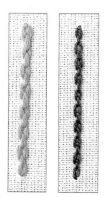

This stitch enables you to make a neatly linked chain with a single movement. It is a pretty border stitch that works well in soft embroidery cotton. Work downwards.

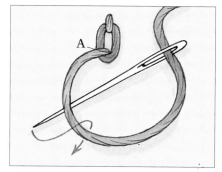

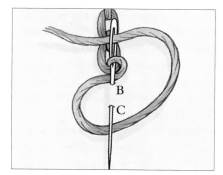

1 *Make one detached chain stitch (page 24). Come up at A, then loop working thread over and under needle from left to right as shown.*

2 *Go down at B and come up at C, looping working thread under needle point from left to right. Pull through to complete the stitch.*

Closed Buttonhole Stitch

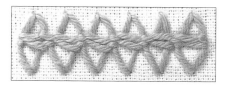

This pretty border stitch can be worked row above row to form a filling stitch. It is a simple variation of basic buttonhole stitch (page 25).

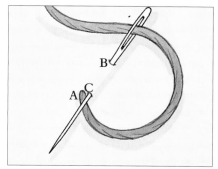

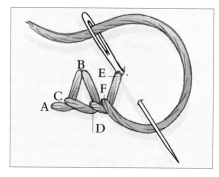

1 *Come up at A, then go down at B and up at C as shown above, keeping needle under working thread. Pull the thread through.*

2 *Go down next to B; come up at D with needle over working thread. Pull through. Go down at E, up at F, down next to E. Repeat from B in Step 1.*

Crossed Buttonhole Stitch

This line stitch features pairs of basic buttonhole stitch (page 25) worked at an angle so that they cross each other. A trellis filling stitch can be created by working a series of rows.

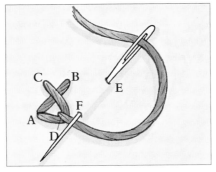

1 *Come up at A, go down at B, up at C. Go down again at A, leaving loop; come up at D through loop. Go down at E and up at F with thread under needle.*

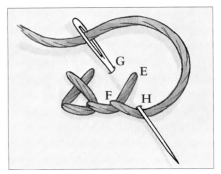

2 *Pull thread through gently. Then loop thread under needle as shown, and go down at G, coming up at H. Repeat along row as desired.*

Petal Stitch
Pendant Chain Stitch

This line stitch looks very attractive when worked in circles. The chain loops hang off a rope of stem stitches (page 31) to create a pendant effect.

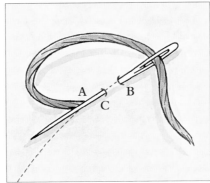

1 *Come up at A, go down at B, and up at C, following guideline and keeping thread to the left as shown.*

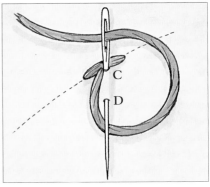

2 *Pull thread through. Go down next to C and come up at D with working thread under needle to create loop.*

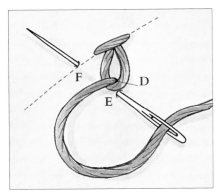

3 *Pull thread through and go down at E, making a small stitch to secure loop. Come up at F.*

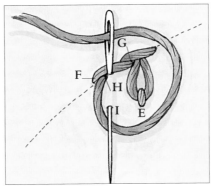

4 *Go down at G (forming stem stitch); come up at H. Pull through. Go down next to H and up at I as shown.*

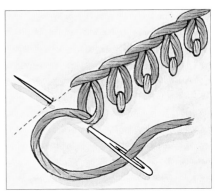

5 *Repeat from Step 3 to form a line of stitches. Work carefully to keep stitching even.*

Sword Edging Stitch

This stitch can be worked in rows to make a pretty edging or as individual stitches scattered across a plain background.

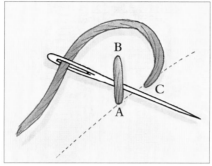

1 *Come up at A, go down at B, up at C. Take thread over stitch A–B and slide needle under it left to right without picking up background fabric.*

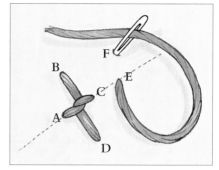

2 *Go down at D, opposite B. Come up at E on guideline as shown. Go down at F to begin next stitch, repeating from C in Step 1 to continue row.*

Ladder Stitch

Open Chain, Step Stitch, Ladder Hemstitch

It is usually best to work this border stitch in a frame in order to keep the loops neat and even. Draw guidelines on the fabric before beginning.

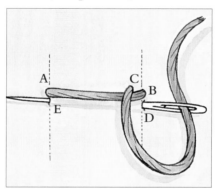

1 *Come up at A, cross over, and go down at B. Come up at C and go down at D, below B. Come up at E as shown.*

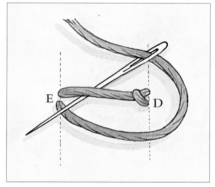

2 *Slide needle top to bottom under long stitch and over working thread. Pull to form knot at left of first long stitch.*

3 *Slide needle from right to left behind right-hand knot. Do not pick up background fabric.*

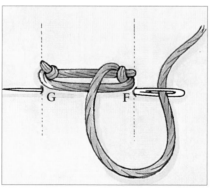

4 *Pull thread through and go down at F, coming up at G. Keep the thread tension even.*

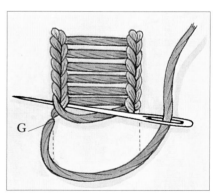

5 *Slide needle behind left-hand knot from right to left. Do not pick up background fabric. Repeat from Step 3.*

Rope Stitch

Good for curves and spirals, these textured line stitches should be close together to give an even effect. As its name suggests, the final stitch has a rope-like texture.

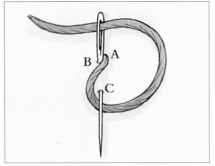

1 *Come up at A. Go down at B, taking thread over needle from right to left. Come up at C, taking thread under needle point from left to right.*

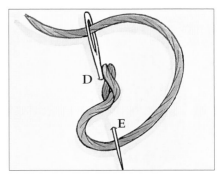

2 *Pull thread through gently. Go down at D and come up at E, looping thread from left to right, over then under needle as shown. Repeat.*

Cretan Stitch

Persian Stitch, Quill Stitch, Long-armed Feather Stitch

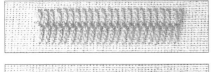

This stitch is particularly useful for filling shapes and creating lines. Work from alternate sides of the shape to fill it. Draw guidelines on your fabric before beginning.

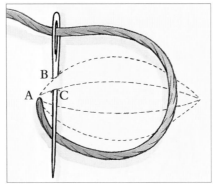

1 *Come up at A, go down at B, and up at C, keeping working thread under needle point.*

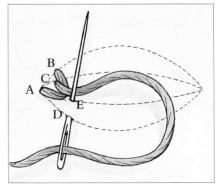

2 *Go down at D, following motif outline, and come up at E, keeping working thread under needle.*

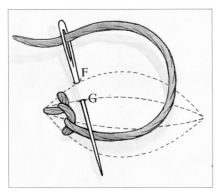

3 *Go down a short distance along at F, coming up at G with thread under needle point as shown.*

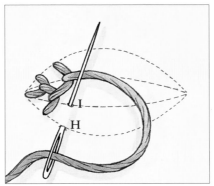

4 *Go down at H and then come up at I, again keeping thread under needle point as shown.*

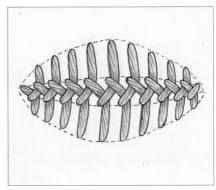

5 *Continue in this way. Vary size of stitch by extending or shortening the central crossover.*

Open Cretan Stitch

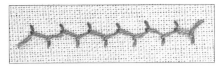

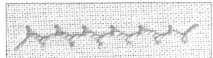

This variation of Cretan stitch is created by spacing the stitches apart. It is excellent for line work and for following curves. Always keep the working thread under the needle.

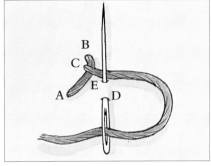

1 *Come up at A, go down at B, and come up just below at C. Cross over and go down at D; come up just above, at E, with working thread under needle.*

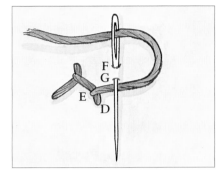

2 *Continue along the row by going down at F and coming up at G, keeping working thread under needle. Repeat from D in Step 1.*

Feathered Chain Stitch

This variation of basic feather stitch is particularly useful for borders. Work from top to bottom. Draw guidelines on the fabric before beginning.

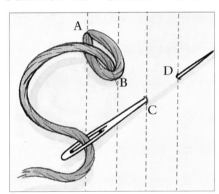

1 *Come up at A. Make a loop and go down next to A, coming up through loop at B. Slant to the right, go down at C, and come up at D.*

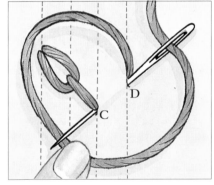

2 *Pull thread through. Go down next to D, then come up at C. Loop thread under point of needle and pull thread through gently.*

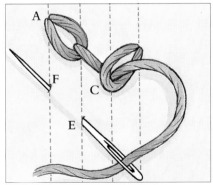

3 *Go down at E and then come up at F (below A) as shown to make straight stitch. Pull thread through.*

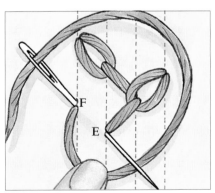

4 *Go down next to F and come up at E, keeping thread under point of needle. Pull thread through.*

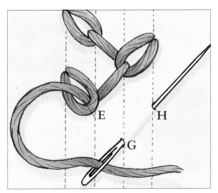

5 *Go down at G and come up at H. Repeat from Step 2 to continue the column, following guidelines.*

Closed Feather Stitch

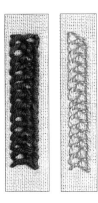

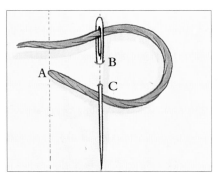

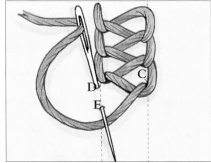

This stitch is worked from top to bottom and creates a wide feathery border. Draw parallel guidelines on your fabric before beginning.

1 *Come up at A, go down at B, and up at C, keeping working thread under needle. Pull thread through.*

2 *Take thread to left; go down at D and up at E. Alternate sides to continue, keeping working thread under needle.*

Double Feather Stitch

Double Coral Stitch, Thorn and Briar Stitch

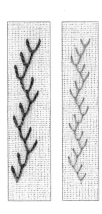

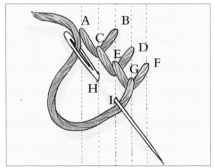

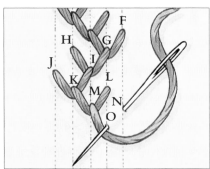

This variation on basic feather stitch is used to create a zigzag of feathery branches. A useful border stitch, it is worked from top to bottom.

1 *Come up at A, down at B, up at C, keeping needle over stitch just made. Repeat, following letter sequence. Then cross to left; go down at H and up at I.*

2 *Repeat, going down at J, up at K, down at L, up at M, down at N, up at O. Continue, working two stitches to left and two to right, keeping loops even.*

Wheatear Stitch

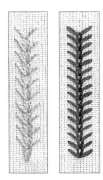

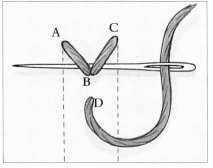

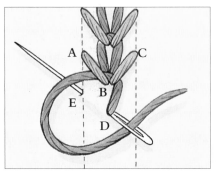

When worked in small columns, this line stitch looks like a stalk of grain. Usually worked in straight rows, this stitch can also follow gentle curves.

1 *Come up at A, go down at B, up at C, down at B again, up at D. Without picking up fabric, slide needle right to left through bottom of the V just made.*

2 *Go down at D and then come up at E, ready for next stitch. Repeat from Step 1 to continue working column of stitches as desired.*

Braid Stitch
Gordian Knot Stitch

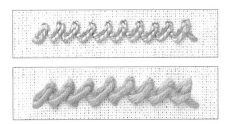

This textured border stitch works well on curves and with a heavy thread such as cotton perlé. Work from right to left, and make sure that you form the loops exactly as shown, with the left side of the loop laid over the right side.

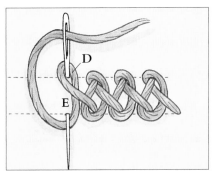

1 *Come up at A. Make loop on fabric as shown, then go down at B through centre of loop. Come up at C with thread under needle point.*

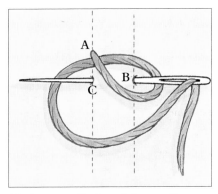

2 *Pull thread through. Then loop thread as in Step 1, go down at D, and come up at E as shown to complete second stitch. Repeat to continue along row.*

Plaited Braid Stitch

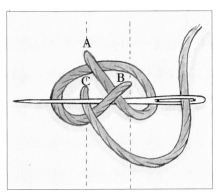

This stitch requires practice but is very effective as a decorative border. Work from the top down and use a heavy thread. Pinning the loops will help you practice.

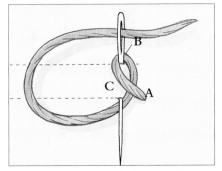

1 *Come up at A and make a loop with working thread, placing loop to the right of A as shown.*

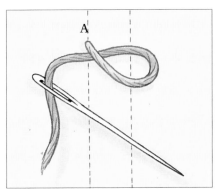

2 *Insert needle through loop at B, coming up at C with working thread under needle point.*

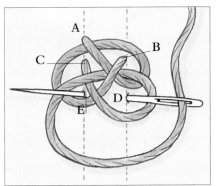

3 *Pull through, holding left-hand loop steady with thumb. Carry thread to right and slide needle right to left as shown. Do not pick up background fabric.*

4 *Go down at D (within bottom right-hand loop); come up at E (within bottom left-hand loop). Keep working thread under needle.*

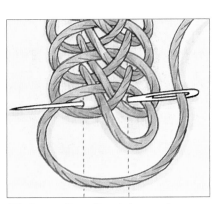

5 *Repeat Steps 3 and 4 to work a row, keeping thread under needle point. Try to make loops even to achieve a neat column of stitches.*

Paisley Shawl

This project uses just three simple stitches worked in varied colour combinations to create a rich pattern. Work as many or as few motifs as you wish.

Size

Finished shawl: 48 in (122 cm) square

Materials and Equipment

49 in (124.5 cm) square of medium or heavyweight silk, or lightweight wool fabric

Medium-sized crewel needle

6 in (15 cm) hoop frame

Tracing paper, transfer pencil

Thread

DMC cotton perlé No. 5, 4 skeins:

■ 792   □ 973
■ 606   ■ 701

Preparation

1 *Make a ½ in (1.3 cm) hem on all four edges of the silk or wool fabric.*

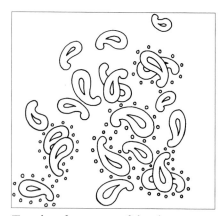

Template for corner of shawl

2 *First enlarge and then trace and transfer whichever sections of the design you choose onto your fabric. The template shows the corner section of the shawl. You also can vary the design by tracing the individual colour motifs and placing them randomly over the fabric. Position the outer motifs about 1½ in (4 cm) in from the vertical and horizontal edges of the fabric. Depending on your design, it may be difficult for you to use a hoop or frame to work the outer sections of the shawl.*

Stitch and Colour Chart

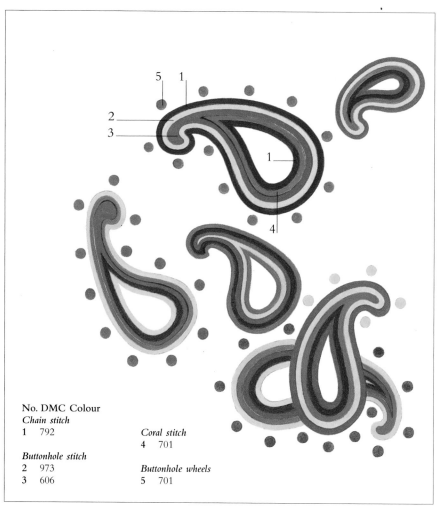

No.	DMC	Colour
Chain stitch		
1	792	
		Coral stitch
		4 701
Buttonhole stitch		
2	973	
3	606	*Buttonhole wheels*
		5 701

Stitching

3 *Colours are shown for only one paisley motif, since the order of the colours changes randomly from one motif to another. Mix and match the order of the colours on the rest of the design to provide an even balance.*

4 *All the paisley motifs have an identical stitch construction. Start with the outer row on each motif and work in towards the centre. Work the outer row of each motif in chain stitch. Work the second row in buttonhole stitch, with the "legs" of each stitch facing towards the centre of the motif. Work the third row in buttonhole stitch with*

the legs facing towards the outer edge of the motif and spaced so that they fall between the legs of the first row of buttonhole stitches. Work the fourth row in coral stitch, and the fifth (inside) row in chain stitch.

5 *Some motifs are framed by a border of circles, created using buttonhole wheels. Each wheel consists of six equally sized buttonhole stitches arranged in a circle. Work from outside edge of circle to a central point.*

Finishing

6 *When complete, press carefully on the reverse side over a soft towel.*

Laced Stitch Family

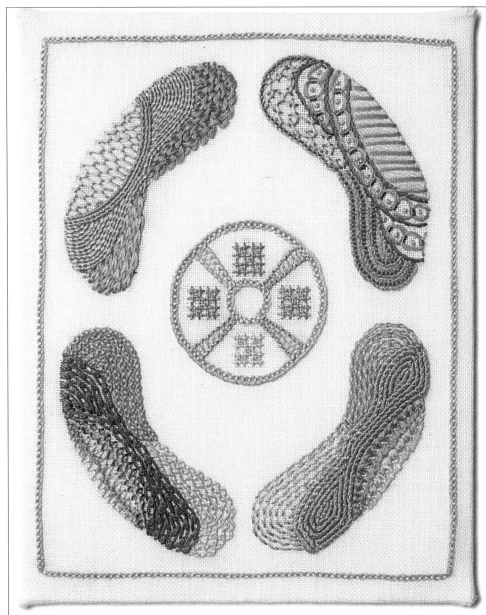

As this sampler shows, the stitches in the laced stitch family are perfect for experimentation with both colour and texture. Whipped satin, raised chevron, and whipped chain stitches add height to the design while an open, ornate effect is created with stitches such as wave stitch. Different coloured foundation stitches add variety to Pekinese stitch and interlaced band. All the foundation stitches have been worked in DMC cotton perlé and all the lacing stitches in DMC stranded cotton.

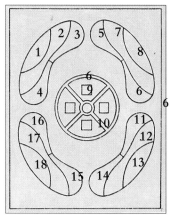

L ACED STITCHES can often appear to be complex arrangements of threads. However, they actually consist of the most basic stitches, which, once completed, are laced through with a contrasting thread – which is why the stitches in this family are often referred to as composite.

Some stitches in this family are very intricate: Pekinese stitch (page 103), for example, was once used extensively in Chinese embroidery. Legend has it that the stitch caused blindness or at least eyestrain, and therefore it was banned – hence its alternative names, *forbidden stitch* and *blind stitch*.

Many laced stitches have become so popular that they have quite singular identities. Guilloche stitch (page 104), for example, is a simple arrangement of three different stitches intertwined with contrasting threads. These composite stitches are often used for decorative bands and filling motifs, especially in crewelwork (page 112).

Laced stitches can also be used to join together two pieces of fabric, since the fabrics can be strengthened by weaving threads over and between the edges.

As this family's name also suggests, you can achieve intricate lacy effects with these stitches. To do this, choose delicate threads, such as flower thread, and carefully work your stitching onto a background fabric with a fine weave.

Threads and Fabrics

Highly decorative effects can be easily achieved with laced stitches, which work well on all fabrics. However, once you have mastered the specific stitching techniques, success or failure depends upon your selection of DMC threads.

In theory your chosen thread can be anything from the finest silk to ribbon or even string, but the row of base stitches must be strong and supple enough to support the contrasting thread(s). For example, if you lace ribbon through a row of stitches worked in delicate flower thread, you will completely lose the value of the flower thread stitches. Choose threads of equal weight for the best effect, and always try a practice stitch first.

Experiment with different DMC threads, textures, and colours: laced stitches are intended to be ornate.

Techniques

Two basic techniques are used in this stitch family.

Whipping Whipping wraps the thread repeatedly over and under a row or motif made up from a basic stitch, such as whipped satin stitch (page 102).

Weaving Weaving intertwines contrasting thread around crossed sections of each stitch to form a pattern, such as Maltese cross stitch (page 107).

In both whipping and weaving, always use a blunt tapestry needle to avoid picking up the background fabric. Never let the needle enter the fabric except at the beginning and end of each group of stitches.

To start a row of whipping or weaving, come up at one end of the row or section to be worked, using a thread long enough to finish the row or section. To finish, take the thread to the back of the fabric at a convenient point and then tie off. Work from left to right or right to left – whichever is more comfortable or convenient.

To use laced stitches to fill an area of a motif, simply work the stitches in rows, making sure that the base of one stitch touches the top of the stitch below and so on.

See Also:
Embroidery threads *page 9*
Basic stitches *pages 20–43*
Rooster wall hanging *page 108*
Crewelwork *pages 112–127*
Couching and goldwork *pages 128–141*

Whipped Running Stitch
Cordonnet Stitch

Whipped running stitch is a neat decorative alternative to plain running stitch and extremely useful for outlining curved motifs.

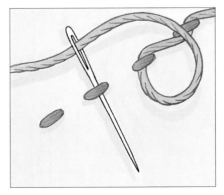

1 *Work a row of running stitch (page 28). With contrasting thread, whip in and out of each stitch, top to bottom, without picking up background fabric.*

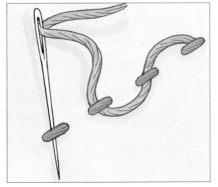

Double whipped running stitch
Weave in and out as shown, making rounder loops. For a denser effect, work loops on both sides.

Whipped Chain Stitch

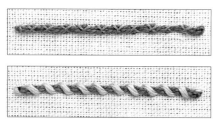

This decorative line stitch is particularly useful for outlining work. The whipped effect can be created using contrasting coloured or textured thread. You can also whip two rows of chain stitch together to create a filling stitch.

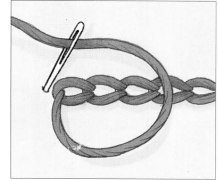

1 *Work a row of chain stitch (page 24), making stitches slightly larger than normal. End with a small straight stitch.*

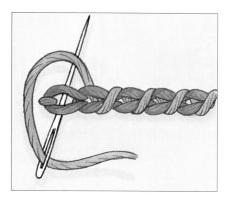

2 *Using contrasting thread, whip needle over and under each stitch as shown. Do not pick up background fabric.*

Whipped Satin Stitch

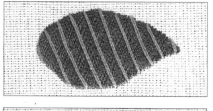

This variation of satin stitch (page 32) gives an embossed effect and is useful for corded lines, narrow shapes, and stems. A satin stitch foundation is worked, then evenly spaced stitches are whipped at angles across the top.

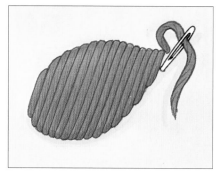

1 *Fill a shape or work a band with a foundation of satin stitch (page 32), taking care to graduate edges gently.*

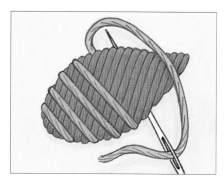

2 *Whip contrasting stitches at a different angle across and under motif, taking care to space stitches evenly.*

Whipped Stem Stitch

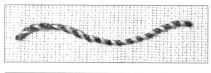

This very simple stitch is a weightier version of basic stem stitch (page 31) with the appearance of a fine cord. It follows curved lines easily.

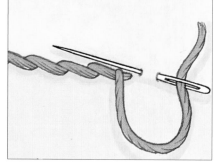

1 *Work a foundation row of stem stitch (page 31) with your base thread, following the motif outline.*

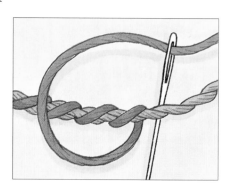

2 *With a contrasting thread, whip needle over and under each stitch in row. Do not pick up background fabric.*

Pekinese Stitch

Chinese Stitch, Blind Stitch, Forbidden Stitch

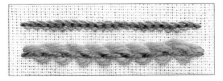

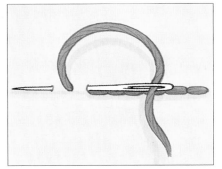

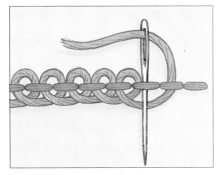

This composite line stitch is popularly used as a border, particularly for lacy edgings on collars and cuffs.

1 *Work a foundation row of backstitch (page 30) following guideline or outline of motif. Tie thread at back of fabric.*

2 *Whip contrasting thread in circular motion, looping in and out of backstitches, keeping loops even.*

Wave Stitch

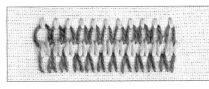

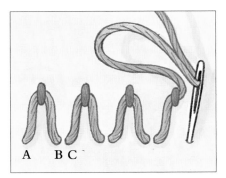

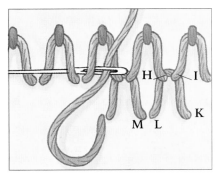

This versatile line and filling stitch can produce different effects according to the length and positions you choose for the base row of stitches.

1 *Work a row of vertical straight stitches. Fasten off. Bring a new thread up at A and slide under first stitch. Go down at B; come up at C. Repeat along row.*

2 *As a filling stitch: come up at K; slide thread through base of H and I; go down at L, up at M; repeat. Pierce fabric only at base of row being worked.*

Threaded Backstitch

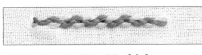

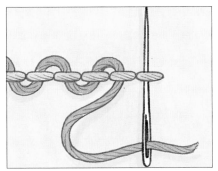

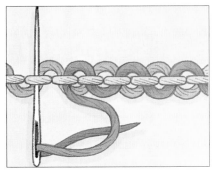

Useful for outlining, this stitch can be worked in one, two, or three colours. Size the backstitches according to the weight of thread to be whipped or laced through row.

1 *Work row of backstitch (page 30), making stitches slightly longer. Use contrasting thread to weave in and out.*

2 *For double threaded backstitch, weave as before in opposite direction. Be careful not to split threads already worked.*

Threaded Detached Chain Stitch

This easy stitch is made with a row of detached chain stitches (page 24) spaced evenly apart, then laced with contrasting threads.

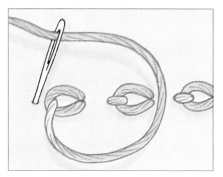

1 *Working from right to left, work a row of evenly spaced detached chain stitches (page 24) as shown.*

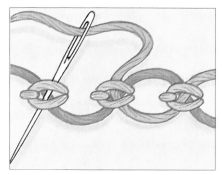

2 *With contrasting thread, weave up and down through main body of each chain. Repeat in opposite direction.*

Guilloche Stitch

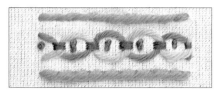

The name derives from a term used in architecture for an ornamental border containing two or more interwoven wavy lines. Used to create a decorative band, guilloche stitch can include several different thread types.

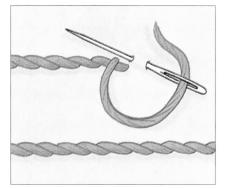

1 *Work two parallel lines of stem stitch (page 31), keeping stitching even. You may want to use guidelines.*

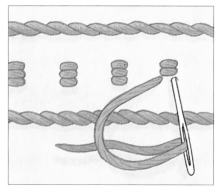

2 *Between lines, work evenly spaced vertical bands, each consisting of three satin stitches (page 32).*

3 *Starting at the left, lace contrasting thread through first band and then through second, without picking up background fabric. Continue across row.*

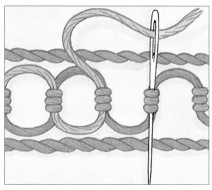

4 *Repeat in opposite direction, taking care not to split existing threads. If you wish, choose a contrasting thread to add interest to the design.*

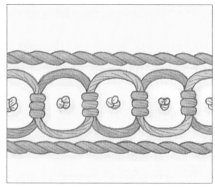

5 *Work a French knot (page 33) at the centre of each circle formed by the lacing as shown, using a new thread colour if desired.*

Tied Herringbone Stitch
Coral Knotted Herringbone Stitch

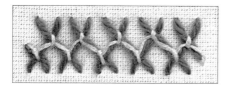

This simple border and filling stitch is made with herringbone and coral stitches (pages 26, 74). When used as a filling, place foundation stitches directly above each other so the tips touch.

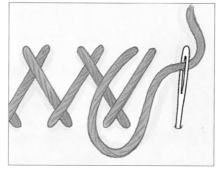

1 Work a foundation row of herringbone stitches (page 26). Keep stitches same length and evenly spaced.

2 With contrasting thread, work coral stitches (page 74) over herringbone stitches, making knot at each intersection.

Raised Chain Band

This composite stitch is made up of horizontal straight stitches linked with chain stitches (page 24) worked with a contrasting thread. Begin by making a vertical column of horizontal straight stitches.

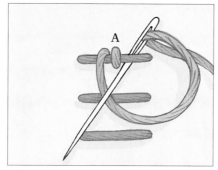

1 With contrasting thread, come up at A, take thread over horizontal stitch; come up to left of A. Slide needle under stitch with thread under needle point.

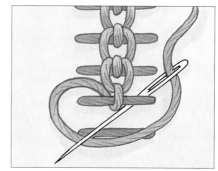

2 Pull thread through. Take thread over and under next horizontal stitch, and slide needle under stitch to the left as shown. Pull thread through. Repeat.

Interlaced Band
Herringbone Ladder Filling Stitch, Double Pekinese Stitch, Laced Cretan Stitch

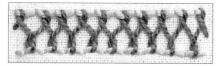

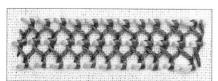

This lacy border and filling stitch is worked on a foundation of two parallel alternating rows of backstitch (page 30). Draw guidelines on the fabric before beginning.

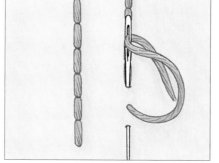

1 Work a row of backstitch (page 30). Then work parallel row of backstitches, positioning stitches opposite stitch breaks on first row as shown.

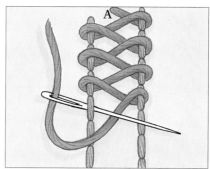

2 Using contrasting thread, come up at A. Lace right to left through top right-hand stitch, keeping working thread under needle. Repeat to left as shown.

Threaded Herringbone Stitch

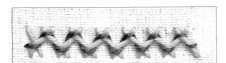

This stitch is made up of a row of herringbone stitches (page 26) laced with one or two contrasting intertwining threads.

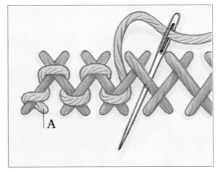

1 *Work a row of herringbone stitch (page 26) from left to right. Tie off. Using contrasting thread, come up at A.*

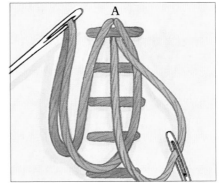

2 *Working from left to right, lace thread under and over row of herringbone stitches as shown.*

Chequered Chain Band

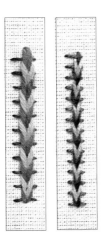

This stitch is worked downwards to create a band. Use as a border, or place bands of stitches side by side as a filling stitch. Create the bi-colour effect by using two needles threaded in different colours and worked alternately down the band.

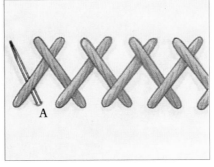

1 *Work column of horizontal straight stitches as shown. Tie off. Then thread two needles with doubled length of thread in each, one light, one dark.*

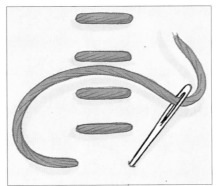

2 *Bring dark thread out at A; bring out light thread under horizontal stitch and between two dark strands. Carry dark thread to left, under light thread.*

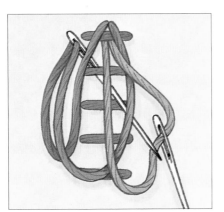

3 *Insert needle with dark thread under second horizontal stitch as shown, and then carry it under dark thread but over light thread.*

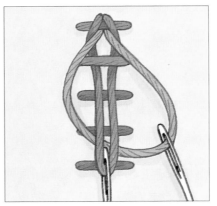

4 *Pull needle through. The band should now look like this. As you work, always keep dark thread to left and light thread to right.*

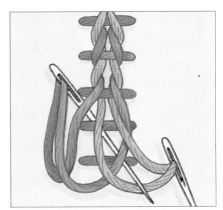

5 *Repeat Steps 3 and 4, this time inserting needle with light thread under horizontal stitch and dark thread. Continue, alternating two needles.*

Raised Chevron Stitch

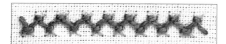

This bold raised border is particularly effective worked in a heavy thread. The foundation rows consist of simple Vs. Work these carefully. Draw three parallel guidelines on your fabric before beginning.

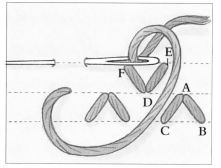

1 Come up on centre line at A. Go down at B, come up at C, then down at A again, up at D. Work next V: down at E, up at F, down at D again. Repeat, spacing stitches evenly.

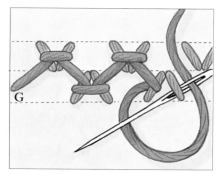

2 Come up at G. Slide over and under first leg of V, right to left, without going through fabric. Slide behind second leg of V, right to left, to form horizontal stitch. Repeat for bottom V and continue.

Maltese Cross Stitch

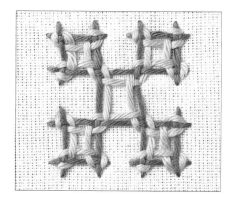

This laced motif can be used alone or as a border. The stitch consists of a grid of interwoven straight stitches with a contrasting thread that is laced through each section.

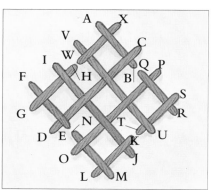

1 Come up at A, go down at B, and up at C. Continue following letters as shown, and complete grid by taking needle down at X.

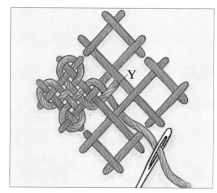

2 Using contrasting thread, come up at Y and under opposite diagonal thread. Weave thread around each crossed section as shown.

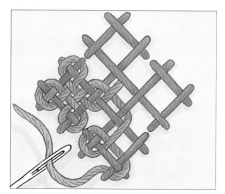

3 When first square is complete, carry thread down to bottom quadrant and continue weaving as shown, finishing in centre of grid.

4 Carry thread to right-hand quadrant and continue in the same manner, weaving threads in between straight stitches as shown.

5 Weave around last square of grid, finishing at starting point. Then take needle through fabric to back of work and fasten thread.

Rooster Wall Hanging

Laced stitches do not always need to look fancy – take a simple motif such as this rooster and stitch onto a natural background fabric for an earthy, ethnic effect.

Size
Panel: 10½ x 7¾ in (26.5 x 19.5 cm)

Materials and Equipment
24 in (60 cm) square Rustico
 14-count Aida
Size 7 crewel needle
Size 24 tapestry needle
14 x 12 in (35.5 x 30.5 cm) frame
13 in (33 cm) hanging rod
Tracing paper, transfer pencil

Thread
DMC coton à broder, 2 skeins:

666		435	
743		434	
741		823	
946			

Preparation

1 *Cut 12 x 14 in (30.5 x 35.5 cm) of fabric and mount on frame. Tack an area 8 x 10½ in (20.5 x 26.5 cm) on fabric centre. Where several colour numbers appear together, use the first to work a laced-stitch foundation row. For areas 12, 13, work three consecutive rows in colours indicated.*

Stitching

2 *Count five blocks of fabric at each corner from each edge; stitch Maltese crosses, working grid over 11 blocks. Work interlaced-band border over two blocks.*

3 *Count three blocks towards centre. Work chequered chain band over three blocks, spacing stitches two blocks apart.*

4 *Trace design, enlarge to 220 per cent, and transfer. Follow chart to work stitching.*

5 *Enlarge the triangle pattern to scale; transfer to fabric, cut out six. Stitch the diamond in the center of three. Sew stitched and plain triangles right sides together, leaving top open. Turn right side out.*

6 *Cut four fabric pieces measuring 2¾ x 6 in (7 x 15 cm). For the hangers, stitch vertical raised chain band on centre of two. Stitch wrong sides together, sewing side seams only. Turn right side out.*

Finishing

7 *Leaving five blocks of free fabric at each edge, fold back the remaining fabric. Fold right side of each hanger in half lengthwise, position at top, four blocks in from the edges. Tack to back of fabric. Place central triangle in position, tack to back of design, repeat for other triangles. Stitch into position. Use leftover fabric to back main panel. Turn in selvedges. Tack, wrong sides together, and stitch around outer edges. For tassels and twisted cord see pages 182, 183.*

Stitch and Colour Chart

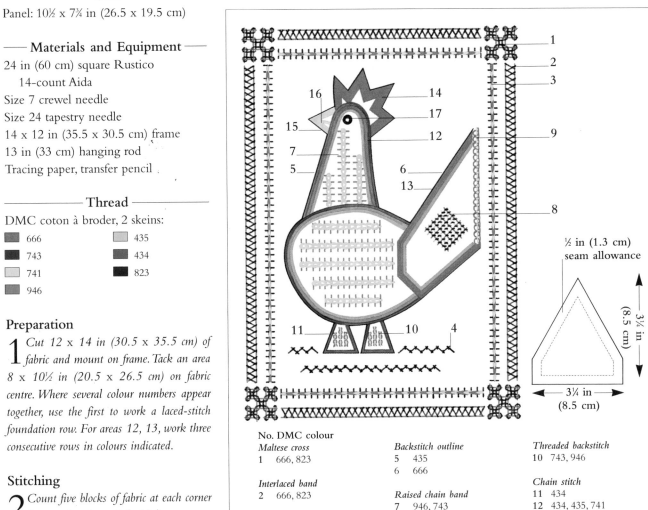

½ in (1.3 cm) seam allowance

3¼ in (8.5 cm)

3¼ in (8.5 cm)

No. DMC colour		
Maltese cross	**Backstitch outline**	**Threaded backstitch**
1 666, 823	5 435	10 743, 946
	6 666	
Interlaced band		**Chain stitch**
2 666, 823	**Raised chain band**	11 434
	7 946, 743	12 434, 435, 741
Chequered chain band		13 666, 946, 741
3 823, 666, 743	**Threaded herringbone stitch**	14 666 (3 rows)
	8 666, 743, 823	15 743 (2 rows)
Tied herringbone stitch		16 743 (1 row)
4 823	**Pekinese stitch**	17 823 (1 row)
	9 743, 946	

Special Skills

Crewelwork, beads and embellishments, monogramming, couching and goldwork, and ribbon embroidery are techniques that can enhance your projects with extra interest and texture.

Here is valuable information on special threads, fabrics, stitches, and techniques. Many are useful for creating a three-dimensional look, and some make use of eye-catching materials such as shisha mirrors and gold threads.

Crewelwork

Crewelwork is embroidery stitched with wool, and the fine, two-ply yarn that is used in crewelwork is known as crewel wool. Crewelwork is also known as Jacobean work, from the embroidered wall hangings popular in England during the late 17th-century reign of King James I.

FOR THE BEGINNER, crewelwork is a perfect opportunity to practise new stitches and to experiment with colour shading. The thickness of wool yarn allows you to cover the fabric quickly, and the texture of the thread will hide minor imperfections.

Traditional crewelwork designs usually feature simple, freestanding images, gently shaded and textured with a variety of stitches. These motifs can be combined to create complex borders, intertwined and repeated to make an all-over pattern on a large piece of fabric, or worked as a corner motif.

Fabrics

Traditionally, crewelwork is stitched onto a heavyweight, natural-coloured linen, provided it is sturdy enough to support the wool embroidery threads. A densely stitched area is quite heavy, so the weave of the fabric should be firm. You can, however, use any plain or evenweave fabric. Modern crewel designs are found on woven wool fabrics, on calico, drill, and on rough, heavyweight silk slub, which gives the contrast of wool thread on silken sheen.

When selecting your fabric, consider your palette of threads and choose a colour that will offset the subtle shading of your stitching.

Frames

Crewelwork should be worked with the fabric stretched taut across a frame to minimize puckering of the background fabric and to help keep your stitching even. A simple embroidery hoop (page 10) will be perfectly adequate for holding small pieces. However, you might prefer to mount your work on a standing frame. Alternatively, for larger pieces, secure with a scroll (slate) frame (page 10) which you could lay over two trestles to form a table top.

Needles

Crewel needles (pages 8, 113) are widely used in embroidery, and particularly for crewelwork. They have a larger eye than sewing needles, but are similar in length and point. Crewel needles are available in a variety of sizes, but sizes 3, 4, and 5 are essential; you will use No. 4 for most of your work, No. 3 for working two strands of yarn together, and No. 5 for very fine work.

Chenille needles (page 8) are also used in crewelwork. These are shorter than crewel needles, sizes 22 and 24 are most often used for crewelwork.

Crewelwork box lid, 1650-75

This traditional, Jacobean-style crewelwork box lid typifies an embroidery technique that was used in ecclesiastical work as well as for furnishings. It is widely believed that designs like this derived originally from the Orient and India. Stitches used include satin stitch (page 32), bullion knots (page 75), and French knots (page 33).

A tapestry (blunt-ended) needle is also very useful, since many of the stitches used in crewelwork involve laidwork (page 115).

Threading wool yarn through a needle can be tricky for beginners. First fold the thread around the needle, flatten the fold with your fingers, and then slide the needle down over the fold of thread. Alternatively, you may find it easier to use a needle threader (page 18).

Threads

You can work crewelwork motifs (pages 116–119) using stranded cotton and fine silks to create pleasing crisp, clear images. However, traditional crewelwork uses crewel wool.

Crewel wool DMC crewel wool (broder medicis) is a two-ply, non-divisible, twisted, worsted wool yarn created specifically for traditional crewelwork.

Because crewel wool is produced from finely spun threads, it has the advantage of allowing you to stitch with two or more shades in your needle at the same time (see below).

You can create fine lines and delicate shapes with single threads, but these threads do have a tendency to break, so use them with care. They are also prone to tangle and to become thin from the action of repeatedly pulling them through the fabric. It is advisable to cut threads to a maximum working length of 12 in (30.5 cm).

You will also find it helpful to store coordinating threads together as a colour palette (page 114).

Tapestry wool Thicker than crewel wool and spun to a rounded shape, DMC tapestry (tapisserie) wool enables you to cover large areas quickly. Because tapestry wool is thicker, it is also stronger and it works well on coarse fabrics.

However, tapestry wool is unsuitable for use on any background fabric that has a very fine weave, as this yarn is certainly not fine enough to pass through the delicate weave of the fabric without damaging it.

Contemporary crewelwork floral design
Stitches used include chain (page 24), stem (page 31), and satin (page 32).

Needles and Threads

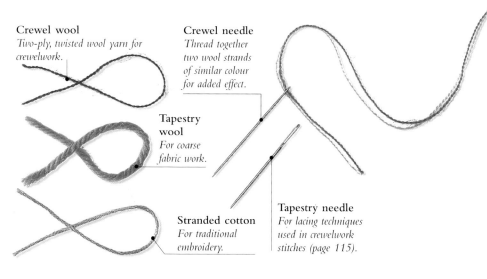

Crewel wool
Two-ply, twisted wool yarn for crewelwork.

Crewel needle
Thread together two wool strands of similar colour for added effect.

Tapestry wool
For coarse fabric work.

Stranded cotton
For traditional embroidery.

Tapestry needle
For lacing techniques used in crewelwork stitches (page 115).

How to Select Colours

You should aim to harmonize all the colours within each motif and balance the colours of your overall design.

Crewel wools can be arranged into six colour families: red, yellow, blue, green, purple, and brown, and then divided into shades, numbered from 1 to 5, with 5 being the darkest shade and 1 being the lightest.

Arrangements of colour values can be considerably more complex than this, but for beginners this system is certainly a good starting point. Beginners may also find it helpful to work their first crewelwork design using values from just one family of colours.

To work with two or more colour families, try selecting one colour from each colour family, then increase values by one or two numbers – for example, you could place yarn colours 1 and 3 together successfully, but not yarn colours 1 and 5.

In some cases, strong colour contrasts work brilliantly – a screaming yellow with a sizzling violet, for example. One of the beauties of experimenting with colour is in the surprising results that can come from using favourite colours.

Crewel Wool Colour Groups

Colour selection is an essential element in crewel embroidery. Here are some traditional colour combinations for crewelwork motifs and designs.

DMC colours *(top to bottom):* 8314, 8407, 8151, 8123, 8895, 8122.

DMC colours *(top to bottom):* 8418, 8331, 8332, 8817, 8514, 8505.

DMC colours *(top to bottom):* 8224, 8223, 8225, 8402, 8309.

DMC colours *(top to bottom):* 8407, 8173, 8175, 8129, 8128.

DMC colours *(top to bottom):* 8223, 8224, 8331, 8326, 8321.

DMC colours *(top to bottom):* 8223, 8203, 8206, 8326, 8207.

Crewelwork Stitches

There is no limit to the stitches that you can use to create crewelwork images. However, the nature of crewelwork designs means you must select at least one outlining stitch – see basic stitches (page 20) and the straight stitch family (page 46) – plus a selection of various filling stitches.

Stem stitch (page 31), split stitch (page 48), and chain stitch (page 24), are all particularly useful for outlining motifs, and satin stitch (page 32) and its variations – see the satin stitch family (page 56) – are excellent choices for creating flat, filled areas within a design.

Many of the filling stitches used in crewelwork use a couching technique (page 131) or lay stitches inside a motif to create intricate trellis patterns.

Light, open effects can also be achieved by scattering seed stitches or working selections of cross or knotted stitches individually within an enclosed area of a design. Many of the stitches described in the stitch library section can be placed together in rows to form attractive fillings within crewelwork motifs. A selection of traditional trace-off motifs for crewelwork is shown on pages 116–119. All the motifs are annotated and illustrated with stitch suggestions to show the potential effect of different stitch combinations

Two popular crewelwork filling stitches are Jacobean laidwork and cloud filling stitch (see opposite), which are both used to create the crewelwork cushion project (page 124).

See Also:
Basic stitches *pages 20–43*
Straight stitch family *pages 46–55*
Satin stitch family *pages 56–63*
Cross stitch family *pages 64–71*
Knotted stitch family *pages 72–85*
Pomegranate needlecase *page 120*
Couching and goldwork *pages 128–141*

T*HESE TWO FILLING stitches make a Jacobean-style trellis that is popular in crewelwork. They belong to the laced stitch family (page 100), where contrasting threads are woven through base stitches to create textural effects.*

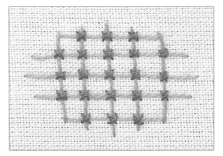

Jacobean laidwork

Also known as trellis couching, this filling stitch can be worked in a square shape or in a circle or oval, as illustrated here.

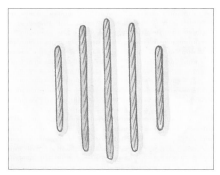

1 *Fill the motif with single, parallel, vertical stitches as shown, working from top to bottom, bottom to top.*

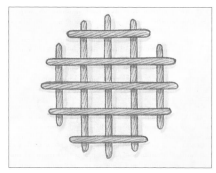

2 *Work long horizontal stitches over the vertical stitches to form a grid. Work from left to right, right to left.*

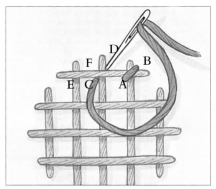

3 *Using a contrasting thread, come up at A, go down at B, up at C, down at D, and up at E. Go down at F.*

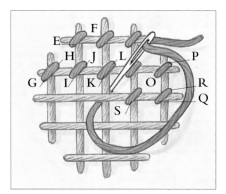

4 *Come up at G, go down at H. Continue back and forth across motif, following letter sequence.*

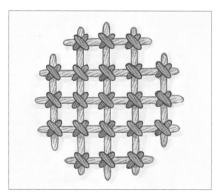

5 *Repeat Step 3, working diagonal stitches in opposite direction to form crosses, and complete the trellis effect.*

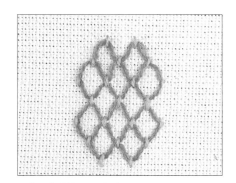

Cloud filling stitch

This stitch is an alternative filling stitch, again traditionally used to fill crewelwork motifs. Use a contrasting thread for lacing to add depth and colour.

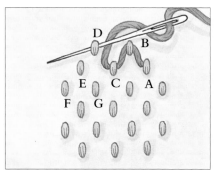

1 *Work rows of evenly spaced, small vertical stitches. Come up to right of A, carry thread through vertical stitch (A) and B and across row, and go down under E. Do not pick up background fabric.*

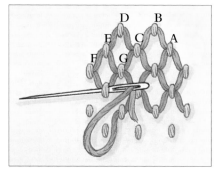

2 *Come up at F, weaving up through E, down through G, up through C and so on. Continue working back and forth across each row.*

115

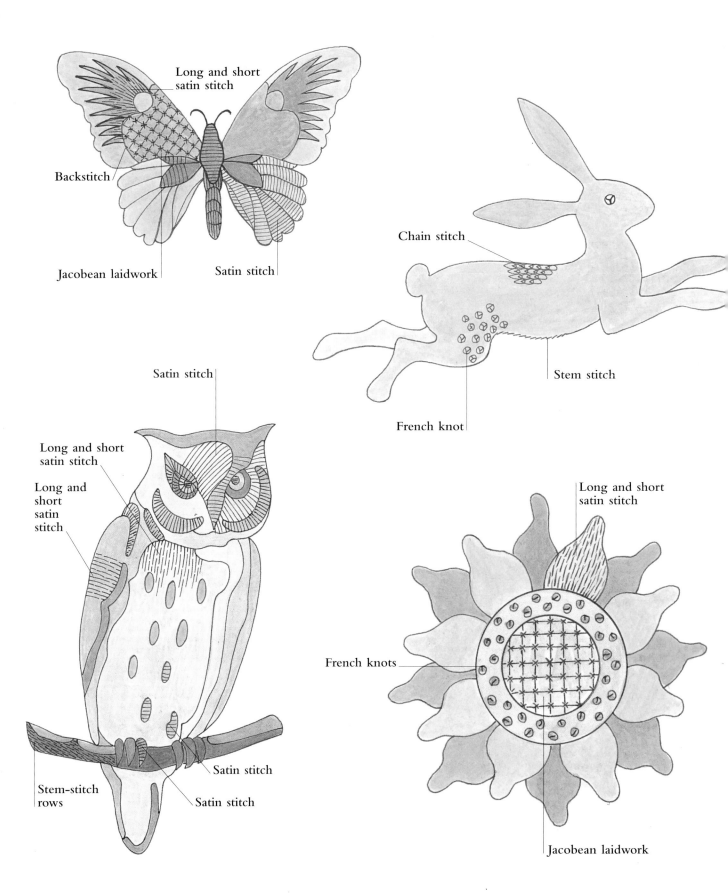

Long and short
satin stitch

Backstitch

Jacobean laidwork

Satin stitch

Chain stitch

Stem stitch

French knot

Satin stitch

Long and short
satin stitch

Long and
short
satin
stitch

Long and short
satin stitch

French knots

Stem-stitch
rows

Satin stitch

Satin stitch

Jacobean laidwork

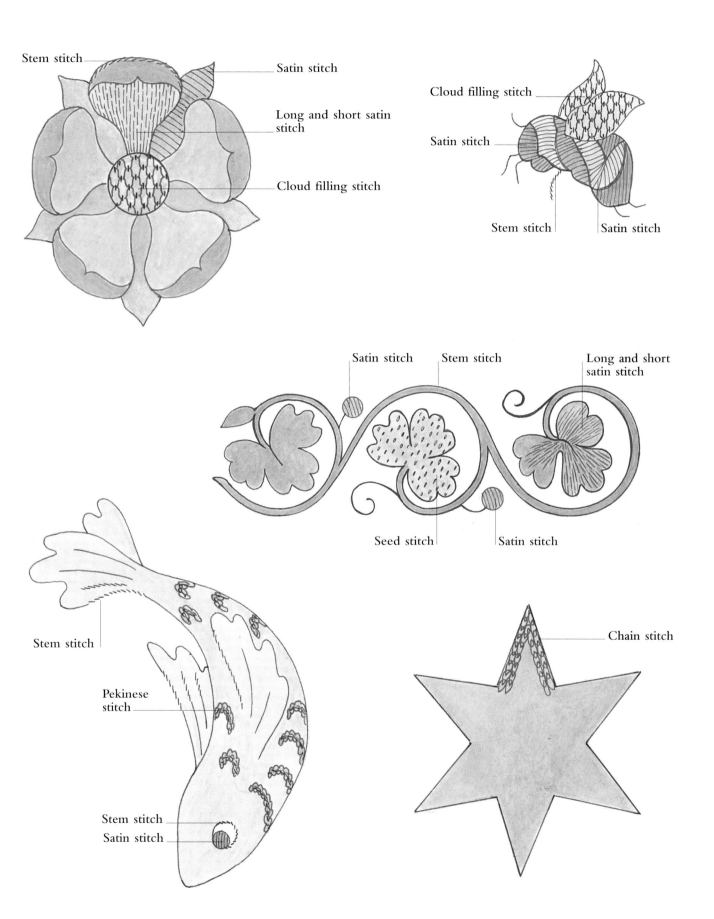

Stem stitch

Satin stitch

Long and short satin stitch

Cloud filling stitch

Cloud filling stitch

Satin stitch

Stem stitch

Satin stitch

Satin stitch

Stem stitch

Long and short satin stitch

Seed stitch

Satin stitch

Stem stitch

Pekinese stitch

Stem stitch

Satin stitch

Chain stitch

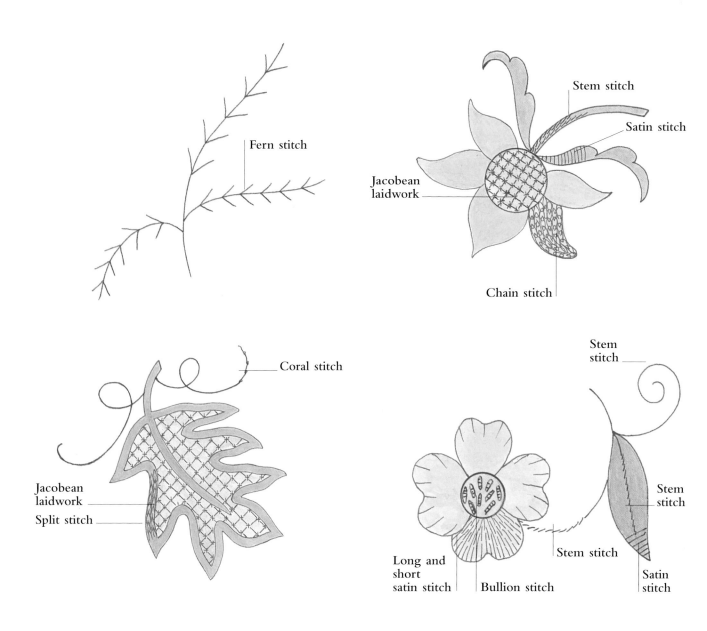

Fern stitch

Stem stitch

Satin stitch

Jacobean laidwork

Chain stitch

Coral stitch

Jacobean laidwork

Split stitch

Stem stitch

Stem stitch

Long and short satin stitch

Bullion stitch

Stem stitch

Satin stitch

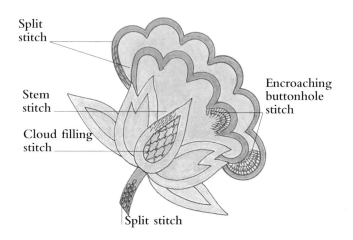

Split stitch

Stem stitch

Cloud filling stitch

Encroaching buttonhole stitch

Split stitch

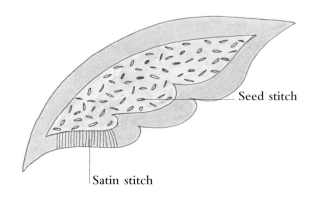

Seed stitch

Satin stitch

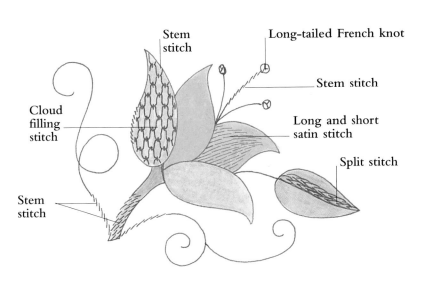

Stem stitch

Long-tailed French knot

Stem stitch

Cloud filling stitch

Long and short satin stitch

Split stitch

Stem stitch

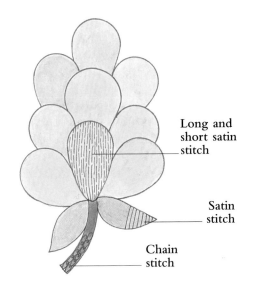

Long and short satin stitch

Satin stitch

Chain stitch

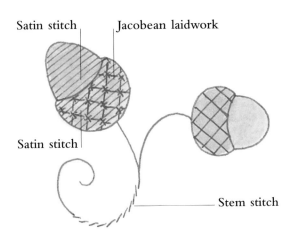

Satin stitch

Jacobean laidwork

Satin stitch

Stem stitch

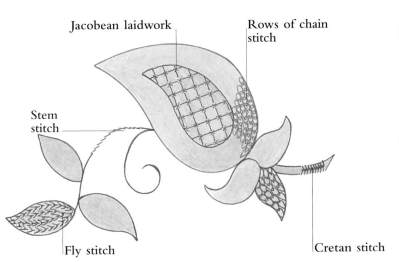

Jacobean laidwork

Rows of chain stitch

Stem stitch

Fly stitch

Cretan stitch

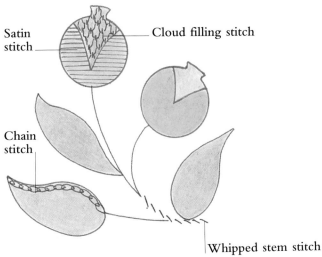

Satin stitch

Cloud filling stitch

Chain stitch

Whipped stem stitch

119

Pomegranate Needlecase

This traditional Jacobean-style design is embroidered with crewel wool, using basic and composite crewelwork stitches in rich, earthy colours.

Size

4½ x 8½ (11.5 x 21.5 cm)

Materials and Equipment

Two 5½ x 9½ in (14 x 24 cm) pieces of fine linen union, or a similar firm fabric (allow enough extra fabric to use a small hoop)

5½ x 9½ in (14 x 24 cm) medium-weight interfacing

Two 4½ x 7 in (11.5 x 18 cm) pieces felt

No. 7 crewel needle

Fine tapestry needle

Small embroidery hoop

Tracing paper, pencil

Transfer pencil

Thread

DMC broder medicis, 1 skein:

- 8407
- 8415
- 8405
- 8412
- 8164
- 8166
- 8104
- 8125
- 8313
- 8417
- 8302

Template

Preparation

1 Trace the outline of the design from the tracing plan (right); reduce to 89 per cent. Fold one piece of the linen union in half, then centre and transfer the design onto the right half of the linen. This will form front cover of needlecase. Mount your fabric in a hoop ready for stitching.

Stitching

2 Begin with the large green leaves. Using medium green wool (8412) to outline the curled tips and dark green wool (8417) to outline the main body of the leaves, work a single row of split stitch around the leaf edges. The split-stitch rows make it easier to work a straight edge in the first row of long and short satin stitches, which will cover the split stitch outlines. The split stitches also define and raise the edges of the leaves.

3 Working towards the central vein and over the split stitches, shade in long and short satin stitch from dark green (8417) at the outer edge to light green (8405) in the centre. Shade the curled tips of the leaves from medium green (8412) to light green.

4 For the small leaves at the base and top of the fruit, first work a row of split stitches as for the leaves, and work over these, shading in fly stitch in dark blue-green (8415) and pale blue-green (8407). Keep the fly stitches adjacent so the loop forms the central vein and the outer edges graduate to fill the leaf shapes.

5 To work the stem, work chain stitch using dark green wool (8417). Start by chain-stitching the outline of the teardrop shape at

the end of the stem. Beginning at the tip of the curled tendril, stitch another row, continuing it to form a double line around the teardrop shape. Then fill the centre with tightly packed French knots in dark gold wool (8302). Starting just below this motif, work two rows of chain stitch in dark green wool (8417) up the stem and through the centre of the top leaf. Carry one of these rows on to form the curled tendril.

6 Complete the leaf and stem part of the design by working another two rows of chain stitch to complete the main stem, and then work two more rows of chain stitch to form the stem and the central vein of the lower leaf. Work another row of chain stitch along the curled area of this leaf, and then continue it to form the tendril.

Stitch and Colour Chart

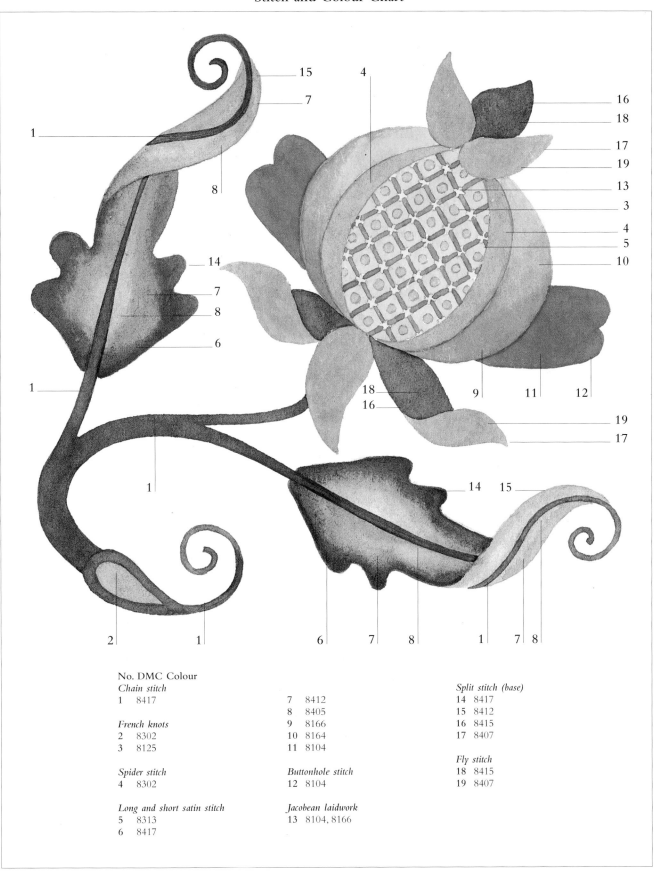

No. DMC Colour

Chain stitch
1   8417

French knots
2   8302
3   8125

Spider stitch
4   8302

Long and short satin stitch
5   8313
6   8417

7   8412
8   8405
9   8166
10   8164
11   8104

Buttonhole stitch
12   8104

Jacobean laidwork
13   8104, 8166

Split stitch (base)
14   8417
15   8412
16   8415
17   8407

Fly stitch
18   8415
19   8407

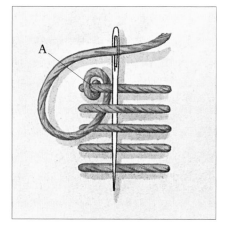

7 To work the fruit, begin with the two central borders, worked in dark-gold spider stitch (8302). Work this as follows: lay a column of horizontal threads, then use the tapestry needle to come up with a new thread at A (see above). Whip thread under and over the first vertical stitch as shown. Then go behind the next two horizontal stitches. Pull through.

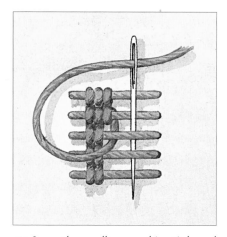

8 Loop the needle over this stitch and continue to bottom of column. Repeat in tight rows until horizontal stitches are completely covered with thread.

9 Add extra threads at centre as needed to fill the broader sweep of the curves. Whipping the threads tightly will also give a raised, bead-like effect on the surface of the fabric.

10 Fill the centre with long and short stitches in pale gold (8313). Then work Jacobean laidwork, laying a trellis of terracotta threads (8104) over the long and

Detail of Needlecase

short stitches. Using dark pink (8166), work a tiny cross stitch at each junction to hold the threads in place. Work a single mauve French knot (8125) at the centre of each couched diamond.

11 Working the outer areas of the pomegranate in long and short satin stitch, shade in dark pink (8166) at the base and pale pink (8164) at the top. Outline the outer "wings" of the fruit in terracotta buttonhole stitch (8104) and fill with terracotta long and short satin stitch. The buttonhole stitches should form a hard, crisp edge.

Finishing

12 Remove the completed work from the hoop, then press or block your work (page 181). With the interfacing at the back of the embroidery, place the embroidery right

sides together with the remaining piece of linen. Using a seam allowance of ½ in (1.3 cm), stitch around all edges, leaving a 2 in (5 cm) opening at the centre bottom for turning right side out.

13 Trim the seam and turn right side out. Next, close the opening with slipstitches. Place the felt pages on top of embroidery cover and fold in half to make needlecase. Stitch to hold along folded spine.

14 Make a twisted cord from the leftover threads (page 182) and sew the cord to the edge of the book (page 182). Make another length of twisted cord 12 in (30 cm) long, and loop it around the spine of the needlecase. Tie the twisted cord at the bottom of the spine, and tie each end 1 in (2.5 cm) from the bottom of the needlecase. Separate these final sections to form tassels.

Crewelwork Cushion

This cushion is worked in a traditional Jacobean style and has rich, subtle colour shading. Create the simple motifs first.

Size

Finished cushion: 14 x 14 in
(35.5 x 35.5 cm)

Materials and Equipment

18 in (45.5 cm) square heavyweight
cotton fabric
White cotton backing fabric, three
pieces:
15½ x 13½ in (39.5 x 34.5 cm)
15½ x 9½ in (39.5 x 24 cm)
15½ x 15½ in (39.5 x 39.5 cm)
Cushion pad 14 in (35.5 cm) square
Medium-sized crewel needle
18 in (45.5 cm) embroidery hoop
or frame
2 yd (1.8 m) piping cord (ours is grey)
White cotton sewing thread
Tracing paper, transfer pencil

Threads

DMC broder medicis, 1 skein in each
of the following colours:

☐	8211	☐	8401
☐	8417	☐	8402
☐	8208	☐	8403
☐	8207	☐	8871
☐	8799	☐	8798
☐	8507	☐	8800
☐	8508	☐	8210
☐	8509	☐	8418
☐	8406	☐	8419
☐	8407	☐	8420
☐	8426	☐	8309
☐	8427		
☐	8369		

Stitch Direction Chart

Preparation

1 *The stitch and colour chart opposite shows the stitches to work and the colours to use for every motif of this design. The key is arranged into types of stitches, and the broder medicis colour numbers are listed next to the key number. Unless stated otherwise, use only one strand of wool throughout the project.*

2 *The chart above shows the direction in which the stitches should be worked. This direction usually mirrors the plant's growth. You can work from base to tip or tip to base of a motif, whichever is the most comfortable.*

3 *First place the stitch and colour chart opposite on a photocopier and enlarge it to 210 per cent. This will give you a template that is actual size. Then press the fabric and transfer the outline of the design from the photocopy to the centre of the fabric. To do this, use the photocopy transfer method, described in the introduction on page 14. After this, stretch the heavyweight cotton fabric on to a hoop or a frame, ready to begin stitching.*

Stitching

4 *Start with one of the simpler motifs such as a bud. Work the stem-stitch stem as shown on the stitch and colour chart, then fill the stem tops in satin stitch.*

Detail of stitch direction chart

Stitch and Colour Chart

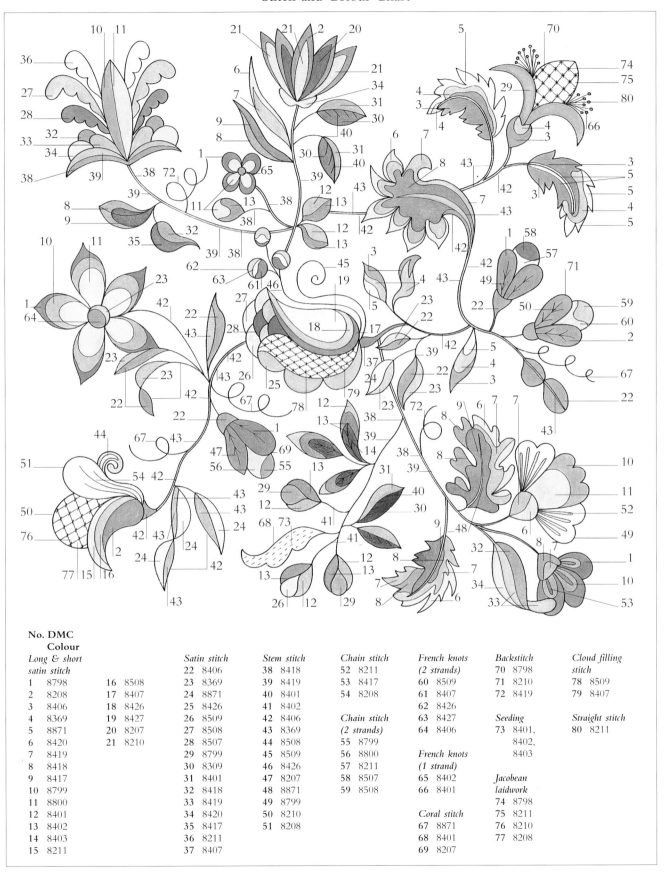

No. DMC
Colour

Long & short			*Satin stitch*		*Stem stitch*		*Chain stitch*		*French knots*		*Backstitch*		*Cloud filling*
satin stitch			22	8406	38	8418	52	8211	*(2 strands)*		70	8798	*stitch*
1	8798	16	8508	23	8369	39	8419	53	8417	60	8509	71	8210	78	8509
2	8208	17	8407	24	8871	40	8401	54	8208	61	8407	72	8419	79	8407
3	8406	18	8426	25	8426	41	8402			62	8426			
4	8369	19	8427	26	8509	42	8406	*Chain stitch*		63	8427	*Seeding*		*Straight stitch*
5	8871	20	8207	27	8508	43	8369	*(2 strands)*		64	8406	73	8401,	80	8211
6	8420	21	8210	28	8507	44	8508	55	8799				8402,		
7	8419			29	8799	45	8509	56	8800	*French knots*			8403		
8	8418			30	8309	46	8426	57	8211	*(1 strand)*					
9	8417			31	8401	47	8207	58	8507	65	8402	*Jacobean*			
10	8799			32	8418	48	8871	59	8508	66	8401	*laidwork*			
11	8800			33	8419	49	8799					74	8798		
12	8401			34	8420	50	8210			*Coral stitch*		75	8211		
13	8402			35	8417	51	8208			67	8871	76	8210		
14	8403			36	8211					68	8401	77	8208		
15	8211			37	8407					69	8207				

5 To stitch the bud petals, first outline the petal shapes using backstitch. Stitch carefully to give a smooth, regular shape to the petal edges.

6 Then work rows of long and short satin stitch over the body of the petals, keeping within the backstitch outlines.

7 When working in long and short satin stitch, do not pull the threads too tightly or the fabric may pucker. Graduate the colour gently to form subtle shading; it may help to practise colour shading with this stitch before you begin.

8 Next, work the leaf veins using stem stitch. Always work the leaf veins after the bodies of the leaves are complete. Fill the inner area above the petal tips with tightly packed French knots.

9 Complete the tip of the bud with rows of chain stitch, worked with two strands of crewel wool.

10 Continue working the flower and the leaf motifs one by one, following the stitch and colour chart on page 125. There are no repeat patterns of stitches and colours on any leaf motifs, so beware of duplicating – the differences between some motifs are very subtle.

11 Where appropriate, stitch the outlines first before moving onto filling stitches, particularly for the trellis stitches, such as Jacobean laidwork and cloud filling stitch, which form the central areas of some of the larger blooms.

12 The main stems of the flowers are made up of two adjacent rows of stem stitch, in dark green and light green yarn. Work the rows very close together so that they form a neat, dense line.

13 Pack groups of French knots tightly together and wrap the wool around the needle twice before completing the knot. Work the single French knots at the end of

Detail of Cushion

the stamens on the top right-hand flowers in the same way (see the stitch and colour chart on page 125).

Finishing

14 Block or press completed piece face down on a soft towel, checking that the iron is set at the correct temperature for both the fabric and the wool yarn.

15 Then trim the fabric carefully to make a 15½ in (39.5 cm) square, making sure that the embroidered area is centred. Take the 15½ in (39.5 cm) square piece of white cotton backing fabric and place

the embroidery over it, right side up. Then take the two remaining pieces of backing fabric, and make a ¾ in (1.9 cm) seam on one of the longest edges of each piece. Position them over the cushion front, wrong side up, with the seamed edges overlapping in the centre. These will form the "envelope" at the back of the cushion.

16 Pin, tack, and stitch all three layers of the fabric together, using a ¾ in (1.9 cm) seam allowance. Turn right side out and attach the gray piping around the cushion edges to complete (page 182). Insert cushion pad.

Couching and Goldwork

Couching is the technique of laying thread on the fabric surface and stitching it down with another thread. Goldwork is the embroidery technique that uses metal threads, which are stitched or couched on fabric depending on their weight.

IN ADDITION to the pleasures of creating intricate patterns in lustrous metal threads, couching has also allowed contemporary embroiderers to explore several new areas. There are many modern designers who like to work with an abundance of textural resources, creating multimedia images on painted, treated, and even burnt background materials.

The technique of couching, both by hand and by machine, gives the stitcher the freedom to include threads, decorative knitting yarns, strips of fabric, ribbons, even plastic tubing and bubble wrap in a design.

With a clever choice of stitches, the couching thread itself can decorate the surface elaborately, adding a three-dimensional quality to your work.

Fabrics

The most popular background fabric for goldwork is silk or satin, but upholstery fabrics, dress fabrics, or organzas can all be used to great effect. First decide if the fabric will be a backdrop for your design or a part of the actual composition. Also consider the effect of light and shadow on both the threads and fabric.

Frames and Other Tools

When you are couching, it is important to hold the fabric taut in order to avoid puckering. You will usually need to use a scroll (slate) frame, or a hoop large enough for the whole design.

This is because the edges of the hoop can crush or damage delicate goldwork threads. If you unhoop your work when it is in progress, the tension of the work will be affected and the finished piece may look uneven.

A sharp pair of short thick-bladed scissors is essential for cutting your goldwork threads. Keep these scissors separate from fabric scissors, as goldwork threads will blunt the blades. You will also need a mellor, an instrument that resembles a sharp-ended paddle, for teasing the goldwork threads into place.

It is advisable to cut hollow threads such as purls (page 129) on a cutting board, which you should first cover with a piece of felt. The felt will stop the snaky threads from jumping in the air as you cut them.

Keep a supply of acid-free tissue paper with which to wrap unused threads and to cover those in work. This will preserve the quality of the threads. Also, try to avoid direct sunlight and damp, humid conditions, which can destroy the threads.

Needles

The long, narrow eye and sharp point of the crewel needle (pages 8, 113) make it ideal for goldwork. The No. 10 is a popular size, but do keep a variety of crewel needles on hand and use the one that feels most comfortable.

The chenille needle (page 8) has a larger eye than the crewel needle and a very sharp point; this makes it a useful tool for taking the ends of goldwork threads through to the back of the fabric. Chenille needles also have a multitude of uses in general couching techniques (page 131).

You may find that a quilting needle, also known as a "between" (page 8), is helpful for working the finer areas of your embroidery.

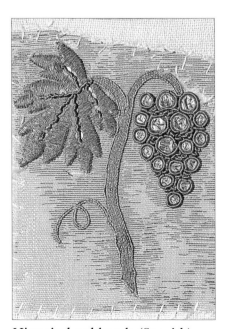

Historical goldwork (Spanish)
This couched vine comprises a padded leaf and grape cluster, created from a range of goldwork threads (page 129).

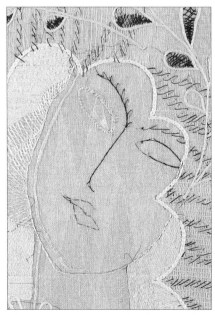

Contemporary couched portrait
Cotton threads are laid and couched to give this graceful, flowing effect around the hairline.

Goldwork Threads

Goldwork threads can be grouped into two main families: hollow (h), and couched (c).
Smooth passing thread and some fine twists can also be threaded in a needle and stitched through fabric.

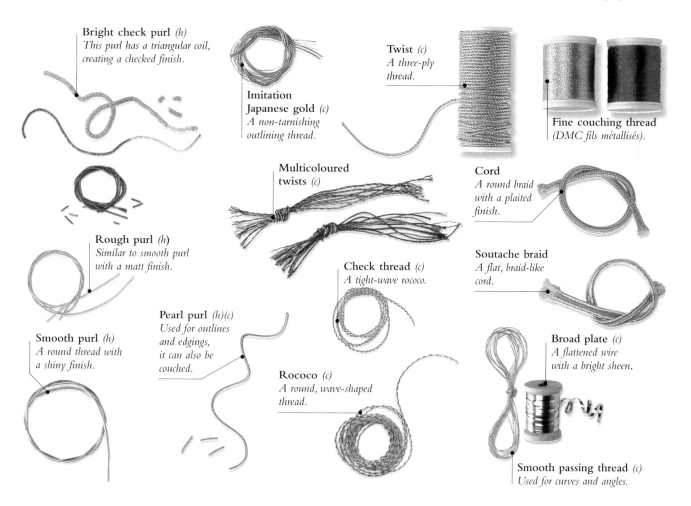

Bright check purl *(h)*
This purl has a triangular coil, creating a checked finish.

Imitation Japanese gold *(c)*
A non-tarnishing outlining thread.

Twist *(c)*
A three-ply thread.

Fine couching thread
(DMC fils métallisés).

Rough purl *(h)*
Similar to smooth purl with a matt finish.

Multicoloured twists *(c)*

Cord
A round braid with a plaited finish.

Check thread *(c)*
A tight-wave rococo.

Soutache braid
A flat, braid-like cord.

Pearl purl *(h)(c)*
Used for outlines and edgings, it can also be couched.

Smooth purl *(h)*
A round thread with a shiny finish.

Rococo *(c)*
A round, wave-shaped thread.

Broad plate *(c)*
A flattened wire with a bright sheen.

Smooth passing thread *(c)*
Used for curves and angles.

Goldwork Threads

Goldwork threads are sold by weight and can be purchased in a variety of thicknesses on spools or in skeins. Traditional finishes include gold plate, silver plate, and copper alloy; modern thread finishes use metallized polyester strips to reproduce this effect. Many other colours can be obtained, including aluminium and synthetic copper, which are usually available from specialist thread suppliers (page 191).

Goldwork threads can be divided into two main families: hollow and couched. The following list of goldwork threads is a good starting point for the beginner, and they are illustrated above. *Hollow threads* are designed to be cut

and threaded through the centre. To use them, cut into lengths and insert a fine thread through the hollow centre of the thread as you would a bead. Suitable threads include purls, which are made from very tightly coiled wires and are often used to fill areas of a motif. *Couched threads* are designed to be stitched down on top of your fabric with a fine thread. Good for working outlines and edges, they include smooth passing, imitation Japanese gold, broad plate, twist, check thread, and rococo.

In addition to hollow and couched threads, there are braids and cords, which are sewn onto the fabric by passing a fine thread through the braid or cord itself. Cord and soutache (above) belong to

this category. For decorative work, such as piping on cushions or clothing, light cords and soutache braid can be attached by hand or machine.

Couching Threads

In addition to a goldwork thread, you will also need to use a couching thread; there are a number of different couching threads available for you to choose from. Traditionalists suggest working with a fine silk, but you can also use a polyester thread in an appropriate colour.

In addition, DMC has a selection of fine metal threads called fils métallisés (above); some of the threads in this selection are substantial enough to be couched onto the surface of the fabric.

Contemporary goldwork bloom
This elaborate goldwork bloom is worked on moiré silk, using a variety of goldwork threads. The outlines and veins of the petals are also couched, designed to echo the direction of the flower's growth.

Couching Stitches

The basic couching techniques that you will need are described and illustrated opposite, along with Bokhara couching, a dense filling technique.

When you are couching fabrics and thick threads, you can enhance your design with another embroidery stitch. Many of the stitches in the stitch library are suitable, particularly the stitches from the laced stitch family (page 100) which can be worked in attractive bicolour or tricolour combinations.

You can also work cross or chain stitches over your couching thread (see the couched Art Nouveau pincushion project, page 136) or try couching your thread onto the fabric using buttonhole stitch or one of its variations (page 25). You could also select a textured thread, such as a cotton perlé, to create an interesting contrast with the laid thread.

Variations

Romanian couching This stitch is worked using a single thread in the same way as Bokhara couching (opposite), except that the couching stitches are closer together to cover more of the couched line.

Hints and Tips

Transferring a design Trace the design and then mount your fabric in a frame (pages 10–18).

Then place the tracing over the design and tack over all the design lines. Next, tear away the tracing paper to leave clear, tacked design lines on the fabric over which to lay your thread (page 14). Select the thread you wish to couch and thread a fine crewel needle with silk or polyester sewing thread.

Always draw threads over beeswax (page 156) before use to protect them from friction as they rub against the metal threads. Beeswax darkens the colour of the threads slightly, therefore it is always best to select couching threads that are lighter than the final colour that you want to work with.

Raised Work

Using padding under threads (page 167) will raise selected areas of a design, maximizing the brilliant effect of light and shadow that goldwork threads can create. You can pad your work with a number of media: string, for example, can be laid onto the surface of your fabric to create a padding for goldwork threads, which can be laid over it and couched down, or wound around the string itself.

Shapes cut from lightweight, acid-free cardboard can be wrapped with thread and then couched onto your work. Pieces of felt – yellow for gold, gray for silver, for example – can also be cut to the required shape and then several thicknesses tacked down on top of one another, so that a mound is formed over which to couch.

See Also:
Cross stitch *page 29*
Chain stitch *page 24*
Buttonhole stitch *page 25*
Laced stitch family *pages 100–109*
Couched Art Nouveau pincushion
page 136

*B*ASIC COUCHING *uses two threads: one laid on the fabric surface, and another to stitch it down. Bokhara couching, used for working dense areas of couching, uses the same thread for laying and couching.*

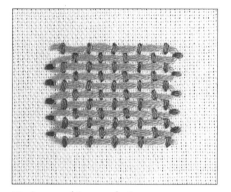

Basic couching technique

Basic couching uses two different threads: one laid thread and a second thread to couch it down onto the fabric.

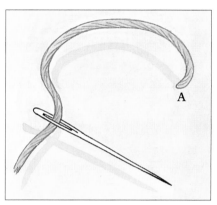

1 *To couch a medium thread, bring it through fabric at A. To couch a thick thread, lay it on fabric over design line.*

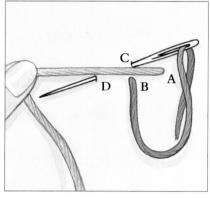

2 *Using fine couching thread, come up at B; go down at C, covering laid thread; and come up at D.*

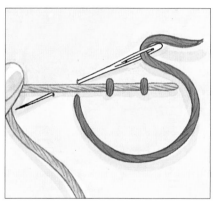

3 *Repeat along row, forming small stitches at right angles to laid thread.*

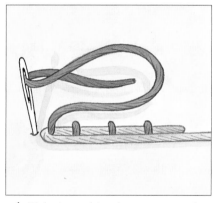

4 *To begin couching the next row, work a horizontal stitch on the bend as shown.*

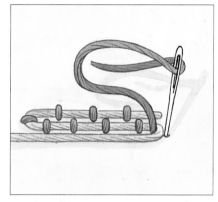

5 *On subsequent rows, position couching stitches between those of row above.*

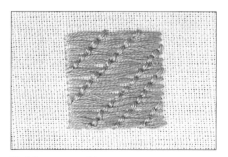

Bokhara couching

This technique is used to lay down dense areas of couching and, unlike basic couching, a continuous thread is used for both. Here stitches form a diagonal pattern, but you could also work random lines.

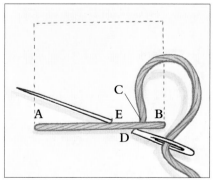

1 *Come up at A and lay thread across shape to be filled. Go down at B, up at C, down at D, and up at E, forming small slanted stitches.*

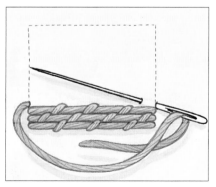

2 *Repeat across row, spacing stitches evenly. Working one row at a time, lay thread from left to right and couch down as in Step 1.*

Couching

Satin stitch

Satin stitch

Satin stitch

Satin stitch

Couching

Padded
satin stitch

Shisha
mirror

Padded
satin stitch

Couching

Couching

Rows of
chain stitch

Couching

Satin stitch

Long and short
satin stitch

Satin stitch

Satin
stitch

Beading

Couching

Couching

Padded satin
stitch

Couching

Darning stitch

Couching

Couching

Couching

Couching

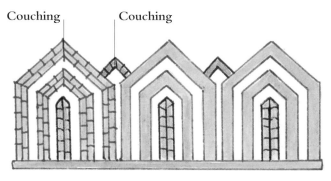

Couching

Couching

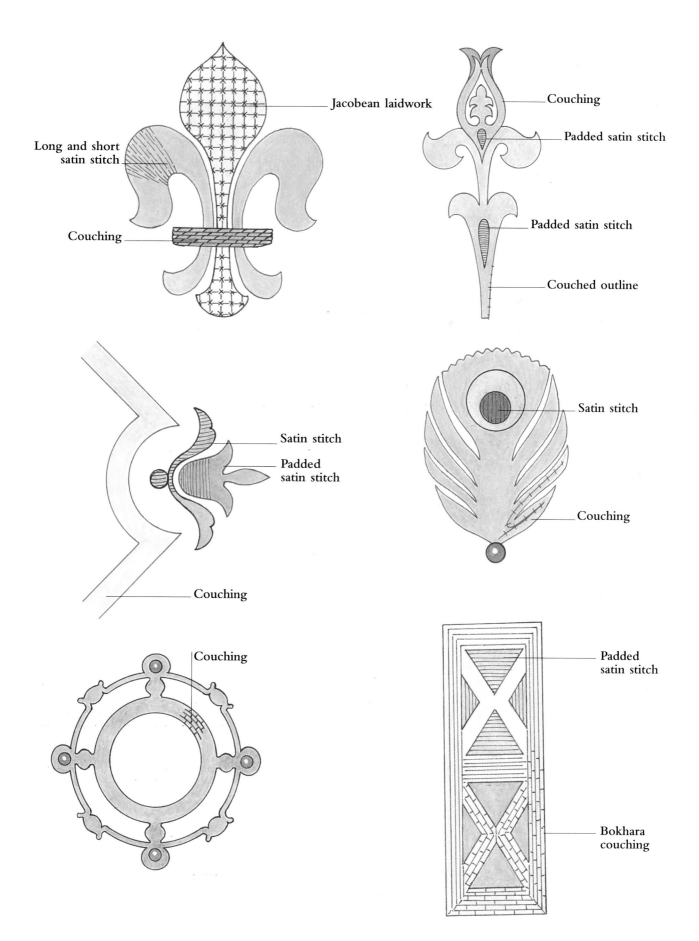

Jacobean laidwork

Long and short satin stitch

Couching

Couching

Padded satin stitch

Padded satin stitch

Couched outline

Satin stitch
Padded satin stitch

Couching

Satin stitch

Couching

Couching

Padded satin stitch

Bokhara couching

Couched Art Nouveau Pincushion

This floral design uses wool, stranded cotton, cotton perlé, and gold metallic threads, couched in elegant flowing lines to characterize Art Nouveau style.

Size

5 x 5 in (13 x 13 cm)

Materials

8 in (20.5 cm) square fine linen union
(or similar firm fabric)
6 in (15 cm) square deep-blue velvet
(for back) or desired colour
Sewing thread to match velvet
No. 7 crewel needle
No. 20 tapestry needle
Polyester wadding for filling
Tracing paper

Thread

DMC tapestry wool, 1 skein:
■ 7297   ■ 7428

DMC stranded cotton, 1 skein:
■ 930   □ 834
■ 3362

DMC cotton perlé No. 5, 1 skein:
■ 930   □ 832

DMC gold divisible metallic thread,
1 reel

Template

Preparation

1 *Trace design from the template above, and transfer to the centre of the fabric.*

Stitching

2 *Work the left-hand leaf first. Thread the tapestry needle with the dark green wool and come up at 'Start,' marked where the leaf stem joins the fruit shape on the chart opposite. Thread the crewel needle with a strand of dark green stranded cotton, and come up next to the wool. Lay the wool along the design line and couch down, using small, evenly spaced straight stitches.*

3 *Continue around the outline, finishing at the fruit shape. Fasten off both threads. Repeat Steps 1 and 2 for the right-hand leaf, overlapping the left-hand stem and the lower part of the left-hand leaf.*

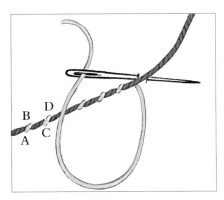

Cross-stitch couching Step 1

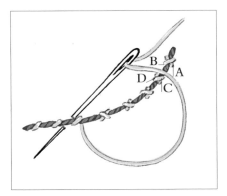

Cross-stitch couching Step 2

4 *Use cross-stitch couching (above) for the leaf veins. Lay dark blue wool (7297) on design line and bring one strand of gold metallic thread up at A, down at B, up at C, down at D, and so on to complete.*

5 *When row is complete, work from other end of the row, still using the same thread. Come up at A, go down at B, up at C, down at D, and so on, slanting stitches over those already worked to form crosses.*

Stitch and Colour Chart

No. DMC Colour

Basic couching
1 7428
2 3362
3 832
4 930 (stranded cotton,
   1 strand)
5 7297

Cross-stitch couching
6 7297
7 Metallic thread (1 strand)

Jacobean laidwork
8 Metallic thread (4 strands)
9 930 (cotton perlé)

Satin couching
10 7297
11 834 (6 strands)

French knots
12 7297

6 Couch down the outer outline of the fruits with small, straight stitches, using gold cotton perlé for both the laid and couching thread. Couch the dark blue inner line in the same way. Begin at the tip of each motif, and lay a length of dark blue wool along the design line. Then couch down the blue wool, using just one strand of dark blue cotton. When the couching is complete, go down through the hole made at the beginning and fasten off the laid thread and the couching thread.

7 Now fill the inner fruit shapes using Jacobean laidwork. To work the two lower fruits, lay a lattice with four strands of the gold metallic thread. Fasten off, then complete the lattice by couching down each thread intersection with a single diagonal stitch worked in blue cotton perlé.

8 To complete the upper fruit shape, work a reverse lattice pattern to that of the lower fruits. First lay a blue cotton perlé lattice and fasten off. Then couch down each thread intersection with a single cross stitch, worked using four strands of the gold metallic thread.

Detail of Pincushion

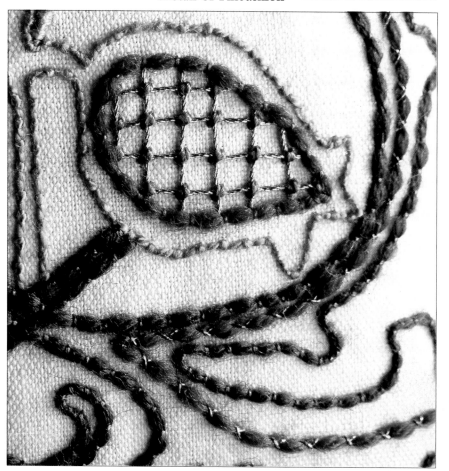

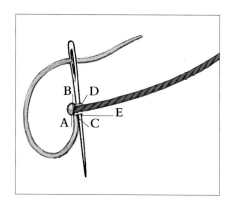

Satin couching Step 1

9 To work the stamens, use satin couching as shown above. Beginning at stem end, couch down dark blue wool with tightly spaced stitches in six strands of gold stranded cotton. Lay thread on design line and bring contrasting thread up at A. Go down at B directly above laid thread, come up next to A at C. Go down at D next to B, come up at E as shown.

Satin couching Step 2

10 Continue working in this way until the laid thread is completely covered and it cannot be seen under the couched threads. Pack the stitches tightly and evenly together, keeping the edges regular. Then take the gold thread through to the back of the fabric and fasten off. The surface should be smooth and regular, so that the final effect is that of a satin-like raised cord.

11 Finally, work three French knots in dark blue wool to form a triangle at the end of each stamen. Then take wool to back and fasten off.

Finishing

12 Lay the completed embroidery face down on a towel. Block the piece or press it, with the iron on steam setting. Alternatively, set the iron to a non-steam setting and then press over a damp cloth. Trim the piece to a 6 in (15 cm) square.

13 Lay the piece of velvet (we used dark blue) on the top of the embroidery, right sides together, and then stitch a ½ in (1.3 cm) seam around the edge, leaving a 3½ in (9 cm) opening on one side for turning. Turn right side out, and then stuff it with the polyester wadding. Finally, complete the pincushion by slipstitching the opening closed.

Goldwork Box Top

This sun and stars design uses couched goldwork threads for the central motif, and couched sequin waste to form the surrounding stars.

Size

Panel: 5½ in (14 cm) square

Materials and Equipment

Box with panel for mounting
Square of tightly woven black cotton
    fabric to match box panel (ours is 12
    in /30.5 cm)
Small amount sequin waste
7½ in (19 cm) square wooden frame
Drawing pins
No. 10 crewel needle (or suitable for
    selected fabric)
Chenille needle
Strong sewing thread for lacing
1 reel yellow polyester sewing thread
Tracing paper, pencil, beeswax

Thread

1 reel fine imitation Japanese gold thread
24 in (61 cm) No. 6 bright check purl

Preparation

1 *Trace design (shown actual size). Stretch fabric over frame using staples or drawing pins. Cover the heads of the drawing pins with cloth tape to avoid snagging the threads. Place tracing over centre of fabric and tack all design lines in yellow running stitch. Tear away tracing.*

Stitching

2 *Cut a length of sewing thread and slide it over the beeswax. Cut 2 yd (1.8 m) of imitation Japanese gold thread and double it to form a loop. Starting at the inner circle of the sun centre, come up inside the loop and go down outside the loop to secure gold thread to fabric.*

3 *Come up on the inside edge of inner circle. Take the needle over the two gold threads and down through the fabric, with needle slanting under gold thread, towards circle centre. Repeat, placing each double row tight against the next.*

Stitch and Thread Chart

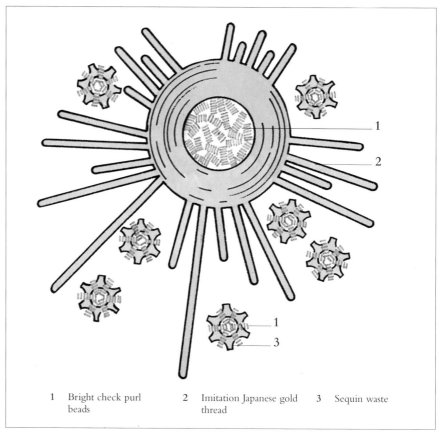

| 1 | Bright check purl beads | 2 | Imitation Japanese gold thread | 3 | Sequin waste |

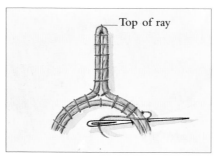

Working the ray

4 *To work the rays, carry the inside gold thread around the circle and use the outside thread to form the ray shapes. Do this by laying the gold thread along the ray, then anchor it at the top of the ray with a stitch. (This will leave a stitch the length of the ray at the back of your work but this will be secured as you couch along the ray.)*

5 *At the point where the ray joins the circle, stitch over the thread at each side (see left). Continue to complete the rays. With chenille needle, take gold thread to the back. Trim then oversew ends with sewing thread.*

6 *To work the seeded centre, cut ¼ in (6 mm) lengths of bright check purl. Stitch on as beads, packing tightly to fill centre.*

7 *Cut star shapes from sequin waste, plus six ¼ in (6 mm) lengths of bright check purl for each and stitch as beads.*

Finishing

8 *Trim to match panel, adding 2 in (5 cm) to each edge. Place over panel and mount, using lacing method (page 181).*

Ribbon Embroidery

The decoration of embroidery with ribbons made from different types of material originated in 18th-century France. Embroidery ribbons can be threaded through needles and stitched directly onto fabric, or folded and stitched with thread to form delicate rosettes and bows.

RIBBONS CAN provide a perfect medium for any design that requires an element of raised detail. They can be used in conjunction with threads and, in particular, with variegated silks and cotton perlé, since these provide a rich textural contrast. Ribbons can be worked to create a whole design, but they are also a useful addition to crazy patchwork.

One of the best advantages of ribbon embroidery is that it can be produced quickly. Unlike many other embroidery techniques, it lends itself to a freestyle approach and does not require a high level of precision.

The most popular use for silk ribbons is within floral embroideries, because the natural flow of the silk makes it perfect for forming petal shapes. In addition to stitching the ribbons into your fabric, you can create blooms separately and then apply them to your design. This method is preferable when you are working with wide ribbons that will not pass easily through the fabric.

Fabrics

Ribbon embroidery can be worked on fabrics such as moiré, velvet, silk taffeta, jersey, and on evenweave fabrics. If you are using lightweight silk ribbons, you could work on a fine fabric such as silk. However, more elaborate compositions need a fabric that is sturdy enough to support them. If it is not, you need to back it with a more stable fabric that will hold the stitches firmly in place.

Needles

The needles you choose for your ribbon embroidery depend on the background fabric and the particular stitches in your design. The eye of the needle must be large enough to accommodate the ribbon, and also to create a large enough hole in the fabric so that when delicate, easily frayed silk ribbon is passed through it during stitching, any friction and wear is minimized. To cover these circumstances, your sewing basket should contain a selection of tapestry, chenille, darning, and crewel needles (page 8), and beading needles (page 157).

Silk taffeta dress, *c.* 1924

Here ribbons decorate the join between taffeta and a Chantilly lace frill. On the taffeta the ribbon is couched (page 131) so it is only seen on the front of the fabric; on the lace frill, the ribbon is threaded through the fabric, like thread through a needle. Stem stitch (page 31) links the motifs, and French knots (page 33) are used as a filling stitch.

The origins of ribbon embroidery can be traced to France and the rococo period of the 1700s, when elaborate decoration was fashionable. Ribbons were folded into flowers, ruched, and stitched (pages 145, 146) to embellish the gowns of the rich and royal.

Embroidery Ribbons

Select ribbons that thread easily through your needle, or choose broader ribbon for individual blooms, and attach to your work.

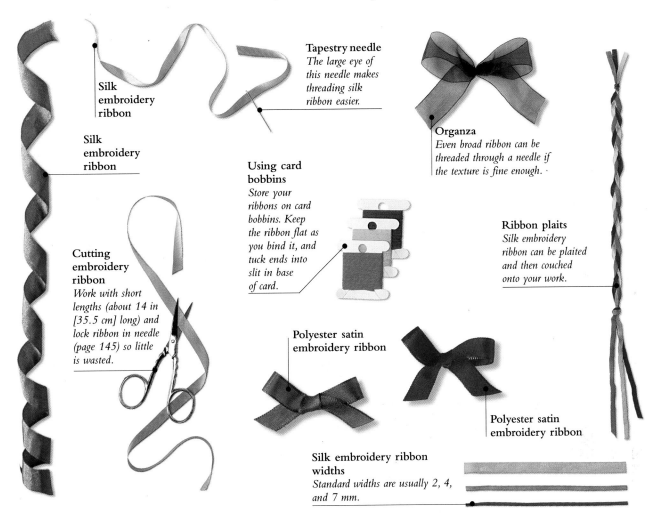

Silk embroidery ribbon

Silk embroidery ribbon

Tapestry needle
The large eye of this needle makes threading silk ribbon easier.

Using card bobbins
Store your ribbons on card bobbins. Keep the ribbon flat as you bind it, and tuck ends into slit in base of card.

Organza
Even broad ribbon can be threaded through a needle if the texture is fine enough. ·

Cutting embroidery ribbon
Work with short lengths (about 14 in [35.5 cm] long) and lock ribbon in needle (page 145) so little is wasted.

Ribbon plaits
Silk embroidery ribbon can be plaited and then couched onto your work.

Polyester satin embroidery ribbon

Polyester satin embroidery ribbon

Silk embroidery ribbon widths
Standard widths are usually 2, 4, and 7 mm.

If you are planning to work on heavy fabrics like leather or denim, you will also need a sharp, pointed tool such as a stiletto with which to make holes.

Types of Ribbon

Ribbons suitable for embroidery come in many colours and textures, from rich velvets to delicate organzas. Select ribbons that easily curve and twist into the shapes you require, and those that thread through your needle.

If you prefer, use a broader ribbon that is more suitable for creating larger individual flowers that you can make separately and fasten onto your design. Ribbons should also complement your background fabric, and both ribbon and fabric need similar care requirements.

There is a wide range of ribbons on the market:

Silk ribbon Although costly, silk ribbon is designed specifically to be used in embroidery. Silk ribbon is available in a broad range of colours, and widths start from a fine 2 mm. Silk ribbon is usually the most popular choice for the ribbon embroiderer.

A viable alternative to silk ribbon is to use a selection of narrow man-made embroidery ribbon, which has been introduced by a number of the major manufacturers. Although this ribbon is not available in a wide range of colours, it does have a texture similar to that of genuine silk ribbon.

Polyester satin ribbon This is suitable for stitching on evenweave fabrics such as Aida cloth (page 185) or tapestry canvas. However, polyester satin ribbon is too stiff to make gentle folds and soft-edged petal shapes.

Knitting ribbon Ribbon that is designed primarily for knitting can also be used in embroidery. Knitting ribbon can be purchased by the ounce (25 g) ball, and this category also includes specialist threads in variegated colours and metallic finishes. Use knitting ribbon with pure silk embroidery ribbon to create an interesting contrast in textures.

Ribbon Embroidery Stitches

Contemporary ribbon garden design

This cottage garden design uses an imaginative range of stitches to achieve its grace and texture. Pink gathered rosettes (page 145) are applied to the right of the vine, which is decorated with ribbon stitch and stranded cotton stem stitch (page 31).
The irises use chain stitch (page 24), and French knots (page 33) form the hyacinths and delphiniums; the crocuses have ribbon-stitch leaves. Two ribbons are threaded together in the same needle to stitch the peach-and-white tulips. The honey bee (left) is a single stitch that has been wrapped.

Many stitches in the stitch library are suitable for ribbon embroidery, but they need to be worked with a looser tension than in other embroidery techniques. Practise working various stitches in a circular motif to create flower heads and refer particularly to the knotted and looped stitch families (pages 72, 86). French and Chinese knots (pages 33, 74), worked individually or in clusters, can produce stunning results. Fly stitch (page 88) and detached chain stitch (page 24) are perfect for individual petals. If you intend to decorate an item of clothing, beware of loose, loopy stitches that can catch and snag. In addition to using traditional stitches, many ribbon embroideries incorporate composite stitches, such as those in the laced stitch family (page 100).

Hints and Tips

Using ribbon economically Given the costly nature of some types of embroidery ribbon, it is important to get maximum use from each length. Work with short lengths – around 14 in (35.5 cm) – and lock the end of the ribbon with the point of the needle to make sure the complete length is used (page 145).
Keeping the ribbon flat One problem with ribbon embroidery is that the ribbon length tends to twist as you work. In order to keep the ribbon sitting flat on the surface of your fabric, use either the shank of a pin or a trolley needle to straighten out the ribbon as you pull it through the fabric.

See Also:
Using a hoop *page 18*
Knotted stitch family *pages 72–85*
Looped stitch family *pages 86–99*
Laced stitch family *pages 100–109*
Flower spray cardigan *page 148*
Cottage garden picture *page 152*

Frames

When you are embroidering with silk ribbon, it is extremely important that your background fabric is held taut at all times during the stitching process.

Use a regular hoop for small areas of ribbonwork and for some thicker fabrics that cannot be worked easily in a frame. However, it is not advisable to re-hoop when work is in progress, as previously worked stitches can be flattened or damaged. It is best to choose a hoop that is large enough to hold the entire area to be worked. If you do have to re-hoop, do take great care when repositioning the hoop in order to avoid spoiling your ribbon embroidery.

Therefore, if the background fabric you are working on is unsuitable to be stitched in a hoop, or the area to be worked is too large, try using Q-Snaps™ (page 10) or a quilting frame.

*T*HESE FLOWER *forms can be created using the techniques shown below, which also use a few simple stitches from the stitch library. Silk blooms are intended to be soft and flowing, so avoid harsh, geometric effects. Vary the ribbon width to vary the size of the bloom.*

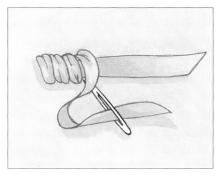

How to start

Make knot at ribbon end or leave a tail on back of fabric as shown. Hold the tail as you stitch, until stitching secures tail.

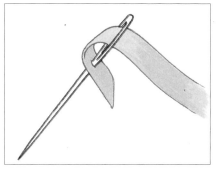

How to lock the ribbon

Thread needle and insert needle point ¼ in (6 mm) from ribbon end as shown. Pull long end down, catching ribbon in needle eye.

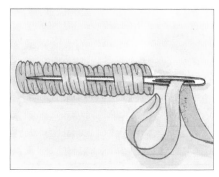

How to finish

Weave the ribbon through a few stitches on back of fabric as shown above. Or, anchor tail end to another stitch with sewing thread.

Straight stitch rose

This stitch consists of a Chinese knot (page 74) surrounded by loosely worked straight stitches. Enlarge by adding more "rounds" of straight stitch. Work counterclockwise or clockwise, whichever is more comfortable.

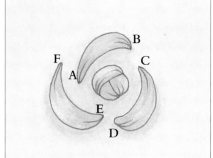

1 *Make a Chinese knot (page 74) for the rose centre. Come up at A then go down at B, forming a loose, straight stitch. Repeat, following letter sequence.*

2 *Make another round of straight stitches, spacing them alternately. Stitches can be placed more closely together, depending on ribbon width and desired fullness of rose.*

Gathered rosette

This simple rosette can be applied in layers to make a full-blown rose. You can also vary the shade and width of the ribbon, working the base rosette in the widest ribbon.

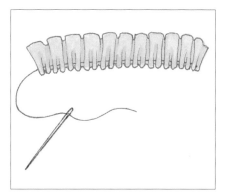

1 *Cut a length of ribbon 3 to 4 in (7.5 to 10 cm) long. Make a row of running stitch (page 28) along one long edge. Pull gently to gather ribbon as shown.*

2 *Starting in the centre, tack ribbon to fabric to form a spiral. Ends are tucked under. Add more loops in the spiral to make a fuller rosette.*

R*IBBON STITCH is a favourite for simple leaf and petal shapes, whereas the spider web rose creates a dense, lustrous effect. Allow the ribbon to twist and turn naturally as you work.*

Ribbon stitch

Ideal for petals and leaves, this is worked by folding ribbon back on itself. The ribbon should lie flat, but do not pull too tightly.

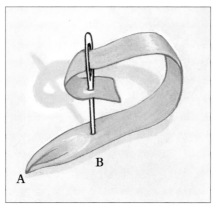

1 *With ribbon locked in needle head (page 145) come up at A, and go down at B through ribbon and fabric.*

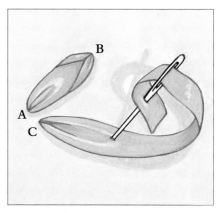

2 *Pull ribbon through loosely and come up at C, ready to begin next stitch. Repeat Step 1 to form a flower head shape.*

Spider web rose

This rose is built on a network of straight stitches worked with embroidery thread.

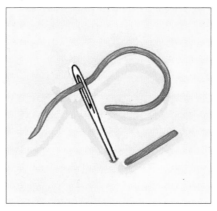

1 *Work a straight stitch (page 47) with cotton perlé or stranded cotton.*

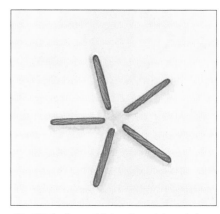

2 *Work four additional straight stitches, radiating from a central point.*

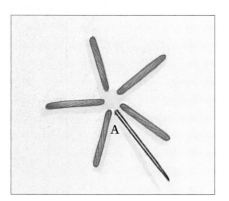

3 *When web is complete, lock ribbon in needle (page 145) and come up through fabric at A.*

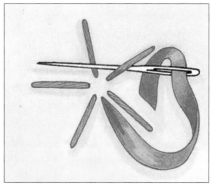

4 *Weave ribbon over and under straight stitches as shown without entering background fabric.*

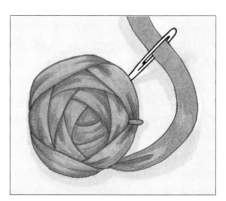

5 *Continue working outward, keeping ribbons loose until "web" is covered. Take needle and ribbon through fabric and tie off.*

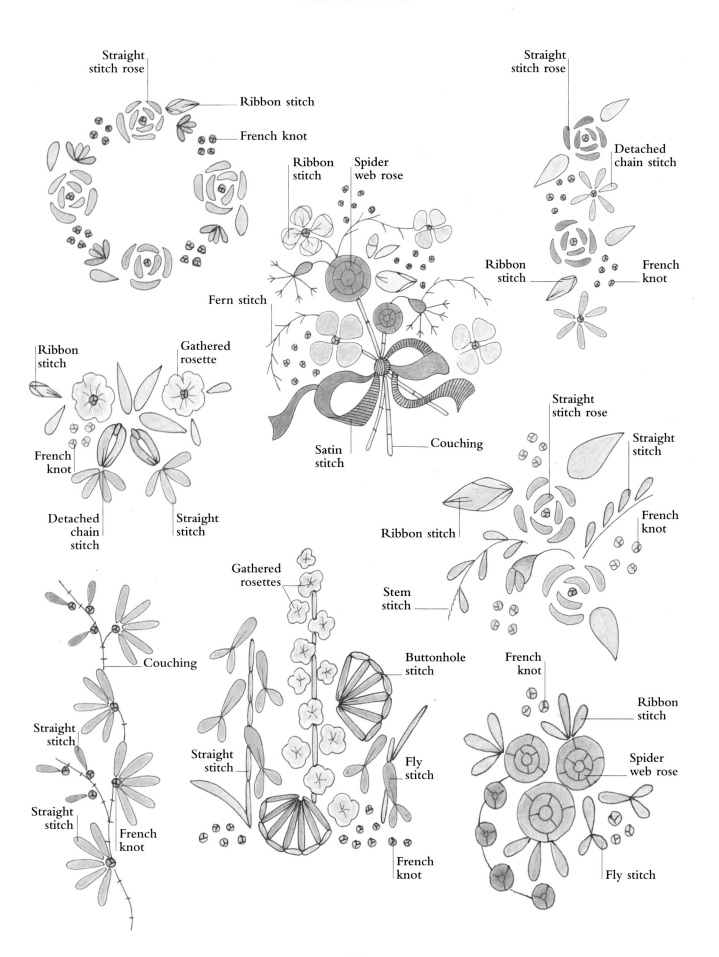

Straight stitch rose
Ribbon stitch
French knot

Straight stitch rose
Detached chain stitch
Ribbon stitch
French knot

Ribbon stitch
Spider web rose
Fern stitch
Satin stitch
Couching

Ribbon stitch
Gathered rosette
French knot
Detached chain stitch
Straight stitch

Straight stitch rose
Straight stitch
French knot
Ribbon stitch
Stem stitch

Couching
Straight stitch
Straight stitch
French knot

Gathered rosettes
Buttonhole stitch
Straight stitch
Fly stitch
French knot

French knot
Ribbon stitch
Spider web rose
Fly stitch

Flower Spray Cardigan

*This stunning ribbonwork project uses a selection of simple silk ribbon
flowers, scattered with French knots for a delicate spray effect.*

Size

Neckline embroidery: 7½ x 4 in
(19 x 10 cm)
Pocket embroidery: 1 x 4¼ in
(2.5 x 11 cm)

Materials and Equipment

1 round-necked cardigan sweater (ours
has patch pockets)
20 in (51 cm) square medium-weight
sew-in interfacing for backing
Two 5 in (13 cm) lengths of 1½ in
(4 cm) wide navy ribbons to back
pocket embroidery
20 in (51 cm) square navy lining fabric
3 yd (2.7 m) of 4 mm silk ribbon,
in seven different shades of peach
3 yd (2.7 m) of green silk ribbon
No. 24 tapestry needle
No. 7 crewel needle
Pale peach sewing thread
Tracing paper, pencil

Thread

DMC coton à broder, 1 skein:

351			469
353			471
746			743

Template for Pocket Top and Neckline

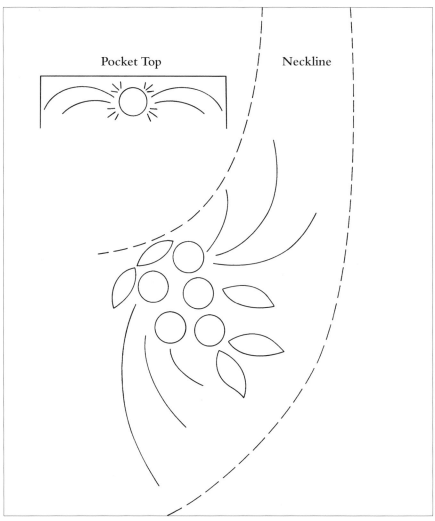

Preparation

1 *Trace a template from the inside edge
of your cardigan neckband and button-
band, and then adapt the design to fit the
template. Cut out interfacing from the
template and tack it into position on the
inside front of your cardigan. Reverse the
template for the opposite side.*

2 *Trace the design onto tracing paper, and
then tack it in position on the outside
front of the cardigan. Repeat, reversing the
design for the opposite front.*

3 *With sewing thread, mark design lines in
running stitch, then carefully tear away
tracing paper. Remove the running stitches as
you complete each section.*

Stitching

4 *Stitch through both cardigan and
interfacing. Use the crewel needle for the
thread work, and the tapestry needle for all
the ribbon work.*

5 *Using pale green thread (471), first work
leaf outlines (area 1 on stitch and colour
chart) using backstitch. Then with the deeper
green thread (469), fill the inner leaves with
feather stitch. Graduate the length of these
stitches to follow the outline. Using pale green
thread, carefully whip over and under the
backstitch outline.*

6 *Work the spider web roses separately in
the ribbon colour indicated on the stitch
and colour chart. Work the ribbon over a
foundation thread "wheel," with seven spokes
for each rose. Complete the roses on both
fronts and pocket tops.*

7 *For the gathered ribbon flowers on the
pocket tops, cut 1¼ in (3 cm) lengths
from palest peach ribbon (one for each flower
head). With pale peach sewing thread, come
up in position for the flower. Lay ribbon
horizontally on fabric and take needle
through ribbon at centre right, then work*

Stitch and Colour Chart

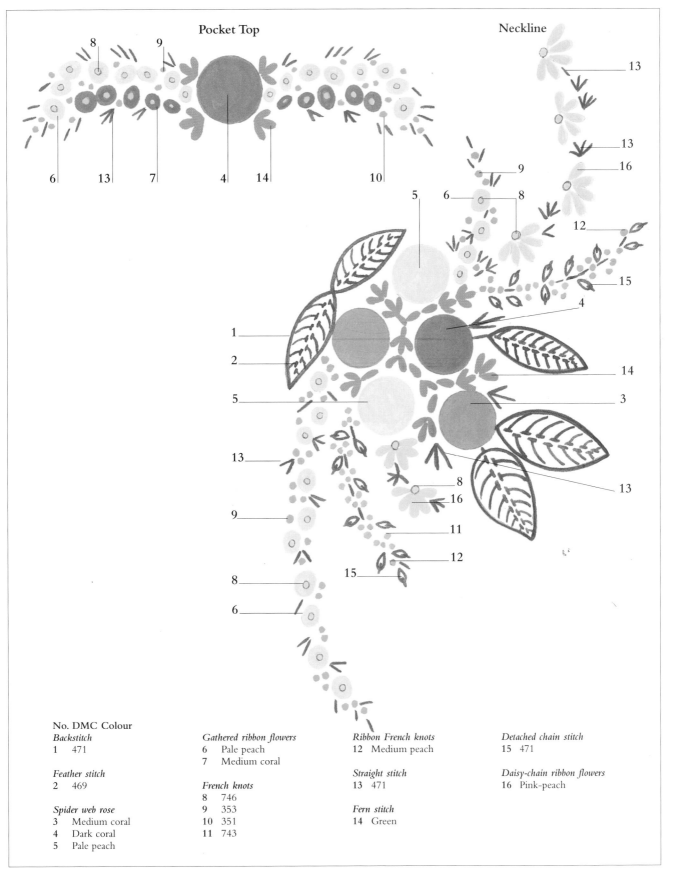

Pocket Top

Neckline

No. DMC Colour

Backstitch
1   471

Feather stitch
2   469

Spider web rose
3   Medium coral
4   Dark coral
5   Pale peach

Gathered ribbon flowers
6   Pale peach
7   Medium coral

French knots
8   746
9   353
10 351
11 743

Ribbon French knots
12 Medium peach

Straight stitch
13 471

Fern stitch
14 Green

Detached chain stitch
15 471

Daisy-chain ribbon flowers
16 Pink-peach

small running stitches along it, spaced ¼ in (6 mm) apart. Push needle down again through the ribbon and fabric at the starting point, pulling ribbon so it gathers. Secure with a stitch, and then come up in position for next flower head.

8 Work an arc of eight of these flower heads on each side of the spider web rose on the pocket top. Using medium coral, work two more arcs of five flower heads (five flower heads for each arc) directly below.

9 Using pale yellow thread (746), make a French knot in centre of each flower. Then change to peach thread (353) and work random French knots along top arcs of flower heads. Repeat along bottom arcs, using a deep peach thread (351). Complete by working small straight stitches in pale green thread (471) for stems and leaves and to link ribbon flowers.

10 The stitch and colour chart (page 149) shows detail for the right front of your cardigan. Thread the tapestry needle with green ribbon and follow the chart, working in fern stitch for the foliage between spider web roses. Hold the needle under the ribbon as you pull the ribbon through so that the ribbon does not twist.

11 Using the palest peach ribbon, work the stem of gathered ribbon flowers at the bottom of the design. In the same way, work the short spray closest to the cardigan neck.

12 Complete the centre of each flower head with a French knot worked in pale yellow thread (746), then intersperse more French knots among the flower heads using peach thread (353). Finish the gathered ribbon spray with small straight stitches in pale green thread (471) to form the stems and leaves.

13 Next, complete the two sprays of ribbon French knots. Work the French knots using medium peach ribbon, and intersperse with French knots worked in

Detail of Neckline Embroidery

deeper yellow thread (743). Then work the leaves using detached chain stitch in pale green thread.

14 Work the two daisy-chain sprays using pink-peach ribbon. Fan out the straight stitches from a central point to form the flowers, and then finish each one with a French-knot centre worked in pale yellow thread (746).

15 Next, join the daisy chains with a stem made from one row of pale green backstitches (471). Then work groups of two or three pale green straight stitches along the spray, placing these stitches at a sharp angle to the stem to form the leaves. Then repeat Steps 6 to 9 in order to work the left front of the cardigan, working a mirror image of the stitch and colour chart on page 149 (see detail, above).

Finishing

16 To line the pockets, first cut ribbon to fit inside width of the pocket, allowing ¼ in (6 mm) to turn under at each end. Pin this to the inside pocket top to cover the embroidered area. Using sewing thread, slipstitch along the top edges, then turn under and slipstitch at the sides.

17 To line the neckline, trace the shape of the template onto the navy lining fabric, allowing a ½ in (1.3 cm) hem around the edge. Turn this hem under, stitch it into place, and then press. Pin the lining along the shoulder seam, inside the neck edge, and centre front. Then slipstitch the lining into position. Stitch the remaining edge to the interfacing only, using herringbone stitch (page 26). Finally, trace a reversed image and repeat to finish the lining for the opposite front.

Cottage Garden Picture

This project uses vibrant ribbon colours to create daisies, roses, climbing blooms, and rich foliage to frame the simple cottage design. Work as many or as few foreground flowers as you wish.

Size

Finished picture: 9¾ x 8 in
   (25 x 20.5 cm)
Panel: 6 x 4 in (15 x 10 cm)

Materials and Equipment

8 x 10 in (20.5 x 25.5 cm)
   14-count Aida fabric
4½ x 6½ in (11.5 x 16.5 cm)
   heavyweight (pelmet) interfacing
1 yd (0.9 m) of 2 mm wide silk
   ribbons in the following colours:
   black, ecru, royal blue, medium blue,
   bright yellow, dull yellow, deep pink,
   dark peach, pale peach, light green,
   dull green, and leaf green
2 yd (1.8 m) creamy white silk ribbon
Wooden frame (ours measured
   8 x 10 in [20.5 x 25.5 cm])
No. 7 embroidery needle
No. 24 tapestry needle
Pale yellow sewing thread
Tracing paper, pencil

Thread

DMC coton à broder, 1 skein:

☐ 3325   ☐ 822

DMC cotton perlé, 1 skein:

■ Black No. 12   ☐ Ecru No. 8
▨ 702

Preparation

1 *Trace design outline, enlarge to 142 per cent and transfer to centre of fabric, squaring it in line with the holes. Stretch the fabric tightly over frame and secure.*

Stitching

2 *To work the black framework under the roof, lay the black ribbon on the fabric at A as shown on the stitch and colour chart. Then continue, following the order of the lettering. Couch the ribbon down with black cotton perlé, making stitches across the ribbon on every third block of fabric.*

Template

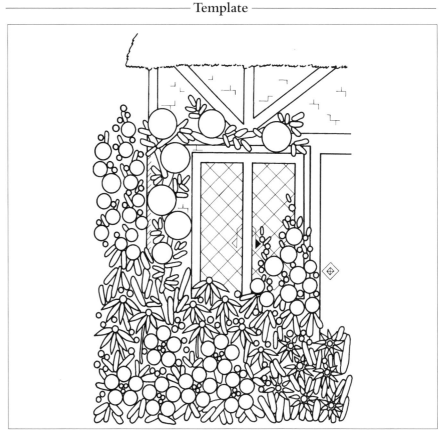

3 *Position and couch the centre post of the window. Then couch down the ribbon for the left and right sides of the window. Next, couch the ribbon for the top of the window and then the door frame.*

4 *Using black cotton perlé and following the detail (see right), backstitch the diagonal lattice window outlines. Then work the window catches, again in backstitch.*

5 *Now work the blue diagonal straight stitches forming the curtains, following the stitch directions on the detail and using pale blue coton à broder (3325).*

6 *Using black cotton perlé, work a vertical row of slanted buttonhole stitches down the left-hand edge of the wall to produce a soft finish.*

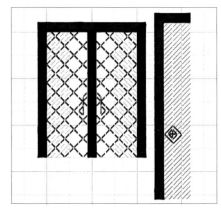

Door and window detail

7 *Follow the detail above for the door. Use green cotton perlé (702) to work three columns of diagonal straight stitches, taking each one over two blocks of fabric. Add the door handle detail in backstitch using black cotton perlé.*

Stitch and Colour Chart

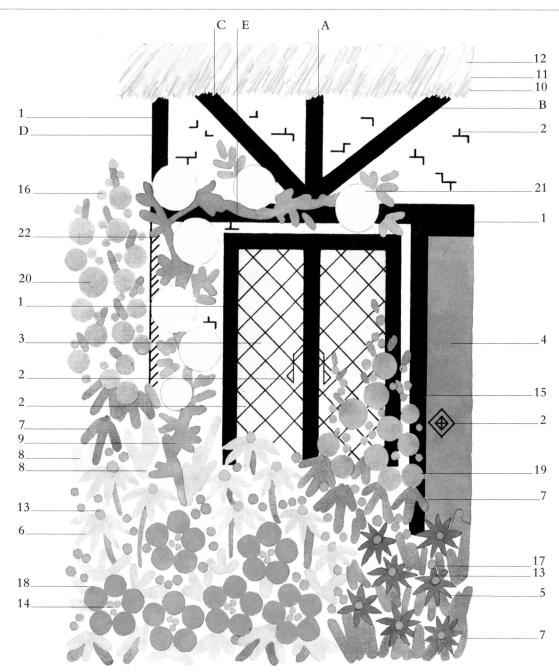

No. DMC Colour

Couching
1   Black No. 12 and black ribbon

Backstitch
2   Black No. 12

Straight stitch
3   3325
4   702
5   Royal blue ribbon
6   Pale peach ribbon
7   Dull green ribbon
8   Light green
9   Leaf green

Long and short satin stitch
10   Ecru No. 8
11   822
12   Ecru ribbon

French knots
13   Dull yellow ribbon
14   Bright yellow ribbon
15   Dark peach ribbon
16   Medium blue ribbon
17   702

Gathered ribbon flowers
18   Deep pink ribbon
19   Dark peach ribbon
20   Medium blue ribbon

Spider web rose
21   Ecru No. 8 and white ribbon

Buttonhole stitch
22   Black No. 12

8 *Now fill in the roof area with slanted long and short stitches, working with light beige coton à broder (822) and then highlighting with ecru cotton perlé and, finally, with ecru ribbon.*

9 *For the blue daisies (5 on chart), use royal blue ribbon to work a downward fan of straight stitches over 2 blocks, with a French knot in dull yellow ribbon at the centre top of each flower.*

10 *To work the peach daisies (6 on chart), use the pale peach ribbon and repeat Step 9.*

11 *For the foreground flowers (18 on chart), make gathered ribbon flowers using deep pink ribbon. Cut ribbon into 1⅛ in (2.8 cm) lengths, five for each flower. Using an embroidery needle and a doubled length of pale yellow sewing thread, bring needle up through the fabric and down into the ribbon, ⅛ in (3 mm) from the end. Make small running stitches ¼ in (6 mm) apart along the ribbon, coming up ⅛ in (3 mm) from the end. Push the needle down through the fabric (in the same position as it originally came up), pulling the ribbon so it gathers. Secure with a single stitch. Tuck in the raw ends of ribbon so they are not visible.*

12 *Repeat this technique to make five gathered ribbons placed in a circle, which creates one complete flower. Complete by working three French knots in bright yellow ribbon at each flower centre.*

13 *For the hollyhocks (shown against window, 19 on chart), work large blossoms as for deep pink flowers, but here use one length of dark peach ribbon to make a complete flower head. The buds are French knots. Complete with groups of three straight stitches in dull green ribbon at the base of the flower to represent foliage.*

14 *For the delphiniums (shown left of house, 20 on chart) work as for hollyhocks, but use medium blue ribbon.*

15 *To work the climbing roses (21 on chart), use ecru cotton perlé as the flower base and weave this with white ribbon, following the instructions for spider web roses (page 146).*

16 *For the foliage (7 and 8 on chart), fill in any foreground areas with random straight stitch in light and dull green, grouping the stitches in various lengths and directions to add interest. Add random French knots in doubled green cotton perlé (702) for extra texture. Then work the rose leaves in the same way using smaller stitches in leaf green.*

17 *When all the other embroidery is complete, give texture to the cottage wall by working small groups of backstitch in black cotton perlé.*

Finishing

18 *Stitch the finished work onto the interfacing and mount it as desired (see page 181 for step-by-step instructions on mounting techniques). Take great care not to crush or damage the delicate ribbons while you are doing this. We have used a cream mount with an inner border of light beige to complement the pastels of the silk embroidery ribbons.*

Beads and Embellishments

*Embellishments such as beads, mirrors, and sequins can add a special texture
and variety to embroidery, and they are available in a wide range of shapes and
sizes in both natural and man-made materials. Long, fine beading needles
are used with strong, flexible thread or thin beading wire.*

BEADS AND EMBELLISHMENTS can be applied to fabric with a needle and thread, or a tambour hook. Some contemporary pieces even use special adhesives. Beads can be used to create a solid beaded fabric, where the shapes and colours create figurative and abstract images, or to highlight outlines on stitched designs. Glass beads (page 158) are particularly useful for adding another dimension to fine tapestry, giving it substance and reflected light.

Fabrics

In theory, beads can be applied to anything a needle will pass through, but in practice your overall design will dictate the type of fabric you should use.

First consider the density of your design. By decorating the fabric surface richly, you are creating a new fabric with new draping capabilities. The weight of the beads is, of course, very important, and you must make sure that your fabric has a weave firm enough to support this weight and that the beads will not slip through the weave to the back of your work. If, for example, you decide upon a very delicate design on net, chiffon, or lace, you may want to line the fabric with a second, heavier-weight fabric to give your piece more body.

Think about the desired effect and whether the beads are to lie flat on a flat surface or nestle in the pile of velvet or wool. Also consider the wear-and-tear

factor. If you want to create a purely decorative panel, you can embroider with any medium. If you want to wear and wash it, you must be guided by the manufacturer's care instructions.

Threads

When applying beads, work with a strong, flexible thread that you can knot. Because the thread passes twice through the bead, choose the strongest thread you can find; waxed nylon beading thread is best. Any thread you use should first be passed over a block of beeswax to strengthen it and minimize fraying caused by friction against the beads. Choose a colour that will blend with the bead and your background fabric.

Beaded net jacket, *c.* 1930

*Decorated with beading, sequins, and tambour embroidery, this beaded jacket was the result of new techniques for manufacturing small glass beads, which made luxurious pieces like this affordable to the middle classes.
The beading is worked on a frame using a tambour hook (page 185) and chain stitch (page 24). The black plastic sequins are concave, and reflect the light from many angles.*

Peacock feather beaded throw

This throw is embroidered with black, purple, and petrol-blue tamboured sequins (paillettes), three cut rocaille and bugle beads and threads, with blue and turquoise faceted embroidery stones.

Needles

The hole in the centre of a bead can vary considerably in size, so select a needle that will pass through it. Special beading needles are available in sizes 10, 12, 13, and 15 (the higher the number, the smaller the needle), but they are quite long and fine and not always ideal. You may prefer to use a quilting needle or a sharp; sizes 10 to 12 usually work.

When threading your needle through tiny holes, thin beading wire is useful. Double a length of wire and catch the thread in the loop. Then push the wire loop, with thread attached, through the hole in the bead. Pushing the thread through the small needle eye can be problematic, so keep a needle threader (page 18) on hand.

Frames and Other Tools

Your fabric needs to be held taut at all times. For small beadwork pieces, a hoop (page 10) is ideal; clamp it to a stand to keep both hands free. When working larger pieces, mount your fabric on a slate (scroll) frame (page 10). Keep a pair of tweezers close at hand for picking up stray beads. If possible, it is also a good idea to collect a selection of small containers for storing beads. Sort your beads according to their type, size, and colour for easy use.

Needles and Threads

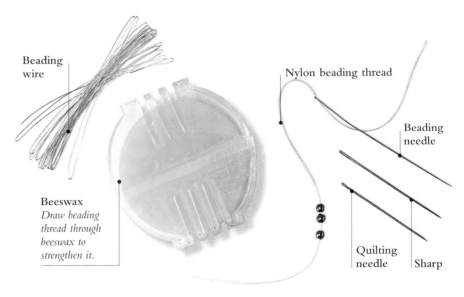

Beading wire

Beeswax
Draw beading thread through beeswax to strengthen it.

Nylon beading thread

Beading needle

Quilting needle

Sharp

Types of Beads and Embellishments

Beads are available in a multitude of shapes, sizes, colours, and materials, and can be threaded or couched onto your fabric.

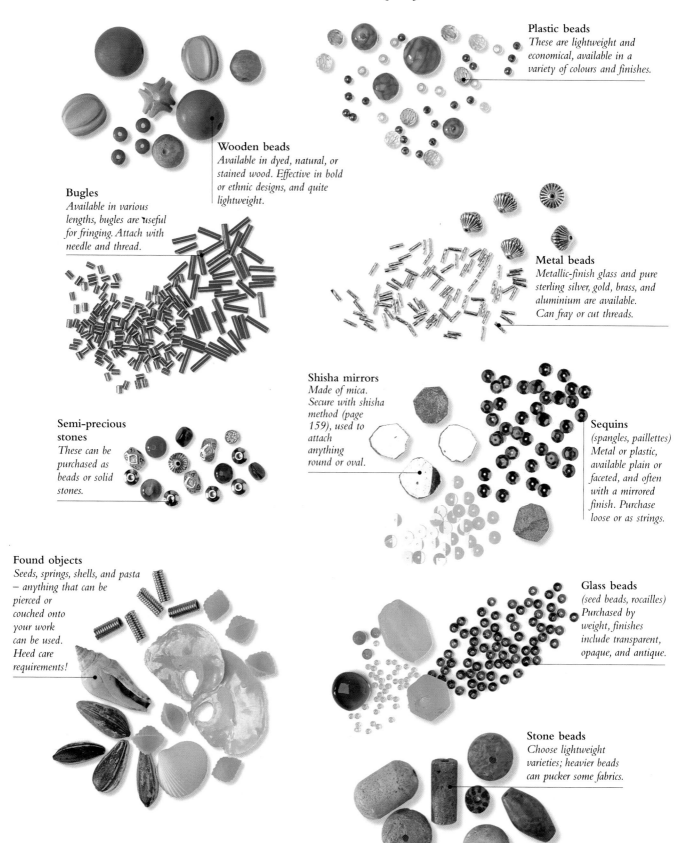

Plastic beads
These are lightweight and economical, available in a variety of colours and finishes.

Wooden beads
Available in dyed, natural, or stained wood. Effective in bold or ethnic designs, and quite lightweight.

Bugles
Available in various lengths, bugles are useful for fringing. Attach with needle and thread.

Metal beads
Metallic-finish glass and pure sterling silver, gold, brass, and aluminium are available. Can fray or cut threads.

Shisha mirrors
Made of mica. Secure with shisha method (page 159), used to attach anything round or oval.

Sequins
(spangles, paillettes) Metal or plastic, available plain or faceted, and often with a mirrored finish. Purchase loose or as strings.

Semi-precious stones
These can be purchased as beads or solid stones.

Found objects
Seeds, springs, shells, and pasta – anything that can be pierced or couched onto your work can be used. Heed care requirements!

Glass beads
(seed beads, rocailles) Purchased by weight, finishes include transparent, opaque, and antique.

Stone beads
Choose lightweight varieties; heavier beads can pucker some fabrics.

Beadwork Stitches

Attach your beads individually, or use a couching technique to stitch on rows of beads at a time. The shisha mirror technique (below) can be used to secure any flat, round, or oval object.

Sewing on beads

There are two main methods for applying beads. Stitch them onto the fabric individually (top) or, if using a pre-threaded row (bottom), use a couching technique.

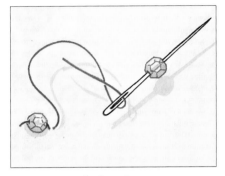

Sewing single beads

Come up through the fabric and bead. Then go down through fabric, come up and place next bead on needle. Repeat, making small backstitch every 4 or 5 stitches for security. Stitching each bead twice also holds bead firmly.

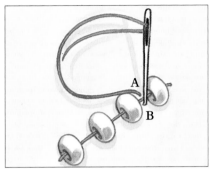

Couching beads

Come up through fabric. Pick up a row of beads, go down at end of row and anchor thread. Come up at A, cross thread between first two beads and go down at B. Repeat along row to secure beads, couching between every third or fourth bead.

Applying shisha mirrors

Use this stitch to attach any round or oval object, such as coins.

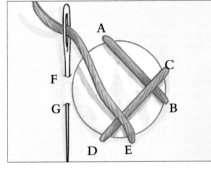

1 *Working over the mirror, come up at A, go down at B, up at C, across and down at D, up at E, down at F, and up at G.*

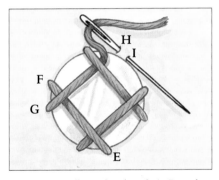

2 *Pass needle under thread A–B and go down at H to form a diamond-shaped grid, coming up at I.*

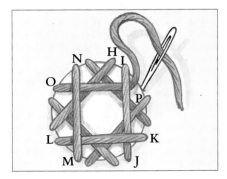

3 *Go down at J, come up at K, down at L, up at M, down at N, and up at O. Pass needle under the parallel vertical threads and go down at P. Fasten off.*

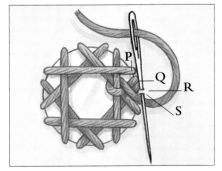

4 *Come up at Q, take needle under and back over intersection of vertical and diagonal stitches. Go down at R, up at S with thread under needle point. Pull through.*

5 *Repeat Step 4, weaving over and under crossed threads until edge of mirror is securely held.*

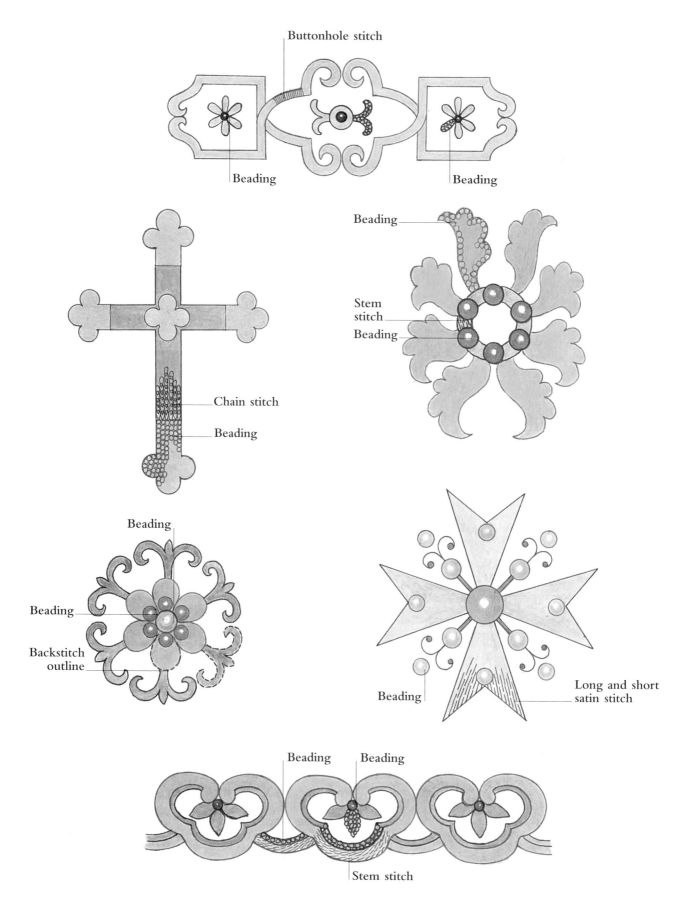

Buttonhole stitch

Beading

Beading

Chain stitch

Beading

Beading

Stem stitch

Beading

Beading

Beading

Backstitch outline

Beading

Long and short satin stitch

Beading

Beading

Stem stitch

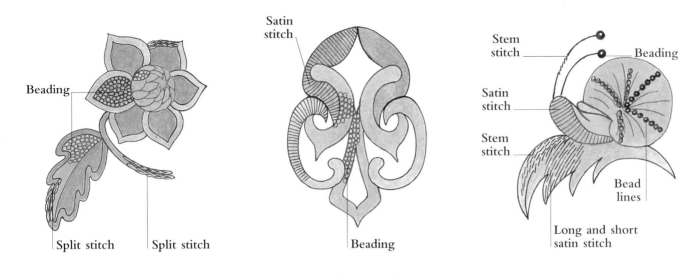

Beading

Split stitch   Split stitch

Satin
stitch

Beading

Stem
stitch

Beading

Satin
stitch

Stem
stitch

Bead
lines

Long and short
satin stitch

Shisha Motifs

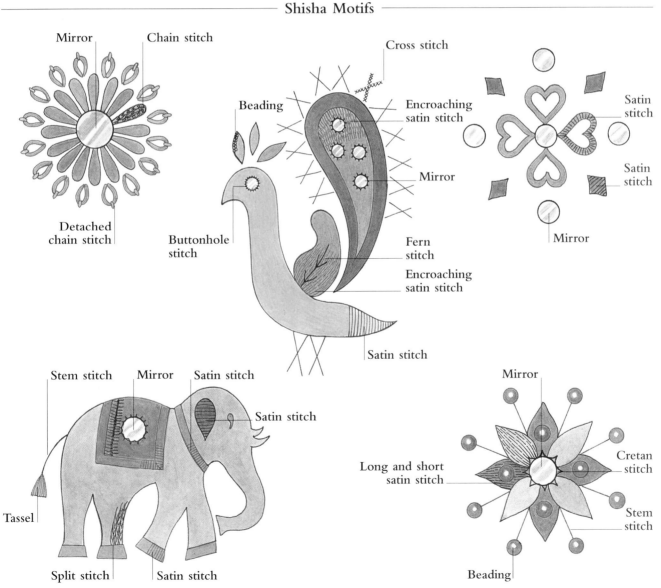

Mirror   Chain stitch

Detached
chain stitch

Cross stitch

Beading

Encroaching
satin stitch

Mirror

Fern
stitch

Encroaching
satin stitch

Buttonhole
stitch

Satin stitch

Satin
stitch

Satin
stitch

Mirror

Stem stitch   Mirror   Satin stitch

Satin stitch

Tassel

Split stitch   Satin stitch

Mirror

Long and short
satin stitch

Cretan
stitch

Stem
stitch

Beading

Beadwork Evening Bag

This simple project uses glass beads in four colours to create a stunning rose design.
The couched gold ribbon complements the iridescence of the beadwork.

Size

Finished bag: 7 x 8 in
  (18 x 20.5 cm)
Motif: 1½ x 7 in (4 x 18 cm)

Materials and Equipment

10 x 20 in (25.5 x 51 cm) each of
  medium-weight black silk,
  lightweight rose-coloured silk,
  lightweight iron-on interfacing
3 yd (2.7 m) gold metallic ribbon, ⅛ in
  (3 mm) wide
¼ oz (7 g) small round glass beads in
  the following colours: bright green,
  red, pale pink, and lemon
Sewing thread to match beads and
  black silk
½ in (1.3 cm) self-cover button
Beading needle, beeswax
Embroidery needle
Tailor's chalk, metal ruler
10 x 20 in (25.5 x 51 cm) tracing paper
10 x 20 in (25.5 x 51 cm) brown paper
  for pattern

Thread

DMC stranded cotton, 1 skein:
■ Black 310

Colour Chart

Cutting Pattern

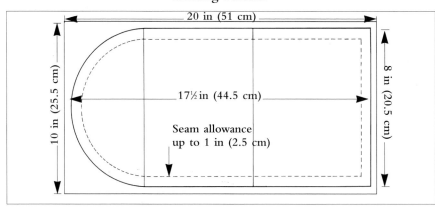

20 in (51 cm)

10 in (25.5 cm)

8 in (20.5 cm)

17½ in (44.5 cm)

Seam allowance
up to 1 in (2.5 cm)

Preparation

1 Iron interfacing onto the wrong side of the black silk fabric. Then cut a pattern from the tracing paper using the measurements shown on cutting pattern, adding a seam allowance of up to 1 in (2.5 cm). Pin the black silk to the pattern and tack around it. (This marks the sewing line.) Remove the tracing paper.

2 Allowing extra ribbon for the seam allowances, lay gold ribbon in diagonal lines across the fabric, starting at the top left-hand corner. Use a ruler and tailor's chalk to mark the lines. Space the ribbons equally, one ruler-width apart. Extend the ribbon beyond the fabric at each end of the pattern outline beyond the seams. Stitch in place along the

centre of each ribbon width by machine or hand, using small backstitches.

3 Trace the rose design from the colour chart and enlarge to 165 per cent. Pin the tracing to the curved end of black silk. With contrasting thread, stitch design lines in running stitch. Tear away the tracing.

Stitching

4 Beginning at the centre of the main rose, stitch on each lemon bead using the beading needle (page 157). Do not pack the beads too tightly and make sure that they sit neatly on the surface of the fabric. After every three or four beads, always make two small backstitches at the back of the work for extra security. Continue following the design, filling in the other colours as indicated on the colour chart shown above.

5 Next, couch over the gold ribbon using herringbone stitch, using two strands of black cotton to secure.

Finishing

6 For the lining, pin and tack the lining to the black bag, right sides together. Join the two pieces, leaving an opening in the top straight edge for turning. Trim seam allowance to ¼ in (6 mm), clip the curved seam, turn to right side. Slipstitch opening.

7 To make up the bag, machine-stitch the side seams with the lining sides out, using a zipper foot for a very narrow seam. The ribbons on the flap should line up with the rows on the front.

8 Cut 3½ in (9 cm) of gold ribbon. Stitch to form loop on centre front of flap.

9 For the button, make a ½ in (1.3 cm) circle in running stitch on a scrap of black silk. Attach beads in a spiral, working out from centre as follows: three red beads, two pink, one lemon until complete. Cover button back with the fabric and sew to front of bag to correspond with loop closure.

Shisha Mirror Waistcoat

Shisha mirrors are secured and decorated with shisha stitch, chain stitch, and herringbone stitch to create these distinctive ethnic motifs.

Size

Motif: 3¾ x 4 in (9.5 x 10 cm)

Materials and Equipment

Waistcoat in plain, closely woven cotton or silk. (Our waistcoat is lined with a shirt-weight cotton fabric and was washed before use in case of shrinkage.)

54 shisha mirrors or mirror sequins, each approximately ½ in (1.3 cm) in diameter

Crewel needle that will pass easily through the fabric and the waistcoat lining

Tracing paper, pencil

Transfer pencil or carbon paper

Thread

DMC stranded cotton:

■ 936, 2 skeins ■ 304, 1 skein

▢ 676, 2 skeins

Preparation

1 *It is possible to buy several different types of mirror for embroidery. Acrylic or machine-cut glass are the least satisfactory, as their depth makes them difficult to use. Genuine Indian shisha mirrors are thin and light, with a faint blue tinge and tiny bubbles, or irregularities. They are unevenly shaped, but this does not matter since your embroidery covers the edges. If you cannot find genuine shisha mirrors, mirror sequins (without a central hole) are an excellent substitute, easy to obtain and use.*

2 *Trace the outline of the motif (shown actual size) six times. Position tracing onto the front pieces of waistcoat, spacing tracings evenly apart. When you are happy with the arrangement, transfer to fabric.*

Stitching

3 *Use two strands of cotton throughout. Working just one motif at a time, use*

Stitch and Colour Chart

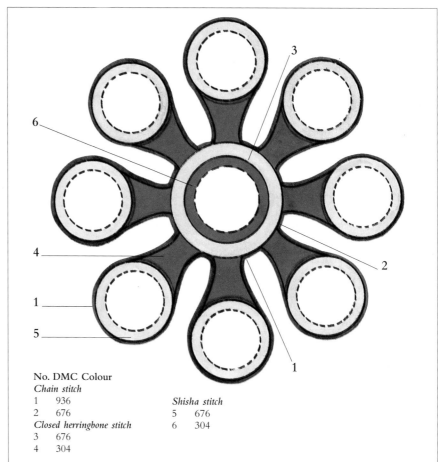

No.	DMC	Colour
Chain stitch		
1	936	
2	676	
Closed herringbone stitch		
3	676	
4	304	
Shisha stitch		
5	676	
6	304	

shisha stitch (page 159) to secure the nine mirrors into position, using two strands of pale gold (676) for outer circle of mirrors and red (304) for central mirror. The foundation mesh of straight stitches needs to be tight and to criss-cross the mirror some distance in from the edge. Practise applying a mirror to a spare piece of fabric.

4 *Using two strands of pale gold (676), work a circle of closed herringbone stitch (page 26) around the central shisha mirror. Next, edge it with an outline of chain stitches, also worked in pale gold.*

5 *Following the design line and using two strands of olive (936), work an outline*

of chain stitch around the whole motif. Finally, fill in the spaces on each "petal" with closed herringbone stitch worked with two strands of red (304). Repeat to complete all six motifs.

Finishing

6 *Carefully press face down over a cloth. Use a warm iron; thin Indian shisha may crack if an iron is pressed too heavily onto it. Mirror sequins (made of flexible plastic) will buckle if the iron is too hot.*

7 *Mirrors and sequins can be gently hand washed in lukewarm water with mild soap. To launder the waistcoat fabric, check the manufacturer's care instructions*

Monogramming

*The art of embroidering letters onto fabric has been used throughout history
for both decoration and identification. Letters can be stitched and applied
individually, joined together to form monograms, or combined
with motifs to personalize a project.*

MANY ITEMS, such as shirts, bed linen, tablewear, and jackets, can be personalized with a single decorative letter. You can add cats, teddy bears, and flowers to convey specific interests, or you can keep the image stylishly simple.

When working bed linen, however, take care to place the design in a corner or on an edge; embroidery is not very comfortable to sleep on.

Letters can be stitched with goldwork threads (page 129) or beads (page 158). They can be cut out from fabric that contrasts with your background fabric and then appliquéd to an item (page 170). Letters can also be worked on a very large scale and strung together to form words on a banner.

Fabrics

There are really no limitations on your choice of fabric. It is simply a question of deciding if you wish to embroider directly onto an item or to work the letter separately and then apply it to your main fabric (see the examples on pages 168 and 169). As a general rule, however, avoid fabrics that stretch, as they can distort the shape of your letters.

Needles

The needle you use will be determined by your choice of fabric and thread. Choose a needle that passes through the fabric with ease and has an eye large enough for the thread (page 8).

Threads

When choosing DMC threads, you should be influenced by the size and the weight of both your background fabric and the design itself. You also need to consider the kind of care your item will require. If it needs to be worn and washed often, then it is best to work with a high-quality stranded thread from DMC.

Create delicate images using single strands of cotton, or make bright, bold statements with tapestry wool or lustrous cotton perlé.

English sampler, 1717

Embroidered monograms have been used to establish ownership, convey messages, and express love, hope, and human virtue. Many royal insignias were lavishly decorated with gold threads (page 129), but simple domestic samplers like this one taught a child patience and provided a proverb or moral for her to learn. This silk-on-linen sampler is signed Isabella Paris.

Sources for Monograms

A vast library of alphabets is available to you with the help of computers and photocopiers. Word processors provide a variety of type fonts, which enables you to select and print out letters in the size and style of your choice. Simply transfer the printed image onto your design (see the introduction for transfer techniques, pages 14, 15) and use it as a basis for embroidered lettering.

If you do not have a word processor, you can select letters from magazines, newspapers, or books and then transfer them in the same way. Experiment with design by placing cut-out letters over each other or linking them together to create monogram patterns.

One of the most important points to consider is legibility. A simple, bold letter can be set in a highly decorative border with scrolls and loops yet still retain its basic purpose.

Letters can also be personalized to convey specific interests. Add favourite motifs, or see the motifs that follow each special skill for fresh inspiration. Trace a favourite flower from a cup or a plate, a teddy bear from a child's nightshirt – in fact, anything that is in or around the home can be used as a motif, then worked into a special composition using your embroidered monogram.

Raised Work

Monograms often benefit from being raised with padding. If you require only a slightly raised effect, fill the design outline with rows of running stitch (page 28) and then work rows of satin stitch (page 32) over the top of the running-stitch rows.

A foundation row of chain stitches (page 24) will produce a slightly more pronounced image. However, for a really bold motif, select a heavy thread and couch it down (page 131), carefully following the lines of the design to form a base for your embroidery. Then stitch over this thread base to complete the raised effect.

Creating Texture and Pattern

These two calligraphic letters were inspired by the patterns and textures of embroidery and fabric prints. You can use stitches to recreate the effect.

Contemporary calligraphy

These calligraphy characters can be embroidered directly onto fabric, using an outline stitch such as trailing stitch (page 169), stem stitch (page 31), or backstitch (page 30). For fabric texture on the D, use whipped satin stitch overlaid with couched ribbons, or couch a fine metallic or a goldwork thread (page 129). For the L, appliqué the letter shape into position on your background fabric (page 170), then decorate with ribbon blooms such as gathered rosettes or spider web roses (pages 145, 146) and add tiny glass beads at the centre of each (page 158).

Design Elements

There are three main design elements to experiment with when you are creating a monogram on fabric: the outline of the letter, the background setting, and the filling of the letter.

A bold letter with a clean, crisp outline can look extremely dramatic left plain, with the outline worked simply in trailing stitch. Or, outline a letter in stem stitch or backstitch and then fill the image with a filling stitch, such as herringbone (page 26) or any other stitch that catches your fancy from the selection in the stitch library (pages 45-109). You might also choose to embroider a plain initial on a fancy background. This background can be created using a filling stitch, such as basic darning stitch (page 49) worked in a block slightly larger than the letter itself. Letters can also provide an excellent subject for cutwork; by cutting away areas of your fabric, you can achieve an attractive, lacy effect. (See the butterfly tablecloth project, page 40.)

Outlining

Whipped running stitch (page 101) is worked here in green and red stranded cotton to give the "A" a simple, bold outline, an easy monogramming technique for beginners.

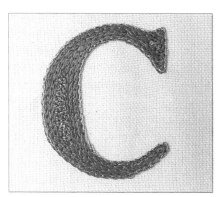

Using a background

Here a dense background is used to define the letter shape. The outline is worked in stem stitch (page 31), the background is filled with Jacobean laidwork (page 115), all worked with woollen threads.

Filling a letter shape

The letter shape is outlined with gold stem stitch (page 31), and the centre is filled with chain stitch (page 24) in stranded cotton and gold French knots (page 33) for a rich, elegant effect.

Monogramming Stitches

The most commonly used stitch for creating monograms is raised satin stitch (page 57), as it gives a silky, professional-looking finish.

Cross stitch (page 29) is also popular and effective, particularly if you are working on an evenweave fabric. Fine lettering and detail can be achieved using basic backstitch or stem stitch (pages 30, 31); these two stitches can also be laced to provide added interest and texture to your design (refer to the laced stitch family, pages 103, 102).

Trailing stitch is another popular choice for monogramming, and this is described and illustrated in the step-by-steps opposite.

Variations

The badge method Embroider the letters in the normal way onto a separate piece of fabric. Next, mark a seam allowance of ⅛ in (3 mm) around the monogram shape, and trim out the monogram. Then turn back the seam allowance, clipping it where necessary, and pin in position on your background fabric. Slipstitch the monogram neatly in place (page 170).

If you prefer, you can disguise the seam by embroidering over it with a decorative stitch such as chain stitch. In addition, you can use one of the border stitches from the stitch library to create a distinctive frame for your letter. This is demonstrated in the monogrammed shirt pocket project (page 174).

M ONOGRAMS CAN BE *stitched directly onto fabric. Two suggested techniques are to use trailing stitch for simple outlining, or work running stitch for padding and to mark design outlines, then complete the body of the letter with a filling stitch, such as satin.*

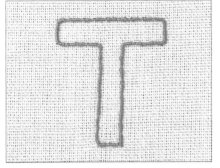

Trailing stitch
This composite stitch will give you an even raised line, so it is ideal for outlining intricate lettering.

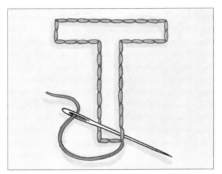

1 *Work a row of backstitch (page 30), covering letter outline. Come up to right of last stitch, slide needle under first running stitch as shown.*

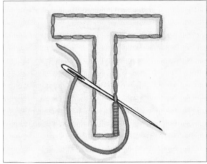

2 *Without picking up background fabric, continue wrapping thread around stitches left to right as shown, until letter outline is completely covered.*

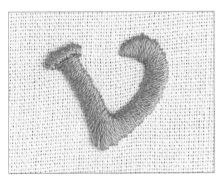

Tissue paper method
This easy transfer method uses running stitch to outline the letter shape, then a filling stitch to work the body of the letter.

1 *Trace letter onto tissue paper and tack tissue paper into position on the background fabric.*

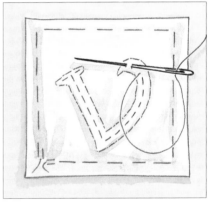

2 *Working through both fabric and tissue, outline then fill in the letter with rows of running stitch (page 28).*

3 *Tear away tissue paper, leaving the running stitch design lines on the fabric as shown. Then add extra lines of running stitch to pad as desired.*

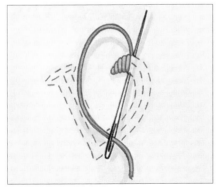

4 *Starting at outside edge of monogram, work over running stitch rows using a filling stitch such as satin stitch (page 32). Be careful to keep edges even.*

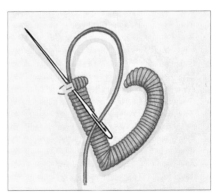

5 *Continue in this way until letter is completely covered. Change stitch direction for extra interest as desired.*

M ONOGRAMS CAN BE *worked separately, then cut out and appliquéd (below). They can also be stitched to a fabric shape and sewn onto your background fabric like a badge (page 168).*

Appliquéing letters
This works best with bold and simple shapes. Trace letter onto a sheet of plastic or cardboard, and cut around outline to form a re-usable template.

1 *Place template on fabric. Trace letter with a graphite pencil. Draw another line about ¼ in (6 mm) outside letter outline to show seam allowance.*

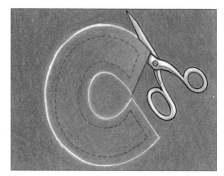

2 *Stitch over letter outline with running stitch (page 28), then cut around seam allowance as shown.*

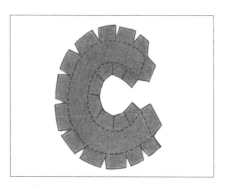

3 *Where necessary, clip around seam allowance up to (but not through) line of running stitches as shown.*

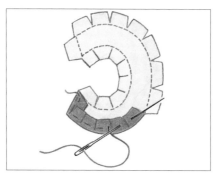

4 *Fold and tack clipped edges on the reverse, over running stitch outline. Press. For simple shapes, fold and press.*

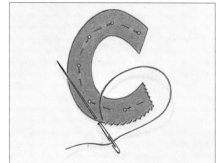

5 *Pin initial to fabric and then slipstitch it in place with invisible slipstitches along folded edge of fabric.*

Variation 1
This appliquéd monogram has a chain-stitch edge (page 24). This creates a fluid effect around the letter outline.

Variation 2
Herringbone stitch (page 26) is used here to give additional texture and depth to the letter outline.

Variation 3
Blanket stitch (page 28) is used here to appliqué the letter, to give a traditional or folk art effect.

Shirt Pocket and Espadrilles

These two projects use two distinctive monogramming styles. The crisp cotton shirt is stitched with a traditional gothic letter, and a cursive monogram decorates the espadrilles.

Shirt Pocket

Size

Finished panel: 2 in (5 cm) square

Materials and Equipment

Cotton shirt with pocket
Medium-sized crewel needle
Tracing paper and transfer pencil

Threads

DMC stranded cotton, 1 skein:

■ 909   ■ 352
■ 350

Preparation

1 *Press the shirt and then transfer the outline of your selected letter (pages 171–3) to the centre of the pocket front.*

Stitching

2 *Using two strands of green thread (909), begin by embroidering the leaves in satin stitch. Take care to gently graduate the edges of these motifs to create a smooth, natural effect.*

3 *Next, stitch the body of the letter in red thread (350), working the solid sections in satin stitch and the single lines in backstitch.*

4 *Embroider the outline of the box in backstitch, again using 350. Then stitch the inner box in satin stitch, using peach thread (352). Stitch precisely on guidelines so that you keep the box shapes as regular as possible.*

5 *Finally, using the green thread (909), backstitch the stems and the tendrils connecting the leaves.*

Finishing

6 *When all the embroidery is complete, block it carefully, or place the work face down on a soft towel and press (page 180).*

— Detail of Shirt Pocket —

Canvas Espadrilles

Size

Finished panel: 2½ in (6.5 cm) square

Materials and Equipment

Canvas espadrilles
Two 4¼ in (11.5 cm) squares of
    medium-weight yellow fabric
    (we have used a slub silk)
Medium-sized crewel needle
Tracing paper
Transfer pencil
Yellow sewing thread (or colour to
    match your chosen fabric)

Threads

DMC stranded cotton, 1 skein:
■ 995

Preparation

1 *Press fabric and transfer design outline (pages 171–3) to centre of fabric.*

Stitching

2 *Using two strands of thread, work along the design lines using a single row of chain stitch. Follow the curves carefully to reflect the flowing, cursive style of the letter. Repeat for the second fabric square.*

Finishing

3 *Trim fabric to a 3½ in (9 cm) square so letter is centred on the fabric. Fold ½ in (1.3 cm) to wrong side on all edges.*

4 *Press the squares face down over a towel and slipstitch them onto espadrilles.*

Silk Scarf

Fine gold thread is used here to stitch a monogram on delicate purple silk. A traditional, Olde English letter style is used to complement the richness of the silk.

Size

Embroidered monogram: 1¼ in (3 cm) square

Materials and Equipment

Light or medium-weight scarf
Fine-sized crewel needle
4 in (10 cm) embroidery hoop
Tracing paper
Transfer pencil

Threads

DMC *fil or* 284, 1 reel

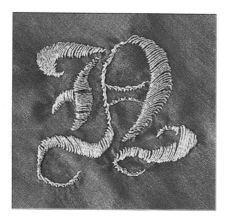

Detail of scarf

Preparation

1 *Begin by tracing the outline of the letter you wish to use. Select the letter from the templates illustrated (pages 171–173).*

2 *Transfer the letter to the corner of the scarf using one of the transfer methods described (pages 14–15). For a dark fabric such as the purple silk used here, you could use tailor's chalk or pounce powder. Position the monogram centrally on the fabric, and place it so that it will be "readable" when displayed or worn on completion.*

3 *Mount this area of fabric in the hoop. Do not remove your work during the stitching process because this can affect the thread tension.*

Stitching

4 *Using a single strand of* fil or, *begin to embroider the design, keeping the fabric taut in the hoop at all times. Begin by working stem stitch for the single lines of the letter, and work this stitch according to the weave of your fabric. For example, if your fabric has a fine, delicate weave, work the stem stitches quite closely together – this will maximize the sheen of the gold thread and also add texture to the design. Work carefully so that the thread does not split or tangle, or damage the weave of the fabric.*

5 *For all the remaining areas of the letter, work neat rows of satin stitch. Place all stitches evenly together to give a smooth,*

lustrous surface to the motif, and graduate the edges of the letter shape very gently to emphasize curves.

Finishing

6 *When the embroidery is complete, press it face down over a cloth. Be sure to set the iron temperature to a cool setting, because too much heat can distort or even "melt" the delicate threads. It is best to test this first by ironing some spare thread lengths and fabric scraps over a towel before you press your finished piece, in order to check that the setting is right. If you wish to store your embroidery, wrap it in acid-free tissue paper (page 184) so that the thread does not tarnish over time.*

Finishing Techniques

Your finished project needs professional
finishing and care. This chapter tells
you how to hem and launder your work,
and make trimmings such as tassels
and fancy cords. There are also
conservation hints and tips to keep your
work looking good, and preserve it
for future generations.

Finishing Techniques

Any needlework that you complete might become an heirloom of the future. If you want to frame your embroidery or to make it into a useful piece of clothing or furnishing, the following information will help you achieve a professional finish.

Hems and Edges

If your embroidery is to be used as a tablecloth or a runner, you need to decide how to finish the raw edges of fabric. The depth of hem should be determined by the weight of your fabric. For example, a very narrow hem is sufficient for a lightweight fabric and can create a pretty rolled edge, whereas a flat, broader edge gives a crisp finish to many heavier fabrics such as linens.

Use the method shown below for working simple hems, and for hemming edges that you wish to be joined with fancy stitches such as insertion or knotted insertion stitch (page 79).

Laundering

The first thing you should do, if your choice of fabric and thread allows, is to launder your completed embroidery. During the stitching process, threads and fabric gather dust and grease – no matter how careful you are to keep your hands clean. Correct laundering will give your finished work a new lease of life.

Cleaning solutions First check out the thread and fabric manufacturers' care instructions. If you can hand-wash your work, use a chemical-free cleaning solution that is pH balanced and contains no bleaching agents. Suitable brands include Purity Needlework Shampoo. Always avoid using strong detergents and products designed for knitwear only, as they are not suitable for needlework.

How to wash your work To wash your embroidery, soak it for five minutes in cool water and cleaning solution. Rinse it thoroughly, gently agitating the fabric. (Never wring the fabric out, handle it roughly, or scrub it.) Then lift it from the water and roll it in a clean white towel to remove excess moisture. Then you can iron or block the fabric. Blocking (page 181) is recommended for raised embroidery, such as knotted, looped or laced stitches, which can be flattened or damaged by conventional ironing.

Pressing your work To press your work, take two clean, thick towels and lay the piece on top, face down. Set your iron to the appropriate temperature for your fabric, then press the fabric until it is dry. Always avoid excessive movement of the iron, because this may disturb and distort your stitches. If your embroidery uses metallic threads or beads, do not let the iron contact the back of the work; place a cloth over it before you press it. After pressing, let your work dry completely overnight before mounting it.

Framing Materials

A glass frame guards against dust and dirt, but can trap moisture and foster mildew, and its reflectiveness can subdue the texture of a piece. You can frame your work without glass, but never use plastic (which traps moisture and air) or clip frames (which press against the piece and destroy its texture). If you do use glass, first insert a mount on top of your work so the glass does not touch the fabric or the thread. Leave openings in the back so that air can circulate. Conservation or ultraviolet glass is the best option.

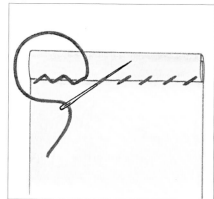

Zigzag hemming

1 *Fold the fabric inwards, then fold it again to make three thicknesses of fabric. Come up through the fold as shown and pull the thread through gently.*

2 *Go down just beneath the fold (making a small stitch) and then come up diagonally through the three thicknesses of fabric. Repeat across the length of the fold, keeping the space between the stitches even.*

3 *Return across the row, working in the same way, but slant diagonals in opposite direction as shown to form a neat row. Herringbone or ladder stitches can also be used as alternatives to zigzag stitch.*

Blocking

You can speed up the drying process by using a hair dryer on the coolest setting or by propping the blocking board in front of a fan. Smaller finished work can be blocked on an ironing board.

Mounting for a Frame

You need to mount your work on a board before you can begin to frame it. First decide the size of frame you require, then select an acid-free, porous white mounting board, which you can buy from good art stores. (Do not use self-adhesive board or cardboard that has any acid content because, over time, this can mark and damage your embroidery.) The board should be about ⅛ in (3 mm) smaller than the frame to allow for the thickness of your mounted fabric. First prepare the fabric edges by machine-stitching with zigzag stitch, or bind the edges with cloth tape. Then follow the method shown below.

Mounting Embroidery on a Cushion

First choose a cushion style and fabric to complement your design. Examine your background fabric. If you have used a relatively lightweight fabric, consider backing it with iron-on interfacing to give it substance and help the area retain its shape. Be aware that the adhesive can harm your fabric over time. Interfacing can be applied to the back of the fabric before you begin or when completed.

Choose a cushion fabric that is the same weight as your embroidery fabric and has the same care instructions. Make sure that zip fastenings or other fastenings will not rust and mark your work. Choose a plastic zip fastening if you think that a metal zip fastening might cause a problem.

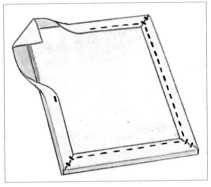

Making a blocking board

1 *Cover board with aluminium foil to protect against moisture, unbleached muslin for padding, then woven gingham for warp and weft guidelines. Stretch and staple cloth to board, mitring corners.*

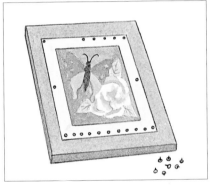

2 *Immerse the completed work in cold water and lay right side up on board. Stretch taut and secure with drawing pins, working from centre to corners. Repeat on all sides. After 1–2 hours, repin damp fabric to remove any more wrinkles. Allow to dry.*

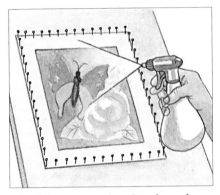

Blocking on an ironing board

Place the finished work right side up on the ironing board. Pin at intervals of ¾ in (1.9 cm). Spray evenly with water from plant mister as shown. Leave to dry completely before removing from board.

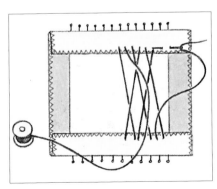

Mounting for a frame

1 *Prepare fabric edges, then centre board on fabric. Fold two opposite edges to back and pin. With strong sewing thread lace edges at 1 in (2.5 cm) intervals. Begin at centre, using large herringbone stitch.*

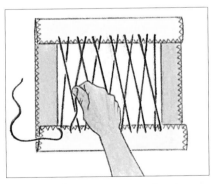

2 *Repeat from centre to opposite edge. Starting at the right, pull each thread to give an even tension. Fasten off. As an alternative, you can work from the left-hand edge to the right-hand edge.*

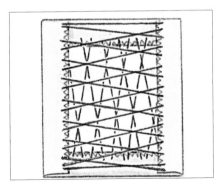

3 *Repeat Steps 1–2 in the same way; fold and pin left and right edges and lace from centre out (or from left to right), again carefully pulling each thread taut. Remove all the pins, ready for framing.*

Trimmings

An imaginative choice of braids or other trimmings can enhance the overall effect of your work. Popular embellishments for cushions include fringes, fancy cords, and tassels, which can all be made easily from leftover embroidery threads.

Fringes Adding a fringe to the edges of your cushion is an alternative to tassels. Fringes can be purchased by the yard or metre in a wide choice of finishes, or you can make your own looped fringe.

Fancy cords Fancy cords can give your work a professional finish. You can purchase fancy cord and attach it (see below), or you can make your own cord.

Fancy cords can easily be made from DMC embroidery thread and can be used to edge cushions instead of piping. Cotton perlé, crewel yarn, and knitting yarn, for example, are all good choices for handmade trimmings. Experiment with a combination of different colours and textures for added effect.

To make a short cord, pin the thread loop to the side of an upholstered chair. To make a longer cord, use the cuphook method illustrated below. You can save time by looping the other end of the thread into a second cuphook attached to a hand drill.

If you are making a very long cord, try hanging a fishing weight from an S-hook in the centre of the cord as you twist it. This helps control the twist and acts as a useful centre marker.

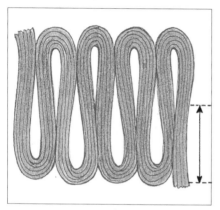

Fringes

1 *Begin by taking several lengths of your chosen thread and then fold in zigzag fashion so that loops are twice the desired depth of fringe. Try to keep all folds regular and do not allow thread to tangle.*

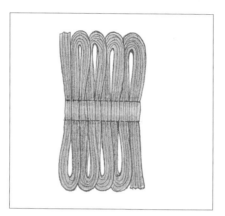

2 *Then work two parallel rows of machine stitching, about ½ in (1.2 cm) apart as shown, right across the centre of the loops. Work carefully so that all the threads are firmly secured and the machine-stitched rows are straight.*

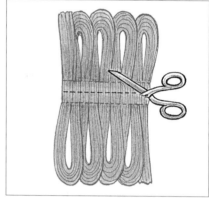

3 *Next, cut between the rows of stitching using dressmaker's scissors to form two lengths of fringe. Insert the cut edge between the back and front edges of your cushion and topstitch through layers to secure. Cut loops if desired.*

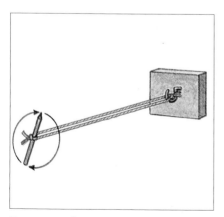

Fancy cords

1 *Cut thread to three times desired length of cord. Knot strand ends together at each end, then loop around a cup hook. Insert a pencil in other end and twist in clockwise direction. Remove, holding ends tightly.*

2 *Fold twisted thread in half. Allow the two halves to intertwine and form a cord, controlling the twist carefully with your free hand. Knot doubled ends and trim. Wrap tape around ends of cord to keep it from unravelling.*

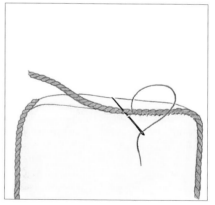

3 *To attach cord to cushion seam, cut cord about 2 in (5 cm) longer than distance around cushion. Use a single thread to sew through both cord and fabric. Finish near a corner, cross cord ends, and then tuck them into the cushion seam.*

Tassels Tassel-making is an art form of its own and it can be very addictive! Tassels can be used to decorate more than just cushions; you can use them to adorn bags, such as the pochette bag (page 34), and to decorate wallhangings (see the rooster wall hanging, page 108) as well as throws, tie-backs for curtains, personal garments, page markers, and embroidered bookmarks.

Before you begin, think about the colours you have used in your finished needlework and then select similar or complementary colours; this is very important for all trimmings used in embroidery. Strong contrasts can work well too, but be careful to make sure that you balance the overall design of the finished piece; a subtle mix of thread colours used to create a finished piece can be dominated easily by bold tassel colours. Equally, bright colours can add a splash of colour to enhance and enliven your work. Always remember that any trimming you use will become an integral part of the finished project so it needs equal consideration. To make your own tassels, choose threads or yarns that contrast or complement those used in your design.

If you are a beginner, you could simply use a varied selection of the same embroidery threads that you have used to work your project. Before you begin, first decide how thick you want your tassels to be, and then check that you will have enough thread in order to make them.

Using dressmaker's scissors, start by cutting a piece of cardboard to twice the depth of the tassel you require, fold it in half, and then follow the step-by-step instructions below.

Variations

Fancy tassels Having mastered the basic tassel, experiment by adding metallic threads and beads to make your finished piece look even more unique. Vary the textures and finishes to add a really individual touch to your projects.

Fancy hems Fancy hems can be created using basic buttonhole stitch (page 25). By varying the lengths of the stitches, you can create a staggered pattern or a triangular pattern along the straight edges of a cloth.

You could also cut the fabric to form a scalloped hem (see the illustration, right) and then work over the cut edges

of the fabric using basic buttonhole stitch. You can buy special scissors, available from needlework stores, that will cut a scalloped edge.

Alternatively, you can draw scallop shapes on your fabric edges. Work over the outline in buttonhole stitch, and then carefully cut away the fabric. Take great care not to cut or damage the existing stitches.

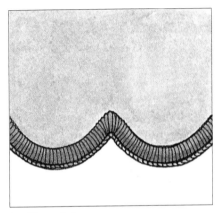

Scalloped hems

Create a scalloped hem by using special scissors to cut the fabric first. Then work basic buttonhole stitch over the fabric edges. For fabric that frays easily, draw scallops on fabric, work the stitching first, then cut away the unwanted fabric with normal scissors.

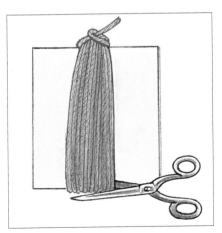

Making a tassel

1 *Cut a piece of DMC thread, double it, and lay across top edge of folded cardboard. Wind body thread around cardboard to required thickness. Make slip knot in securing thread and pull tightly. Cut through thread loops.*

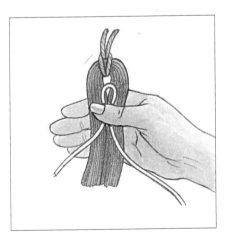

2 *Take a long length of thread and loop it. Then position it vertically as shown, just under the slip knot, holding it in place with your right thumb. Bind the tassel tightly from bottom to top so that this loop is almost covered. Keep the binding neat and regular.*

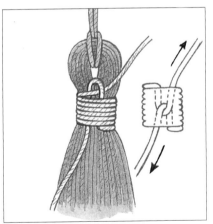

3 *Thread the loose end through the vertical loop. Pull bottom thread to secure loop inside binding and then trim bottom threads to level them. Cut the tassels down to size if necessary, then use sewing thread to stitch them to your finished design.*

Conservation Hints and Tips

These precautions will help to preserve your embroidery over the years.

Laundering Make sure that your finished piece is washed and blocked or pressed before you store it; see the instructions on pages 180–181.

Storage Wrap your work in acid-free tissue paper before storing. It also best to keep your work rolled up rather than folded, as dust and dirt tend to gather on sharp folds, and folding weakens the fibres at the fold.

If you intend to store your work in a wooden chest, seal the wood with three coats of polyurethane varnish, then line the wooden chest with acid-free tissue paper. Wood, especially softwoods such as pine, exudes oils that will eventually mark your fabric. It is also advisable to pack a moth repellant alongside your stored needlework.

Do not store your work in plastic, which retains moisture and releases chemicals that will eventually damage the fabric. Also, keep your embroidery away from metal objects, such as pins and fasteners, which can leave rust marks on the piece.

Displaying your work Direct sunlight will inevitably fade the colours of your work, so it is best not to display your work in direct sunlight.

The final touch Sign and date your work. This might not be important to you, but it will be to future generations. Sign using either a permanent marker pen, or embroider your name and the date with one strand of thread. The signature could appear in the main body of the design or on an edge. When dating your work, include the century. Who knows how long it may be around!

Troubleshooting

Prevention is better than cure, but if the worst happens, refer to this list of common problems and their remedies.

Colour bleeds While manufacturers do all they can to make sure their threads are colourfast, accidents do happen, and there can be occasional problems with reds and blacks. When colour runs or bleeds, it is usually only a residue of unprocessed dye remaining in the thread. This can be remedied simply by running the fabric under cold water until it is clear. It is important not to let your fabric remain damp for any length of time as this will aggravate the problem of loose dyes. Always block your fabric dry after washing (page 181).

Insufficient border If you find that you have not left enough fabric at the edges of your work for mounting, add a strip of fabric to each edge of the finished piece. Use a matching fabric, or try a contrasting fabric that complements the colour or texture of the frame, cushion, or other background being used. Machine-stitch the edges of the two fabrics together, using a ¼ in (6 mm) seam, and then press flat.

Marks and stains If regular cleaning methods already described (page 180) do not remove marks or stains, you may decide to cover the stain with additional stitching. A small appliquéd patch might also work and add to the charm of the finished piece. Stain removers are available to treat specific substances and these can be used as a last resort, but always test the chemical first on a scrap of fabric or a bad situation might turn into a disaster.

Torn fabric There are three possible solutions to this problem.

Apply a patch of iron-on interfacing on the wrong side of your work behind the tear in the fabric.

On linen and coarser fabrics, pull threads from the selvedge, and then weave the threads into the embroidered area to cover the tear, following the weave of the cloth as you work.

Outline the tear with buttonhole stitch (page 25) to create a decorative eyelet that could be incorporated into your overall design.

GLOSSARY

Aida An *evenweave* fabric used particularly in *counted cross stitch*.

Appliqué A method of attaching pieces of material onto fabric for decoration.

Assisi work A *counted thread* technique in which an area is surrounded by stitches, so that the unstitched area becomes the design motif.

Blackwork (Spanish work) A *counted-thread* technique used as a substitute for lace. Stitching is traditionally produced in black thread on white fabric.

Couching (laidwork) A method that involves laying thread on the surface of the fabric and overcasting it in position.

Count The number of fabric threads per inch. Used to describe the fineness or coarseness of fabric.

Counted cross stitch A *counted thread* technique in which a precise number of stitches is needed to complete a design.

Counted thread work A form of embroidery where stitches are worked over given numbers of fabric threads.

Crewelwork A method of *freestyle* stitching using 2-ply, nondivisible wool embroidery threads.

Cutwork Embroidery that involves outlining areas of design with stitching and then cutting away the background fabric to create an openwork pattern.

Evenweave Fabric that has the same number of threads running in both directions.

Freestyle embroidery A type of embroidery that is worked without counting threads on fabric.

Fusible webbing An adhesive material that fuses layers of fabric together when heated by ironing.

Goldwork Embroidery using metal threads which are either stitched or couched onto a fabric surface.

Interfacing Thin non-woven fabric used as a backing to strengthen and stabilize embroidery.

Jacobean embroidery A form of crewelwork in which the design is influenced by Elizabethan motifs, in turn derived from Oriental imagery.

Metal threads Threads made from finely spun lengths of thin metal fibres, including gold, silver, copper, and aluminium.

Metallic threads Fine synthetic threads with a metallic finish commonly used with stranded cotton.

Mitre A corner seam or joint that meets at a 45-degree angle.

Monogramming An embroidery technique in which letters are embroidered or *appliquéd* onto fabric.

Needlepoint (canvas work) Stitching produced on woven canvas of an even count, usually worked in wool yarn. Sometimes misnamed *tapestry*.

Openweave A loosely woven fabric, not necessarily an evenweave.

Overcasting (oversewing) Stitching by hand or machine over a raw edge. This technique is also used to join edges of fabric together.

Petit point A type of needlepoint on fine canvas in which very small stitches are used throughout.

Plain weave The simplest type of fabric weave; the *warp* and *weft* threads go over and under each other singly.

Pouncing A method of transferring an image onto fabric using a fine powder usually known as pounce powder.

Ribbon embroidery Ribbons are used instead of threads, stitched through fabric or attached separately.

Sampler (example) A piece of embroidery consisting of examples of various stitches or motifs. Traditionally used as a practice piece.

Selvedge The firmly woven outside edges of fabric, which should be removed before finishing.

Smocking A method of gathering together widths of evenly folded material with decorative stitching.

Stumpwork A 15th- to 16th-century embroidery technique in which padding is used to create three-dimensional effects.

Tacking Large running stitches are used to hold the fabric in position temporarily. Also used to mark an area of a design.

Tambour work A method of applying beading to a fabric using a small hook called a tambour hook.

Tapestry Often misused to describe *needlepoint*, tapestry is the creation of decorative woven fabric on a loom.

Warp The vertical threads of the fabric weave, running parallel to the *selvedge*.

Weft The horizontal threads of the weave in fabric, running perpendicular to the *selvedge*.

INDEX

Project titles are shown in italic. Numbers in italic refer to illustrations; numbers in bold indicate the most important reference to a subject.

Author's Acknowledgements

The production of a book of this kind requires teamwork of the first order. As the author, my work would not have been possible without the support and enthusiasm of many others, and in this space I would like to extend my appreciation and thanks for all their efforts. The following designers and embroiderers contributed their flair, skill and expertise, together with finished projects which were a joy to receive.

Daphne Ashby Teddy bear bib *(page 36)*, fish motif towel *(page 38)*, seashell tablecloth *(page 62)*, rooster wall hanging *(page 108)*, goldwork box top *(page 140)*, flower spray cardigan *(page 148)*, cottage garden picture *(page 152)*.

Christine Benson Pochette bag *(page 34)*, beadwork evening bag *(page 162)*.

Caroline Crabtree Shisha mirror waistcoat *(page 164)*.

Joan Everard Paisley shawl *(page 98)*. Adaptation of original design by *Dorothy L. Woodsome*.

Sue Hawkins Pomegranate needlecase *(page 120)*, couched Art Nouveau pincushion *(page 136)*.

Vivienne Lavender Cyclamen picture *(page 42)*, crewelwork cushion *(page 124)*.

Sue Whiting Cutwork butterfly tablecloth *(page 40)*, parrot cushion *(page 52)*, geometric place mat *(page 70)*, shirt pocket and espadrilles *(page 174)*, silk scarf *(page 176)*.

Jan Eaton, Liz Elvin, Jane Fox, and *Carolyn Palmer* Extensive know-how, moral support, and stitched samples.

I am also greatly indebted to the following:

DMC, in particular *Cara Ackerman*, for their superb fabric and threads.
Mark Collins, Cameron Brown, and *Roger Bristow* for their know-how, know-what, know-when, and know-where.
Liz Dean, Maggi McCormick, and *Ann Poe*, three terrific editors who motivated me and miraculously put all the pieces in the right places.
Coral Mula and *Amanda Patton* for their beautiful artwork.
Lucinda Symons for her stunning project photography.

Publisher's Acknowledgements

Thanks to *Diana Vernon* for the peacock feather beaded throw *(page 157)*, *Patricia Platt* for the ribbon garden embroidery *(page 144)*, and *Peg Morris* for the stitch family examples *(pages 22, 46, 56, 64, 72, 86, 100)*. Thanks also to *Bill Barnes* of Benton & Johnson, and *Vivienne Wells* for valued consultancy, and to *Sarah Davies* for design input.

Picture Credits

The Victoria and Albert Museum, London *(pages 20–21, 44–45, 112, 128 [left], 166, 178–9)*
The Royal School of Needlework, Hampton Court Palace, Surrey *(pages 113, 130)*
The Embroiderers' Guild, Hampton Court Palace, Surrey *(pages 110–111, 128 [right])*
The Devonshire Collection of Period Costume, Totnes, Devon *(pages 142, 156 [photographed by Paul Biddle])*
Peter Smith of Scaionis (author portrait, *back cover*).

We are grateful to the following suppliers:

Barclay & Bodie *(for the sewing basket on page 139)*
7–9 Blenheim Terrace
London
NW8 0EH
Tel: 0171 372 5705

De L'Isle *(for the cupboard shown on page 165)*
287 Lillie Road
London
SW6 7LL
Tel: 0171 385 6760

Tridias *(for the toys shown on page 53)*
124 Walcot Street
Bath
BA1 5BG
Tel: 01225 469455

Suppliers

The following suppliers all offer a mail order service:

Threads and Fabrics

DMC Creative World Ltd.
For the name of your local stockist contact:
DMC Creative World Ltd.
Pullman Road
Wigston
Leicestershire
LE18 2DY
U.K.
Tel: 0116 281 1040

The Campden Needlecraft Centre
High Street
Chipping Campden
Gloucestershire
GL55 6AG
U.K.
Tel: 01386 840583

Creativity
45 New Oxford Street
London
WC1A 1BH
U.K.
Tel: 0171 240 2945

John Lewis
278–306 Oxford Street
London
W1A 1EX
U.K.
Tel: 0171 629 7711

Liberty
210–220 Regent Street
London
W1R 6AH
U.K.
Tel: 0171 734 1234

Mace & Nairn
89 Crane Street
Salisbury
Wiltshire
SP1 2PY
U.K.
Tel: 01722 336903

The Stitch Shop
15 The Podium
Bath
Avon
BA1 5AL
U.K.
Tel: 01225 481134

Voirrey Embroidery Centre
Brimstage Hall
Brimstage
Wirral
L63 6JA
U.K.
Tel: 0151 342 3514

Beads

Creative Beadcraft Ltd.
Denmark Works
Sheepcote Cell Road
Beamond End
Near Amersham
Buckinghamshire
HP7 0RX
U.K.
Tel: 01494 715606

Custom-made Wooden Boxes

Canopia
P.O. Box 420
Uxbridge
Middlesex
UB8 2GW
U.K.
Tel: 01923 672008

Goldwork Threads

Benton & Johnson Ltd.
26 Marshalsea Road
London
SE1 1HF
U.K.
Tel: 0171 407 8646

Pure Wool Blanketing

Melinda Coss Designs
Ty'r Waun Bach
Gwernogle
Carmarthenshire
West Wales
SA32 7RY
U.K.
Tel: 01267 202386

Shisha Mirrors

The World Embroidery Shop
2 Woodlands
Kirby Misperton
Malton
North Yorkshire
YO17 0XW
U.K.
Tel: 01653 668419

Silk Ribbons

Ribbon Designs
42 Lake View
Edgware
Middlesex
HA8 7RU
U.K.
Tel: 0181 958 4966